More praise for *Dare to Be Yourself*

"Thank you, Alan—I love how you celebrate bliss as the guide on our road home!"

—Terry Cole-Whittaker
Author of *Love and Power in a World Without Limits*

"Alan Cohen is one of the most gentle and powerful guiding lights of the profound transition now occurring on earth. His writing will give you courage to release all fear and allow yourself to be lifted naturally to the next stage of human evolution."

—Barbara Marx Hubbard
Peace activist

"Alan's work is very insightful and helpful. Many people have told me how they have grown as a result of his books and tapes. They have brought peace and fulfillment to thousands and I heartily endorse them."

—Wally "Famous" Amos
Cookie magnate and motivational teacher

"From one who has truly learned the art of daring to be himself, Alan Cohen shares his great gifts of deep insight and inspiration. You'll laugh, you'll cry, you'll awaken to who you really are, and you'll never be quite the same again."

—Mary Manin Boggs
Director of Living Enrichment Center
International New Thought Alliance

D0181621

DARE TO BE YOURSELF

How to Quit Being an Extra in Other People's Movies and Become the Star of Your Own

Alan Cohen

Fawcett Columbine • New York

A Fawcett Columbine Book
Published by Ballantine Books

Grateful acknowledgment is made to Dr. Jerry Fankhauser for permission to reprint an excerpt from *From a Chicken to an Eagle* by Dr. Jerry Fankhauser.

For the readers' reference, the following addresses are given for sources referred to in the text:

Awakening Heart Productions, HCR5 Box 831, Burnet, Texas 78611

The life and teachings of Hilda Charlton, Golden Quest, P.O. Box 190, Lake Hill, New York 12448

A Course in Miracles, Foundation for Inner Peace, P.O. Box 1104, Glen Ellen, California 95442

Robert Fisher, *The Knight in Rusty Armor*, Wilshire Book Co., 12015 Sherman Road, North Hollywood, California 91605

The life and teachings of Paramahansa Yogananda, Self-Realization Fellowship, 3880 San Rafael Avenue, Los Angeles, California 90065

Library of Congress Catalog Card Number: 93-91065

ISBN: 0-449-90839-9

Cover design by Georgia Morrissey
Cover illustration by Rick Lovell

Manufactured in the United States of America

First Ballantine Books Edition: July 1994

10 9 8 7 6

To Karren,
who has dared me to be myself
by seeing the greatness in me.
It takes one to know one.

Acknowledgments

I wish to express my heartfelt appreciation to those who have supported and assisted me in the invitation to dare to be yourself. Their assistance has been a major contribution to the quality and integrity of the material presented in this book.

Noel Capelle, for her word processing, editorial input and her steady, clear, and positive attitude;

Valerie Johnson and Carl Ball, for their consistently willing attitude and meticulous typesetting and electronic transmission skills;

Dr. Susan Smith Jones and Rev. Mary Boggs, for their gentle sincere willingness to support me and endorse this work;

Patt Narrowe, for her dedication to artistic beauty and cooperative adventure in graphic excellence;

Joy Nelson, for her solid appreciation of this work, valuable editorial suggestions, and encouragement;

Charley Thweatt, my partner in song and mischief, who reminds me to not settle for less than peace;

Mark and Dean Tucker of Awakening Heart Productions, for their generous and talented photographic offerings;

All of the teachers and fellow travelers who have shared my movie and brought me the experiences and insights that shaped my life and this book.

Introduction

Many years ago there lived a well-loved Jewish sage named Rabbi Zusya. Rabbi Zusya was renowned throughout the world for his gifted insights as a scholar, teacher, and healer.

When the time came for Rabbi Zusya to leave this world, his students gathered at his bedside. During a tender moment the Rabbi began to weep.

"Why do you cry, Rabbi?" asked one of the disciples. "If anyone is assured a place in Heaven, it is you. You are one of the greatest and most revered spiritual teachers in the world!"

Rabbi Zusya turned his head softly toward the one who spoke, and looked him in the eye. His gaze was piercing, as one who can see through this world to another.

"I will tell you why I weep, my dear one," the sage replied. "If, when I approach the gates of Heaven, the angel who meets me asks, 'Why were you not a Moses?' I shall answer with conviction, 'Because I was not born to be a Moses.'

"And if the angel challenges me, 'But neither did you perform the feats that Elijah did,' I shall firmly respond, 'My mission was not the same one that Elijah was sent to accomplish.'

"But there is one question that I fear being unable to answer: 'Why were you not a Rabbi Zusya?' "

If I had to sum up my adventure here on earth, I would say that it has been a series of lessons in becoming who I truly am. Mahatma Gandhi entitled his autobiography, *The Story of My Experiments with Truth*. Perhaps my autobiography will one day be called, *The Story of My Experiments with Being Myself*.

At one of my workshops an older gentleman raised his hand and stood up to speak. "I tried being myself once," he quipped. "But it didn't work—I realized I didn't have enough experience!"

The entire audience laughed with him, perhaps because there was a poignant truth behind his statement, one with which everyone in that room could identify. All of us are seeking to more fully be ourselves. Sometimes our treasured self comes forth in a joyful moment of self-discovery, and sometimes we find ourself through challenge and apparent conflict. No matter what route we take, we all share the awesome journey to the mountaintop of self-awareness.

Two hundred years after Rabbi Zusya left this world, a little girl came to claim her place in life. At the age of twelve, Jennifer Capriati knocked the tennis world for a loop. Before she had both feet set in adolescence, Jennifer was competing in first class circles, challenging and defeating some of the most formidable adult stars. Not surprisingly, she created quite a sensation among her colleagues and in the media.

When asked by an interviewer if she hoped to be the next Chris Evert, Jennifer answered, "No, I want to be the first Jennifer Capriati."

Perhaps it is the same unapologetic confidence in herself that Jennifer manifests on the court. She knows that the only way she can truly succeed is to be what she is, rather than an imitation of someone else. Like Jennifer, you and I have come to the earth with a perfectly individual purpose, one which only we can fulfill as unique and gifted beings. It is only when we give way to our own greatness that we find true satisfaction and success in finding our soul's destiny.

It is to this spectacular journey that this book is dedicated. *Dare to Be Yourself* is a celebration of the courage we demonstrate in stretching to discover and claim our own beauty.

Alan Cohen

DARE TO BE YOURSELF

How to Quit Being an Extra in Other People's Movies and Become the Star of Your Own

DARE TO BE YOURSELF

The Return
of the
Golden Buddha

THE GOLDEN BUDDHA

We are stardust. We are golden.
— Joni Mitchell

O nce upon a time in a distant land there was a Golden Buddha. This magnificent being was fashioned out of tons of pure gold, and stood as tall as ten men. The great Buddha sat serenely in lotus position in the garden of a monastery on a hilltop overlooking a peaceful little town. In this tranquil setting many spiritual pilgrims would sit in meditation at the feet of the Golden Buddha, contemplating the depths of their being.

One day word reached the monastery that a belligerent army from a neighboring city was on its way to invade the village. This news disturbed the monks greatly, for they knew that if the army discovered the Golden Buddha, it would be plundered and destroyed. Hastily the monks gathered together to try to find some way to save the Buddha. After considering many ideas, one monk offered a plan: disguise the Buddha. "Let us cover the Buddha with mud and stones and mortar," he suggested. "Then the invaders will believe that the statue is merely a stone sculpture." This idea met with unanimous approval, and the project was begun.

Arduously the monks worked through the night. Bathed in the mystical glow of torchlight, all the men, young and old alike, offered prayer and summoned energy to save the Buddha. Finally, just as the dawn was breaking in the eastern sky, the last pail of concrete was poured over the Buddha's head. The great golden god had become but a cement statue.

And it was good that the monks worked so diligently, for later that very day the pounding footsteps and creaking wheels of the warring army were heard at the town gate. The soldiers marched up the hill toward the monastery and filed past the temple. Anxiously the monks watched the procession, fervently praying that no gold would shine through the Buddha's disguise. The army passed, and hardly any of the soldiers took a second look. The monks breathed a deep sigh of relief—their plan was a success. The Buddha was unrecognized. The monks went back to their activities, satisfied.

Years passed, and after a time the occupying army left the village. But by then, all of the monks who had covered the Buddha had left the monastery or passed away. In fact, there remained no one in the town who remembered that the Buddha's true nature was golden. Everyone in the monastery and village went about their business, and all who looked upon the Buddha believed that he was made only of stone.

Then one day a young monk was sitting on the knee of the Buddha, meditating. As he arose from his prayer he leaned on the Buddha's leg, and a little piece of concrete chipped off the knee and fell to the ground. To his surprise, the monk noticed something shiny underneath the stone on the Buddha's leg. He brushed away the debris and discovered that there was another Buddha underneath the one everyone beheld—and it was golden!

The monk ran to the great hall of the temple, where the others were studying. "Come quickly!" he shouted. "The Buddha is golden!"

The monks dropped what they were doing and flocked out to the Buddha. When they saw that the young monk was speaking the truth, they ran and got their hammers and chisels. Together they began to chip away the stone and mortar that had disguised the Buddha for so many years. Before long all of the facade had been removed, and the Golden Buddha was restored to its original splendor.

The story of the Golden Buddha is true. Now the great Buddha sits majestically in The Temple of the Golden Buddha in Bangkok, Thailand, where once again thousands upon thousands of devotees come to sit at the feet of the Buddha and find refuge in the golden nature within themselves.

And yet there is a deeper meaning to this story. There is a golden one within all of us. Behind the facades, defenses, and images we present to the world, there is a bright and precious soul calling for expression. There is one within us who is strong, wise, and compassionate. This one has a great capacity to give and receive love, and know the deep truths of the heart. This is the one we have been questing for all our life. The Golden Buddha is you and me.

Over years—perhaps lifetimes—we have shielded ourselves from the destruction we feared by covering our true self with plates of protection, masks of bravado, and stone walls of defenses. Layer by layer we overlaid our original nature with illusions and untruths about who we are. At first our intention was to protect ourselves from pain, but in the bargain we kept love at a distance. We thought we could succeed by living up to an image expected of us by the outer world, but our adaptation has been at the dear cost of our inner life. Ironically, in our attempt to make others believe we are something we are not, we have fooled ourselves. If you tell a lie long enough, you begin to believe it; ultimately deception entraps even the liar. We have tricked ourselves into believing that we are other than we are. We have forgotten the beauty and greatness of our true self, and come to believe that we are not worthy of all the good our heart yearns to enjoy, and deserves.

We can hide who we are, but we cannot destroy it; ultimately we must discover and live for our inner truth. The time comes when we must put aside our fears and claim our heart's desire. It does not matter how long the Buddha has been disguised; the noble adventure of reclaiming our identity begins the moment we catch a glimpse of the gold behind the stone. The truth of our wholeness has not been marred as we journeyed through the dream of our mistaken identity. All the while our real self has remained untainted, innocent, and perfect as God created it. We are, and always have been, perfectly safe. The armies of fear have come and gone. They have marched into dust, and we are here to build anew. Let no ancient memories of terror cast their shadow upon the morning at hand. The Golden Buddha lives.

The Golden Buddha

1) Think of a time in your life, perhaps when you were a child, when you felt golden—beautiful, lovable, and whole. In this memory, how old are you? Where are you? Who are you with? What are you doing? What are the sights, smells, and sounds in your world? What feelings do you experience, especially in your heart?

2) Can you remember an event which led you to start protecting yourself? Did someone hurt you, leave you, or deny your goodness? What feelings arose within you, and how did you shield yourself from the pain?

3) How have you continued to protect yourself? What is your pattern of self-defense? How does this pattern *seem* to work for you? How does it hurt you, limit you, or cut you off from what you truly want?

4) How has life chipped away at you? How has the stripping away of your mask revealed more of your golden nature? How have you become stronger as a result of your challenges?

5) If you allowed your true golden self to express more fully, what would you be doing differently?

AWAKENING
FROM THE DREAM

We are told in Genesis that "a deep sleep fell over Adam"—but nowhere does it say in the Bible that he woke up! In essence, all the events that followed Adam's falling asleep are a part of his dream.

Metaphysically, Adam represents all of us. We, too, have entered into a deep sleep. As individuals, nations, and a planet, we have in many ways forgotten where we have come from, who we are, and where we are going. An honest look at the troubles we have created for ourselves as people and a planet reveals that we have painfully lost sight of the visions that once painted our future. What began as a happy dream seems to have tailspun into a nightmare. Struggling in the murky shadows spun by the bony fingers of fear, it appears as if there is no escape from the labyrinth of the problems we perceive. The heaviness of our sleep has drawn dark curtains over the memory of our golden origin.

But nightmares always end with awakening. While the dream may seem overwhelming when you are in it, it becomes as nothing the moment you open your eyes. Sometimes the awakening is gentle, light, and easy. Often it is startling and it feels jarring. But if we are having a painful dream, one in which we see ourselves as powerless, small, or unlovable, is it not worth the shakeup in order to wake up?

The Citadel of Fear

Every sojourner of spirit must face the time when the walls that protected his old world begin to crack. Just as in the story of the Golden Buddha, sooner or later the chisels of life's trials pick away at our armor. And this dismantling is wonderful, for there is no greater tragedy than hiding behind something that we are not, living a life that is less than we are. The universe is continuously working to remind us of our identity and our purpose. If we are living a life that is untrue to our soul's calling, our inner guide will not let us rest until we step back onto our true course.

The time comes when we can no longer find refuge in our defenses. We discover, often with awe, that it is precisely our defenses that have kept us in darkness! We tire of straining to protect ourselves, and we feel stifled and restricted by the walls we have built between our heart and others'. Our defenses are not worth the love we lose in hiding. We cannot afford to maintain a citadel of fear at the cost of peace. In our efforts to keep pain away from our heart, we have also denied entry to joy. The moment arrives when we must break free and make a stand for who we are. *That moment is now.* The time has come to cast aside our cloaks of smallness and don the robes which honor our true magnitude. We must claim the strength to live in the dignity befitting our identity.

Disillusionment is a Step Toward Truth

When I first set onto my path of awakening, I felt as if my whole world was falling apart. Many of the things to which I had devoted my time, attention, and energy, suddenly became meaningless. It can be very startling and unnerving to discover that the values for which you lived no longer seem real. I did not find the same satisfaction or communication with the friends I was used to spending time with. I wondered why I was doing the kind of work I was in. The social pursuits which had formerly brought me pleasure no longer held gifts for me. I felt that most of the goals that I had strived for were no longer true for me and not worthy of my continued attention. My entire sense of purpose had shifted. I had a brief taste of something more and better, but I did not know how to make it a lasting element of my life. I felt lost, sometimes even as if I was going crazy. It was a dark night of the soul.

If you are passing through such a night, or have ever done so, take comfort in knowing that such a void is a very important, helpful, and necessary part of the journey. When planting a garden, the earth must be turned over, tilled, and smoothed out before new seeds can grow; otherwise the old weeds will overtake the seedlings. In the same way, before a new and shining building can be erected, the old, dilapidated, and useless structures standing on the lot must be cleared away. We must make space for something new and better to enter our life. While it may seem that we are out of control or subject to forces greater than ourself, it is important to remember that there is a wisdom in the events that we attract to us. All is for learning, growing, and healing. God is very present, and we are not alone.

Such a time calls for faith, the knowing that everything somehow works out for the best. *It is not your world that is shattering, but your illusions.* God's world can never be shattered, for God's world is founded in love, the only indestructible energy in the entire universe. If you feel disillusioned, then, take heart; *dis-illusion* means the end of an illusion. Disillusionment is the best thing that could happen to anyone. It means that something false has been undone, and the truth behind it is available to be discovered. *The truth is always healing. Only illusions are painful.* Therefore be glad, even proud, that you have had the courage to learn a lesson that would break your illusions and replace them with greater strength and wisdom.

Our pains and tribulations are the chipping of the cement off the Golden Buddha. The armor falls away to reveal the gold. A worthless image is crumbling, and the treasure is coming forth. It is the end of the cover-up and the beginning of the radiance. In such a birth, there is great cause for joy.

Peace Must Come

Once you have begun to awaken, you can never really go to sleep again. Oh, we can doze a wink or two here or there,

9

but once the climber has caught sight of the mountaintop, nothing can stop her from reaching the summit. We have come too far to turn back now. We have played out many of our fantasies and idle wishes. We have been teased, tantalized, titillated, and seduced by the cheap perfume of shallow dreams, and somehow the aroma just doesn't turn our head like it once did. Now we want peace more than idols.

To dare to be yourself means to live in the spirit of power rather than weakness; to proceed from peace instead of clamoring to maintain defenses; to want the reality of love more than the nightmare of fear. And we do.

The time has come for us to be released from the burden of living for dreams other than our own. Armoring is for protection, not expansion. The Golden Buddha must stand in the sunlight. We are living in the age on earth when men and women are stepping forth to claim freedom. There is a great wave of awakening that cannot be denied, suppressed, or reversed. Those who align with the expansion are empowered and uplifted by a Force much larger than themselves. And those who resist or oppose it are gripped in only deeper struggle. We must choose between love and fear, and learn the truth of the one and the uselessness of the other.

Peace must come to those who ask for it. Strength must be given to those who claim it. And love must bring healing to all who open our arms to receive it. The time of awakening is at hand.

Awakening from the Dream

1) List three major disillusionments you have experienced in your life. Then note the truth you learned as the illusions crumbled.

2) Would you, or could you go back to the illusions you once held?

3) How have your disillusionments empowered you to become stronger, clearer, and more alive?

4) What gifts have you been able to share with others because you weathered a storm that brought forth your strength?

DESTINED FOR GREATNESS

Do you ever wonder what you are doing here? Have you ever pondered if you have a purpose for living? Do you believe in destiny? And if there is a plan for your life, where did it come from and how can you live it?

You *do* have a purpose here, and it is a good one. Your sojourn has not been cast upon you by some outside agent who dispassionately chooses your fate. You choose your mission in life, and you will live it.

The first *Superman* movie offers us a marvelous visual image of the process by which we step into our destiny. We meet Superman as an infant on the planet Krypton, which is about to blow up. Just before the final moment of their world, Superman's parents place their child in a space capsule and send him hurtling off into space. The tiny craft is programmed to soar past the stars to the Planet Earth.

During the long voyage, the capsule's automated environment plays an audio tape which educates the child. The voice on the tape teaches Superman of his origin and his identity, and instructs him about his abilities and potential. His talents are clearly described to him, along with all he needs to know to fulfill his mission on earth. He is to participate in this planet's life, learn, and become a force for good. As young Superman flies through galaxies, a wealth of strategically important words are implanted in his open mind.

When Superman finally arrives on earth, he is clear and well prepared to fulfill his function. Remembering his purpose, Superman soon begins to manifest his extraordinary powers and exercise his calling. Although he is adopted by two earthly parents, he remains conscious of his heritage. While he is disguised as an average person, he retains his identity as the hero he was born to be.

We, too, have a heritage from a higher world. Before we arrived on earth, we were united with our source of wisdom and power, and we were aware of our potential. We were, as the Bible tells us, "little less than God." Our vision was merged with that of our Creator, and our sense of purpose was unsullied.

Then we came to earth. We had lessons we wanted to learn, experiences to enjoy, and service to render. Consciously, in co-creative accord with our Source, we set out on our great adventure. We knew our purpose, along with what we were to do to fulfill it. We embarked on our glorious quest and dove into the great ocean of life. We are to be commended for our courage to learn and grow through the experiences we knew this world would bring us.

But then something happened. We encountered a turn of events that Superman escaped: *we forgot*. We came to life and we went to sleep. Almost immediately upon entering this world, we began to take on the programming of our parents, teachers, and friends. Their example might have told us that life is a struggle, some people deserve more love than others, and we had to protect ourselves from people who would hurt us if we told the truth. Perhaps we heard our mother say, "You'll be the death of me," and we began to see ourself not as a child of God, but a murderer. Or a teacher may have told us, "You'll never amount to anything," and we thought we were worthless. Other children might have made fun of us because we were fat, skinny, or the color of our skin was different than theirs. In one way or another we started to believe that we were somehow inferior. We came with love in our heart, enthusiasm in our spirit, and integrity of purpose, but then we began to think that fear was more real than love, and this world was more of a threat than a blessing. We lost our awareness of our mission and exchanged our innocent vision for a mass sense of confusion and separation. The practical result of our hypnosis was that all of the powers and potentials we came with were lost to us—not because they were taken from us, but because we no longer believed they were real. Belief is a very powerful force. You can have the riches of the universe available to you, but if you do not believe they are yours, they will go unnoticed and unused.

Behold, we find ourselves in a life in which we feel powerless, unloved, and lost. We meet other souls in equal or even deeper stupors of fear and loneliness. Desperately we search the eyes we meet in hopes of finding a spark of memory of our purpose or a hope of living a greater destiny than the one that has been shown to us by the teachers of lack. And alas, the eyes we search are as vacant as our own. Moreover, we become terrified to discover that they are probing our own eyes for a glimpse of the strength they have missed.

Could this be the destiny of souls born of an all-powerful Source? Did we come here but to wander in emptiness, stumbling through endless caverns of disappointment, occasionally bumping into another weary traveler on a rocky path, only to find they have wandered even farther from the light than we have?

If you have felt abandoned, alone, or unloved, then take heart. Your history is not your destiny, and your fears of oblivion are unfounded. God has far greater things in store for you than you have known or can imagine. Our Father has not left us to rot on a dung heap devoid of Spirit. Spirit is the only reality, and our journey will not be finished until we find ourself in the Kingdom we once knew.

Like Superman, we have a role to play in the drama we call life on the stage we call earth. And also like him, we are heros. We may not gain world notoriety or have comic books and movies written about us, but we do have a domain to which we have the power to bring healing. We are all healers, and every person and event that comes to our attention is an invitation to bring a richer quality of love to the planet. If one person is happier because you were here, it is all worth it. And if you are that person, God is well pleased.

Destined for Greatness

1) Imagine a time before you were born when you chose your purpose for coming to earth. What was the major life lesson you wanted to master?

2) What gifts in the form of people and experiences have served to help you to learn the lesson? What do you still need to do to master it?

3) What limiting words, phrases, or examples were you given by your parents, teachers, or friends, which led you to believe that you were inferior? What were you told that distracted you from being yourself?

4) What people or experiences reminded you of your talents, strength, and beauty?

5) What steps can you take now to get back on the track of your purpose?

6) What can you do to encourage or support others to recognize and fulfill their purpose?

YOUR LIFE IS CALLING

*C*omedian Richard Pryor starred in a powerful movie called *Jojo Dancer*, in which he courageously and unashamedly portrays the events in his life which led to his attempted suicide. Beginning with his childhood as the son of a prostitute and an abusive father, we see Jojo struggle through a long series of painful encounters as he attempts to establish himself as a respected comedian. As I watched Jojo's confrontations with gangsters in seedy bars, his disappointments with unfaithful friends, and his agonizing relationships with a string of wives, I felt the heartrending hardships of a bright child who got lost in the world.

Finally Jojo tailspins into heavy use of drugs and a series of thicker and deeper lies, until his life is so painful that he wants out. In desperation, Jojo attempts to burn himself to death. But like so much of his life, even his effort to die is a failure. Jojo survives, just barely.

While he is in the hospital, Jojo begins to reconsider the decisions with which he has shaped his life. But now, in contrast to the smoky veil through which he has customarily viewed his interactions, Jojo sees his life from the perspective of his higher self. Through these eyes, Jojo is not a lost and confused little boy in the body of a man, sick of life and steeped in torment. Instead we see a whole and lovable Jojo, clear of mind and attuned to the wisdom of his spirit. This insightful guide (Jojo's higher awareness) assists the burnt and decrepit man to look upon his journey with clarity, love, and deeper understanding. Through the vision of his higher self, Jojo can see past his fears and into his purpose. He recognizes the bigger picture, and this makes all the difference.

At this critical point, Jojo's wife turns to the doctor and anxiously asks, "Is he going to live?"

Silently the doctor looks her in the eye and shakes his head, "No."

Jojo observes his prognosis, and is struck with terror. He has a decision to make. Before, he was unwilling to live. Now he is unwilling to die. Through his introspection he has found compassion for himself and those he loves. Now Jojo has a great deal to live for. He wants another chance. He wants the chance to do it right this time.

Jojo opens his eyes and silently tells his wife that he wants to live. And so he does. Jojo Dancer chooses life, and Richard Pryor is healed to tell his story. The full title of the movie is *Jojo Dancer—Your Life is Calling*.

Back to Your Destiny

Like Jojo, you and I have a life that is calling us. We have a mission that each of us must fulfill in our own way. My life is in my hands, and what you make of your time here is up to you. Others may show me the way to walk and give me inspiration to walk it, but in the final analysis only I can do the walking. And as I fulfill my destiny, I invite everyone who sees me to claim their own.

When you do not follow your call to the life you were born to live, there remains a gap in the universe. There will be a little space in your heart, a tiny ache calling you to be more, for you know that you *are* more. There will be a gift to the world left undelivered. There is an untiring advocate in your soul that will not let you rest content until you have brought your talent to life and walked the way your heart chooses.

Another motion picture, *Back to the Future,* unfolds the story of a teenager who is accidentally cast back into the 1950's. Marty McFly must complete his mission and return to his present life within a certain time frame, or else the world will be as if he had never been here. Marty can tell how much time he has left to return by looking at a family photograph he carries in his wallet. As Marty's time runs out, his image fades from the picture, indicating that the world is coming closer and closer to the way it would be if he had not been born. Day by day the details of his body become lighter and lighter, until there is but the slightest trace of his face in the photo. Marty sees that he must make a last ditch effort to complete his mission, which means risking a dangerous experiment. Marty decides that his presence in this world is worth the risk, and he does make it. Instantly his face and body are restored to full color and presence in the photo and his family.

You, too, have a place in the photograph of life. If you do not fill it, you begin to fade from the picture and there is a gap where you were supposed to be. And just as in *Back to the Future,* there is often a sense of daring or seeming risk about what you need to do to forge ahead into your right place in destiny. And like Marty, you will do it. You are here for a reason, and all of your adventures on earth are a part of learning to express that high purpose.

Is There Life Before Death?

In recent years there has been a great deal of attention paid to near-death experiences. You have probably read or heard some of the many fascinating accounts of people who have been clinically dead for short periods of time, and then returned to life.

I think it might be even more urgent to do a study of near-*life* experiences! The question is not, "Is there life after death?" The question is, "Is there life *before* death?" How many people eat, work, have sex, and die without ever having really lived? It is quite possible to act our way through the postures of living, look really cool, amass many revered symbols, utter the popular catch-words, and not be fully alive. A woman told me that for many years her life script was, "How much pain can I be in, and still look like I have it together?" Life is not about how it looks, but how it is. Inside, that is. In the heart. In the gut. In our sense of purpose, integrity, creativity, expression, vulnerability, outra-geousness, and in our willingness to risk, play, and be fully present.

If you're not fully present, the question is, "Where are you?" Have you escaped into your head, work, past, future, alcohol, joint, bank account, girlfriend, car, or your campaign to be right? I have given my power to all of these psychic crutches at one time or another, and I have discovered one glaring characteristic they all have in common: they are all *not here.*

More than ever before in my life, I want to be here. I want to play this movie out and really see what the adventure is all about. As George Bernard Shaw declared, "My life is no brief candle—I want to be thoroughly used up when I die." I want to look back on my life and say, "Well-lived—from the heart." And I don't have to wait until I die to say that. I can say it now, right in the midst of life.

Living in Color

There was yet another movie character who learned how to live his destiny now. Sergeant Edward Garlick served as Adrian Cronauer's (a.k.a. Robin Williams) assistant in *Good Morning, Vietnam*. After a hair-raising ride on a bicycle without tires, teetering recklessly through the streets of Saigon, Garlick had a few discoveries to share with Cronauer:

"I was almost killed! I fell off that bike and my nose was just inches from the moving tire of a passing truck. While I was lying there, my whole life passed before my eyes. And do you know what scared me more than anything else?—It wasn't even interesting!"

We can live our life in black and white, or we can view it in living color. It's your movie. A black and white life is photographed in right and wrong, good guys and bad guys, "us" and "them." In such a life you feel like a human yoyo, bouncing back and forth between happiness and sadness, winning at times and losing at others, taking turns being a victim and a villain. You can't be at one of those two poles without alternately being at the other. It's a package deal.

A life in color is founded not in judgment, but creative self-expression. People, events, and experiences are here not to be

labeled, but enjoyed and learned from. We do not need to divide
life into either's and or's; we can see the richness of it all. Then
we discover an infinite range of hues, depth, and intensity that
makes our journey joyful. As Carlos Casteneda's Don Juan
explained, "All paths lead nowhere; but those who follow the
path with heart will bless their journey."

Even if we have lived in muddied or muted hues for many
years, we can enter into the colors of our spirit at any moment
we choose. Life is forgiving, kind, and regenerative. There is
always a chance and a way to make a new start. I am amazed
at the way grass grows through the cracks in cement. Recently
I saw an unused tennis court that was becoming a green field
again. Tiny, slender, seemingly fragile blades of grass broke
through the rock and dismantled tons of asphalt. Nature has the
power to heal anything that has been laid over it. We just need
to stop squashing the seedlings of our dreams and give our true
vision a chance to develop. God is not intimidated by our past,
and neither must we allow any dark memory to intrude on the
light of the moment. *There is no life except in the moment.* And
there is no destiny other than full self-expression, which always
begins with a gentle step toward your heart's desire.

Jojo Dancer's life is a dramatic expression of our own. Each
of us began our adventure with a wonderful vision, and we have
all been distracted from it. But we are waking up together. As
each of us claims the right to live our vision, we bring everyone
closer to their dreams. Blessed are all of us who have gone through
difficulties to get where we are, and come closer to being who
we are through developing our spiritual muscles. Each fear and
false idol that we face and cast aside clears a pathway for all who
follow. Our life is calling to us, and we are ready to answer.

Your Life is Calling

1) If your whole life passed before your eyes, what would you say about the movie? What kind of movie would it be? Would it be a comedy, drama, romance, science fiction, musical, biblical epic, cartoon, soap opera, horror, documentary, or another? What would Siskel and Ebert say about your movie, and what would they do with their thumbs?

2) If you left this world tomorrow, what could most accurately be inscribed on your tombstone as a summary of the way you have lived your life and the way you touched the world?

3) Have you accomplished what you wanted to do? What would you need to do to feel a greater sense of accomplishment?

THE EAGLE'S FLIGHT

*Who would attempt to fly with the tiny wings of a
sparrow when the mighty power of an eagle has been
given him?*

— *A Course in Miracles*

One day a naturalist who was passing by a
farm saw in the barnyard a flock of chickens,
and among them was an eagle. The naturalist
inquired of the owner why it was that an eagle, the
king of all birds, should be reduced to living in the
barnyard with the chickens.

"Since I have given it chicken feed and trained
it to be a chicken, it has never learned to fly," replied
the owner. "It behaves as chickens behave, so it no
longer thinks of itself as an eagle."

"Still," insisted the naturalist, "it has the heart of
an eagle and can surely be taught to fly."

After talking it over, the two men agreed to find
out whether this was possible. Gently, the naturalist
took the eagle in his arms and said, "You belong to
the sky and not to the earth. Stretch forth your wings
and fly."

The eagle, however, was confused; he did not
know who he was. Seeing the chickens eating their
food, he jumped down to be with them again.

Undismayed, the naturalist took the eagle up on
the roof of the house and urged him again, saying, "You
are an eagle. Stretch forth your wings and fly." But
the eagle was afraid of his unknown self and the world
and jumped down once more for the chicken food.

On the third day the naturalist rose early and took
the eagle out of the barnyard to a high mountain. There
he held the king of the birds high above him and

23

encouraged him again, saying, "You are an eagle. You belong to the sky as well as the earth. Stretch forth your wings now and fly!"

The eagle looked back towards the barnyard and up to the sky. Still he did not fly. Then the naturalist lifted him straight towards the sun, and it happened: the eagle began to tremble; slowly he stretched his wings. At last, with a triumphant cry he soared into the heavens.[1]

The eagle in this story represents our true identity as beings of unlimited power and potential. The chicken represents the part of our mind that is earthbound by fear, limitation, and the conditioned boundaries which others have suggested to us— and to which we have agreed.

Like the eagle, we have suffered under a case of mistaken identity. We have succumbed to a kind of spiritual amnesia in which we have forgotten our origin and nature as spiritual beings. Our forgetting cannot remove our identity, but it can cause us to act in a way far less creative and powerful than we are—a charade quite unbecoming to a being of divine origin. Our goal, therefore, on the path of awakening is not to change who we are, but to remember who we are. Are you a chicken or an eagle? Were you born to scratch in the dust, or soar in the heavens? In your answer lies your destiny.

Who Are You?

In the tiny town of Tiruvanamili at the foot of the sacred mountain Arunachala in southern India there lived a great sage named Ramana Maharshi. Sri Ramana, as he was called by his devotees, taught one very simple method for attaining enlightenment: Ask and answer the question, *"Who Am I?"*

Many students seeking higher awareness came to Sri Ramana.

---

[1] This story and theme adapted from Jerry Fankhauser's excellent books, *From a Chicken to an Eagle* and *The Way of the Eagle*.

A businessman asked, "How can I find the solution to my financial difficulties?" A young man sought an audience with Sri Ramana to air his questions about his prospective marriage. A tearful woman, diagnosed as barren, came to ask for a blessing so that so she might bear a child. Hundreds, then thousands of sincere aspirants found their way to Sri Ramana so they might hear and feel the wisdom of the ages.

For each and for all, Sri Ramana offered the same prescription for healing. "Meditate on one question," he told them: *"Who am I?"* The master taught, "When you know who you are, you will have the answer to every challenge that life poses. When you do not remember who you are, all of life is a problem. Close your eyes, quiet your mind, and delve into your Source. Deep within you is the awareness that you are a spiritual being, perfect, whole, and one with the Great Mind that created you. Herein lies the source of your healing. It is the way out of your difficulties and into peace."

Though he lived more than a hundred years ago, Ramana Maharshi's message is timeless and bears wisdom that can help us just as powerfully now as it did then. Who are you?

Eagle, Come Forth

Even farther back in time, yet perfectly present now, one walked the earth who demonstrated the power of soaring vision. Jesus was a great eagle. He came to remind us that we, too, can fly. If we read the story of his life and ministry as a lesson in remembering who we are and Who is our Source, we learn a very strong flying lesson indeed. Jesus saw the view from the highest mountaintop, and he chose to walk in the valley to offer his vision to those who wished to rise.

Perhaps the most dramatic lesson in the power of eagle vision was presented at the tomb of Lazarus. Jesus was a friend of Lazarus' family, and when Lazarus was dying, his sisters sent a message to Jesus asking him to come quickly to heal their brother.

Jesus, however, did not arrive until four days after Lazarus had passed on. When Jesus approached, the sisters were distraught.

"Where were you?" they reproached Jesus. "It is too late now—our brother is dead!" But Jesus, being a master eagle and seeing as one, did not live in the consciousness of the limiting concept of death. He knew himself to be an immortal spiritual being, and he knew that his friend Lazarus shared the same identity. Here was a perfect opportunity to demonstrate the power of the eagle's vision to those who were seeing only from the ground.

Jesus approached the tomb, told the people to roll back the stone covering the cave where Lazarus lay, and then prayed to the Father, Jesus' source of vision and power. Jesus knew the truth that Lazarus lived, no matter what the chickens were clucking. Then Jesus faced the tomb, raised his open hand toward the sepulchre, and spoke: *"Lazarus, come forth!"*

Then, to the astonishment of the onlookers, lo and behold, Lazarus did come forth. "It is a miracle!" the crowd shouted. "The master has raised the dead! It is a miracle!"

But miracles can happen only where there has been doubt and fear. A miracle is a demonstration that limitation is not real, and freedom is. Jesus would not be caught dead, and he would not allow Lazarus to be trapped in such a preposterous predicament. To Jesus, the raising of Lazarus was not a miracle; it was natural. A miracle is not an exception to nature, but an affirmation that our true nature is higher than the one in which we have been living. Miracles are not extraordinary; indeed, when we see life from above the treetops we recognize that only healing is natural. A miracle is by no means an illusion; fear is the illusion, and the miracle is the denial of darkness.

The entire lesson hinges on the answer to this question: *To whom was Jesus speaking* when he decreed, "Lazarus, come forth!"? Certainly not to the dead body that the world acknowledged as real. Jesus didn't raise the dead because *Jesus didn't see the dead*. If Jesus saw death as real, he could never have overcome it. To the contrary, Jesus knew Lazarus as a living spirit. Before Jesus had journeyed to Bethany, he told the disciples he was going "to wake Lazarus up." He did not say he was going to raise him from the dead. The dead cannot be raised, but the sleeping can be awakened. It was not a dead Lazarus that the master summoned; it was the Lazarus who lived beyond the illusion of death. Life speaks to life, and death speaks to death, and the two conversations are never mingled. ("Let the dead bury the dead," Jesus advised. "Why do you seek the living among the dead?") One eagle called to another eagle, and together they flew.

Squadrons of Eagles

The power of eagle vision is infinite and immediately practical. The principle that Jesus used to awaken Lazarus is available to us now, if we are open to employ it. Flying lessons are continuously being offered us. We put our wings to their intended use as we shift our focus from our problems to our potential.

Jaime Escalante is a modern eagle. Born of Brazilian parents, Jaime accepted a position as a mathematics teacher in one of the toughest school districts in east Los Angeles. He was given a class of hoodlums, drug addicts, and flunkies, along with few materials and the task of teaching mathematics to a group of kids that were largely written off as unteachable. An onerous task for a chicken—but a fantastic opportunity for an eagle!

Jaime decided that he would not only teach these students math (they were having trouble with fractions), but he would make them proficient in calculus as well—a formidable vision indeed! When Jaime presented his immodest proposal to the Chairwoman of the Math Department, she laughed. When he pursued his intention, she reacted defensively. "I will not have you going beyond the scope of our curriculum," she threatened him. "These kids are the lowest functioning students in the school system."

When he heard her response, Jaime rose from his chair, approached his supervisor, and looked her straight in the eye. There was no doubt about his intention. *"The student will rise to the level of the expectation of the teacher,"* Jaime affirmed.

Dead silence in the room. A long dead silence. Then the Chairwoman responded: "Very well, do what you can."

What can an eagle do? He can see other eagles. He can see the potential for flight where others are stupefied by the thought of grovelling. He can hold his vision far above the petty concerns of littleness. He can push, pull, prod, love, encourage, challenge, and draw forth the dormant greatness in other eagles still caught in the fantasy that they are chickens.

And that is exactly what Jaime Escalante did. He devoted himself entirely to drawing forth the hidden wisdom in those tough kids. He wrangled them to come to school early, stay late, and sweat through a hot summer of voluntary study. It was a consistently challenging task. The students confronted him, attempted to manipulate him, and made every plea they had ever used to keep themselves small. They fought to confirm the world's pitiful vision of who they were. And Jaime refused to fall for any of it. He told them, "Walk out the door and you will be flipping hamburgers for the rest of your life; stay, and learn how to earn a living that will make you proud." They stayed.

When the results of the national advanced placement calculus proficiency exam came in, all of Jaime's students passed. This man had taken a bunch of chickens and transformed them into eagles. Or shall we say he mended their wings and taught them how to be who they were. His class was not just a study of mathematics; it was a course in self-esteem. These floundering flyers were eagles all the while, but they needed an experienced flyer's vision to renew their own. It takes one eagle to know another.

During the concluding frames of *Stand and Deliver*, the motion picture which depicts Jaime's true story, we see a record of the number of students at Garfield High School who passed the calculus exam. Eighteen the first year. Twenty-nine the next. Then forty-five. Then seventy-three. And so on. Entire *squadrons* of eagles! *The student will rise to the level of the expectation of the teacher*. The patient will be renewed in accord with the healer's vision. An eagle who has learned to fly will show many others the way to limitless skies.

Jaime Escalante is not an exception to the rule of limitation, but a mirror of our own freedom and potential. He, like Jesus and the other magnificent wayshowers, shines as a reminder that you and I can accomplish anything we desire if we are willing to see the highest in ourselves and those we touch. We come forth from the tomb of our limiting beliefs as we remember that we are not chickens, but eagles; not bodies, but spiritual beings; not lost souls, but beloved children of an ever-present God. All the lessons of the Bible are the same as those of Jaime Escalante's classes in rising above smallness. We share one purpose that we came here to fulfill: to know ourselves as the eagles that God created us to be, and then to fly.

The power to change your life and the world is in your hands. You have the strength and the opportunity to choose what you want to be, and then become it. We can scratch in the dirt of chicken consciousness or we can raise ourselves above the barnyard and see a vast new world from the mountaintop. Jesus said, "Even greater things than I, shall you do." Another way of teaching the same lesson is, "You and I can and will fly together." As the naturalist told the deluded eagle, "You belong to the sky and not the earth. Stretch forth your wings and fly!"

The Eagle's Flight

1) In what areas, situations, or relationships do you act like the chicken? How do you feel and act when you are a chicken?

2) In what areas, situations, or relationships do you allow your natural eagle to come forth? How do you feel and act as an eagle?

3) What is it that you know, experience, or understand when you are the eagle, that you forget when you are a chicken?

4) Choose one situation in which you have been acting like a chicken, and visualize how you would be thinking, feeling, and acting as an eagle. Record the desired results of your eagle attitude and actions.

Dare to Love Yourself

DARE TO LOVE YOURSELF

*Each day affirm that there is nothing in this world
that can stop you from transforming your life,
opening your heart, loving yourself, and sharing
your love with everyone you encounter.*

— Yogi Amrit Desai

Recently I presented a lecture at the Beverly Hills Hotel. To my amazement, I discovered that the recent bevy of movies about Beverly Hills is not exaggerated. Large denominations of money pass through hands there like Chinese food through an alimentary canal. Perhaps the lesson is the same in both scenarios: enjoy the flow; let it come, and let it go.

My musician partner Charley Thweatt turned our car over to the valet for parking. Charley, in the generous swim of the environs, gave the fellow a five dollar tip. Then we headed for the patio restaurant and sat down to have some breakfast. Overlooking the pleasant garden, Charley scanned the menu for inexpensive items.

"How much is a side order of bacon?" Charley asked our waiter.

"That would be five dollars, sir," answered the man.

Charley thought for a moment and then responded, "I think I'll pass."

As my friend continued to ponder over the menu, I could tell that he really wanted the bacon. "Go ahead, my man," I encouraged Charley. "Go for the bacon."

Charley's face lit up. "Yeah, sure, why not? That's what I'd really like to do." And he ordered it.

As the waiter took our menus and made his way toward the kitchen, Charley's face turned to stun. "I just realized something," he told me, almost looking through me. "I had no problem giving that valet a five dollar tip to park my car. I knew it would make him happy. But when it came to paying the same price for something I like, I was not willing to do it. That shows me how much—or little—I am loving myself. I am more willing to make someone else happy than to take care of myself. What an incredible lesson!"

Jesus taught us to "love thy neighbor as thyself." We usually take this as a reminder to be kind to other people. But what about "as thyself?" Perhaps there is yet a deeper message in Jesus' most famous teaching. He was telling us to give ourself the same love that we would give to someone we care about very much.

You might find this to be a very challenging experiment to undertake. Consider what you would do for the person you most respect and appreciate, and then ask yourself if you would do the same for yourself. Perhaps not. And here is a good starting point for a new direction in your life. Start giving yourself the love you desire.

With the One I Love

My friend Jai Josefs, composer of the popular song, *I Love Myself the Way I Am*, came to visit me in Hawaii. After spending a few rewarding days together, Jai was reflecting aloud on his visit to these resplendent islands. "You know, Alan," he shared with me, "years ago I had two dreams that I always hoped to enjoy with the one I love. I wanted to buy a home with my beloved, and I wanted to vacation in Hawaii with this one closest to my heart. Recently I bought a home, and now I am here in Hawaii, but it is not with a woman I call my beloved. But I have learned something perhaps even more important than fulfilling my vision as I had hoped. I realize that I had to really love and honor myself to buy my house and to vacation in Hawaii. If I didn't value my happiness, I probably would have found ways not to allow these beautiful experiences into my life. So in a way I have shared these important events with the one I love. But, to my surprise, the one I love is me."

Many of us are looking for our soulmate, that special person with whom we want to share our life. Some of us are in a relationship with someone we hoped would be our soulmate, but we feel disappointed that this person is not loving us as much as we would like, or feel we deserve. The most direct way to attract someone who will love us, or to get our partner to love us more, is to love ourself. We draw to us those people who mirror our attitudes about ourself. If we believe we are worthy of love, we will magnetize someone who reflects that vision. If we believe we deserve to be hurt, we will "hire" someone to bring us pain. If we do not wish to be available, we will attract someone else who is not available. And if we desire to be with someone who will nurture and care for us, we must first give ourself that honor. No one "out there" can give us more than we are willing to give ourself or receive.

Author Jerry Waters offers the ultimate test of whether you are ready for your soulmate. He asks, "Would you marry yourself?" Do you believe you are beautiful and attractive? Do you value your gifts? Are you content to spend time with yourself and find it rewarding? If you do not appreciate yourself, how do you expect someone else to honor you? You probably realize by now that it will not work to try to find someone else who will fill you in or be the things to you that you are not. God, in Her great compassion, will not let you hobble through eternity on an external crutch. To get someone else to complete you means that you are not already whole, and such a self-image is a painful lie that denies your identity as a whole being.

Certainly we may enjoy a partner, a companion, a beloved with whom we delight in dancing through life; this is one of the great gifts of living. But the key here is that we have to love ourself enough to be able to allow such a one into our world. Before you can know your soulmate, you must know your soul.

Dare to Take Time for Yourself

One of the ways we can honor the one we love—ourself— is to take the time to nurture ourself spiritually, emotionally, and physically. All too often we cram our life with so many appointments and responsibilities that we lose sight of peace. We are not fulfilling our purpose here unless inner peace is a prime element in our activity. A wise man has said that anyone who is too busy to pray, is too busy. We might also say that anyone who is too busy to take time to relax and enjoy life, is too busy.

If you are such a person, you may be guilty of "resisting a rest." Do not wait until the universe forces you to rest. A hospital is the last resort in God's curriculum. We can avoid unnecessary pain by hearkening unto the gentle voice that tells us we need to slow down and breathe with life. You can choose to relax now and avoid pain later. In other words, you can play now rather than pay later.

Recently I received an important teaching from the events in my life. I have two cars which, within a few weeks time, both had problems overheating. As I was leaning over the engine of one of the cars with my mechanic, who is on the spiritual path, he gave me a valuable insight. "You have two cars, and they're both overheating," he noted. "What do you think is the message here?"

I thought about it. I know that everything in the outer world is a reflection of the dynamics within me. Especially when the same type of problem keeps occurring, there must be a lesson the universe is trying to get my attention to learn. In the case of both cars, not enough water was getting to the engine to cool it. Through this metaphor I saw that my life was "running hot." I needed to cool it. As I considered my activities of the previous few weeks, I recognized that I was on the go almost constantly, trying to get many things done in a short time, without leaving much space for rest or relaxation. Water represents spirit. There was plenty of water available in the cars, but it was not getting to the places that needed it. Taking the symbolism one step further, I understood that I was not allowing enough spirit into my life. I was busy getting the job done at the expense of joy and aliveness. And now, through the teaching medium of my automobiles, life was letting me know it was time to cool out. Once I got the "aha!" of the overheating cars, I took the time to relax and play more, both cars were repaired, and the problem has not recurred. The universe did its job to deliver a timely message, I was open and willing to receive it, and the entire experience was a valuable one indeed.

A Gentle Reminder

A friend of mine is learning a similar lesson in taking the time to honor herself. After many years of a successful practice as a doctor, she decided it was time to nurture her spirit. She sold her practice and set out on a journey of self-discovery which has changed her life entirely. She showed me a letter she was writing to her father, an eighty-year-old retired attorney whose life has been busier than it has been peaceful. This was her message to him:

In the midst of all your ambitiousness, I offer you a gentle reminder to remember and keep in focus all the truly important things in life—quality time with those you love, quality time with yourself, doing the things that bring happiness to your heart, taking some time in nature or communing with God in whatever way satisfies you, or just "taking some time to smell the roses."

I am recovering from an addiction which is perhaps more insidious than any because it is highly sanctioned by society. That is workaholism, or as I call it, "chronic doingness." This malady doesn't have to involve work, as I discovered when I quit my job and still found myself consumed by the addiction—busy every second. I am slowly transforming, and in doing so I am beginning to feel a joy and aliveness that deepens with each passing month. I know that what I am doing may look crazy to the family, but that's OK; it feels very right for me. I am becoming happy again. I am finding peace with myself. Now I see that this is the greatest gift I could give myself and you, my dear family.

Hyacinths for Your Soul

It is a wise person who knows how to balance work and play, action and rest, gravity and humor. Both doing and being are important aspects of our expression on earth. To indulge in one at the neglect of the other creates a serious imbalance which we must learn to restore. In our culture we tend to err in the direction of overdoing and underbeing. Most people do not take the time to enjoy the ride. What is the use of reaching our destination if we miss the journey? The path is as important as the goal. Sometimes the goal as we perceive it is but a motivation for us to walk the path so we may learn the lessons along the way. Thus all of our experiences are valuable.

A Persian poet advised, "If you find yourself with but two pieces of silver, buy a loaf of bread with one, and some hyacinths for your soul with the other." Being in the presence of beauty, keeping our spirits lifted, and enjoying recreational time are just as important as getting the job done. All the accolades of the outer world are meaningless if your heart is empty. To love yourself is to give your soul the food it needs.

I met an airline flight attendant whose spirit affected me deeply. During a long flight we were talking with one another about our lives. She told me that she had been successful in her career, but she was longing for more of a home life. "I want to come home and see flowers on the table," she told me. There was something about the way she said those words that touched my heart. Here was a woman who was yearning for her spirit to be nourished. She reminded me of the part of myself that needs to be in the presence of color, creative expression, and life. If we spend our days muddled with machines, paperwork, and deadlines, we become a dull and bleary soul. Rather than more deadlines, we need more *lifelines*. We push ourselves to produce to a deadly degree. Now it is time to return to the wisdom of the heart. What is the use of accomplishing a feat of prowess for which the world applauds us, if we kill ourself in the process? Jesus asked, "What shall it profit a man if he gains the whole world, but loses his soul?"

Make Space for Joy

I have found it very helpful to schedule playtime and entertainment that nourishes my soul. I have set certain days when I am in the office, and certain days when I go out and recreate. On the office days I work hard, and on the play days I play hard. I do not play when I am working and I do not work when I am playing. Strange as it may sound, I have had to discipline myself to play! I make appointments for massages and I schedule dinners and movies with friends. I build a space for joy into my schedule, and I honor it. I am very glad I do this, for the time I give my inner child enriches my heart. When I return to work I bring a fresh creativity to my actions. I am more effective because I took the time for my soul—and I am certainly happier.

You must claim the time for renewal, or it probably will not come to you. If you do not give it to yourself, no one else will do it for you. The first step to taking healing time for yourself is to recognize that you deserve it. When you know your worth, you do the things that honor your right to be happy. Renewal is doing the things you truly enjoy—taking a walk in the woods, dancing, setting out on a weekend jaunt; the form is not as important as the feeling it leaves you with. Shift your goal from worldly achievement to inner peace, and you will wake up one morning to find that you have both.

You do not have to defend, explain, or justify your joy time to anyone else. If your program to nurture yourself brings you greater peace, it is worthwhile. "Mental health" days are just as important as physical health days, perhaps even more so. One well-deserved mental health day can prevent a need for many days of physical convalescence. When you give your soul the time it needs, you will gain so much energy and enthusiasm that everything else you do will become more successful because of it.

You cannot be effective if you are burnt out. You owe it to your clients, students, or associates to bring them a fresh spirit. But even more important, you owe it to yourself. Wouldn't it be a tragedy if you went though life and missed out on the fun? Barbara Bush, the wife of the President of the United States, told students at the Wellesley College commencement, "life is supposed to be fun." So there you have it.

Jesus explained that "man does not live by bread alone, but by every word that proceeds from the mouth of God." The word of God is anything that nourishes our spirit. Our first and foremost responsibility in life is to keep our light shining. Then we are a lamp to all the world.

Ignite Your Heart and Light the World

It is not selfish or narcissistic to love yourself. It is your first and foremost responsibility. Doing the things that make you happy will not take away from the happiness of others; it will add to it. One whose cup is brimming with happiness can overflow into the cups of others.

Airline safety instructions clearly advise that in the event of a need to use oxygen masks, parents should put their masks on before assisting their children to do so. The reasoning is clear: if the parent is not around to help the child, the child will have a far greater problem than simply waiting for the parent to put their mask on. When you care for yourself, you enhance your ability to serve others.

We live in an age in which many of us have come from dysfunctional families. We are learning to become the parents to ourselves that we did not find when we were children. If others are leaning on you for support, you must be sure that you can give them something to lean on, or else both of you will fall down. If we expect to be of any service to our children or the world, we must keep our oxygen supply flowing before attempting to offer assistance to others. The oxygen I refer to here is spirit, the quality of living that lets us breathe with who we are and what we came here to do. We must be peaceful ourself before we can offer peace to others.

Metaphysician Leonard Orr advises us, "Our responsibility is to learn to take care of ourself, and then teach others how to take care of themselves." A heart full of joy shines brightly in a darkened world and lights the spirits of those who need to look upon models of peace. To see the light you must be the light. The first step on the path of world transformation is self-appreciation. When you love yourself, all of the succeeding steps will be shown to you in the right way and time. Then all of your actions will bring true healing to yourself and everyone you meet because your life springs from a well that never runs dry.

Dare to Love Yourself

1) List three things that you would do, or have done for other people that you would not do for yourself.

2) What cherished activities are you waiting to do with someone else, or have someone else do for you, that you could do for yourself now?

3) List several areas of your life in which you may be guilty of "resisting a rest."

4) What are the hyacinths for *your* soul? List three things you could do for yourself that would uplift your spirit and keep greater beauty in your life.

5) List three things that you can schedule today that would create space for more joy in your life (Example: massage, dinner, movie, vacation):

DARE TO
BELIEVE IN YOURSELF

If you do not get it from yourself,
where will you go for it?

— The Buddha

The 1990 World Series flaunted one of the great upsets in baseball history. The bold and confident world champion Oakland A's, sporting a long string of post-season victories, were a shoe-in to trounce the underdog Cincinnati Reds. Sportswriters and fans alike were annunciating their fear that the series would be the most boring in decades. Reds fans hoped their team would win at least a game or two.

Around the time of the series, a radio story announced that Charlie Housler, a devoted Reds fan, had bet $50,000 on the Reds to *sweep the series*—to win in four games flat. The odds against him? Thirty to one.

In October, 1990, it was hard to miss the headlines. The Reds won the first two games in Cincinnati, and then had to go into the lion's lair to face the A's in their home ballpark, where the team was backed by a zealous hometown crowd. But that did not stop the Reds. In two more games they prevailed and emerged with one of the most unexpected world championships in history.

And Charlie Housler? It was reported that he emerged with 1.5 million dollars—the payoff on thirty-to-one odds against him.

I learned from the wins by the Reds and Charlie that faith in ourselves is far more powerful than popular opinion or mass thinking. Prophecies, predictions, and prognostications mean nothing in the face of intuitive guidance that tells us who we are, what we can do, and how we can win.

The odds of the world are determined by the beliefs of the world, and if you do not subscribe to them, you are not subject to them. A true winner creates his own odds by consulting a higher source and trusting his intuition.

Creative, Not Reactive

The world as it is usually depicted by the media, public institutions, and popular opinion is filled with fear, sorrow, horror and drama. But is this the real world? Is this the way we, as spiritual beings, were intended to live? It is not. We were born to be creative, not reactive. We have the freedom and responsibility to choose, not panic.

Consider the stock market, for example. The activities of this important economic institution are almost entirely reactive. One day there surfaces a rumor purporting bad news, and traders start selling. The next day an optimistic news report appears, and the Dow Jones Index goes up. Like the stock market, the events that shape many of our social institutions are dictated not by inner strength, conviction, or vision beyond circumstances. They are governed by outer events and the choices that other people make. All too often, fear is the ruler of mass consciousness.

Our greatest need now, as individuals and a planetary family, is for each of us to have the faith and willingness to turn within for guidance, and act on our inner wisdom with courage and confidence. We need to believe in ourselves more than what we read in the newspapers or what Uncle Morris tells us we should be doing with our life. We cannot afford to allow anyone or anything outside of ourself to limit us. We can try advice on for size to see if it corresponds with our heart's calling, but in the end it is our own self to which we must be true. Each of us has a destiny, and it is only when we believe in ourself that we can live it.

The God in You

There is a magnificent wisdom that guides the entire universe, and you and I are a part of it. The mind of God lives in you, and the heart of God expresses through your being. When you trust the inherent goodness of your dreams, visions, and intuitions, you give God an open door to manifest happiness and success in your life.

Recently I visited Discovery Island at Disney World in Florida.

There I observed the nesting habits of the Brush Turkey. I saw a huge mound of leaves eight feet long and six feet high, into which the female Brush Turkey burrows when she is ready to lay her eggs. While she is nesting, the male stays outside the nest and maintains a constant temperature of the mound by adding or removing leaves. Reading the guidebook at the site of the mound, I came upon a most fascinating fact: due to the male's close monitoring, the temperature of the nest *never varies more than one degree* from the optimum temperature of ninety-one degrees fahrenheit. How, I wondered, does he know how to do this? Surely the universe must bear a great intelligence that guides this creature to take care of his family.

There is perhaps an even more astounding example of the wisdom of the big picture. Monarch butterflies, the beautiful orange and black beauties that we love to behold fluttering through our gardens and forests, do not simply die off when the cold weather arrives. They migrate. At the appointed time, all the Monarch butterflies in the continental United States set off for *a particular glen* in the southwest. Now here is an astounding element of their odyssey: the butterflies that set out for the glen never reach it. But their children do. Along the way, the pregnant females give birth to their offspring and the parents die off. But the children keep flying. Somehow, without ever having been there, the young Monarchs arrive at the exact glade toward which their parents were headed! I saw a film of this area, and the sight was awesome. There were a hundred thousand magnificent Monarch butterflies fluttering about this colorful glade! Can you imagine the beauty and majesty of this sight? I was struck with a deep reverence. All of these butterflies were guided to meet at a place none of them had ever been before. Surely there is God who is wise and compassionate beyond our understanding.

Just as the destiny of the young Monarchs is guided by a plan that is bigger than can be seen in the little picture, so there is a loving and nurturing force in life which takes care of us. Moreover, that power operates *through* us. At this very moment God is pouring ideas and feelings into your mind and heart which will bring richer substance and greater joy into your life if you are willing to act on them. To receive our good, we must acknowledge that there is a Force of Blessing that loves us and wants the best for us, and we then must be willing to act on the instincts, intuitions, and opportunities this Force sends our way. God can only do for us what She can do through us.

The Key Element of Success

I make it a practice to study the lives of successful people. I want to know what is the element that makes people winners. After many years of study, the same answer keeps coming up again and again: *Believing in yourself and what you are doing is the most important rung on the ladder of success.*

I read a review of Ronald Reagan's autobiography. The reviewer noted that readers of these memoirs are likely to feel as if they are reading a fairy tale, a story that seems too perfect to be true. But, the reviewer went on to state, the amazing thing about the fairy tale is that it *is* true. Growing up in a small midwestern town, Ronald Reagan did not have much money or experience, but he had a dream to be an actor. Through hard work and persistence, he became a major movie star, went on to become a strong governor of California and ultimately a powerful President of the United States—beginning at the age of seventy-two. His marriage to Nancy Reagan is described as an ideal, eternally romantic bond, and as far we can see, it is. Nearly everything in Ronald Reagan's life seems to fit and work very nicely. "Mr. Reagan," noted the reviewer, "always comes across as sincere, and he is. He believes everything he says."

Around the same time the autobiography was published, I caught a television news program on which Barbara Walters interviewed the former president. In her confrontive style, Ms. Walters questioned Mr. Reagan on a number of issues for which he was criticized during his presidency, including the sharpest thorn in his side, the Iran Contra scandal. Suavely, deftly, and with a calm and gentlemanly demeanor, Ronald Reagan fielded each question, demonstrating total conviction that he was justified in all of his decisions.

Then I got it. It hit me like a row of flashing lights on a movie marquis: the man believes in himself. He does not doubt himself or question his motives. He decides what he believes is the right thing to do, and he goes with it a hundred percent.

This observation has nothing at all to do with the correctness of Mr. Reagan's political decisions. We can debate those if we wish, and history will ultimately reveal the value of his choices. I am not speaking in political terms now; I am elucidating the dynamics of what it takes to achieve your goals. If you believe in what you are doing, you will probably accomplish your objectives.

As I look over my own life, I notice that I have undermined myself a great deal by driving with my foot on the gas and the brake at the same time. I would get an idea to do something, and then I would doubt its worth or question my intentions. I would mull the idea over in my mind a thousand times until I had reduced the notion to a shred of its original brilliance. Then I wondered why I wasn't more powerful. I see it clearly now—I did not take the ball and run with it. I did not believe in myself a hundred percent, and therefore I created diluted results. Gradually I have learned to reverse that pattern and act on my intuitions with confidence. The difference in the results has been phenomenal.

Perhaps the example *par excellence* of Ronald Reagan's child-like exuberance in playing his role was made public toward the end of his term in office. The President was returning from a surgery for which the entire right side of his head had been shaved. As he and Mrs. Reagan were stepping down the stairs off an airplane, a photographer snapped a photo that said it all. The shot has become a classic in the annals of media pictorial essays. The photo shows Ronald Reagan removing his hat and waving to the assembled greeters. His greeting reveals half a head of his thick (dyed) black hair, and the other half nearly bald, except for a short crop of gray stubble. The President is sporting a huge smile, seeming almost proud of his quasi-punk appearance. Behind him stands Nancy Reagan with the most dreadful look of shock and embarrassment on her face. Her grimace seems to be saying, "My God, Ronald, have you lost your mind? I'm so embarrassed! Put your hat on this minute!" But Ronald is obviously having a good time.

So there we have it, all right there in the photo. A world dignitary who looks very weird, but is having a blast because he likes himself enough to go naked in public. Add to the play an outraged wife with a tremendous investment in protecting the image, and *voila* we can see the elements of our own mind that make us tick.

No matter what controversy follows Ronald Reagan through the hallways of history, he and others like him impart a lesson well worth learning: If you believe in what you are doing, you will probably succeed.

The Success Principle Can Be Used by Anyone

The universe does not restrict the principle of success to any particular kind of person, act, or purpose. You can succeed at anything you choose. Success, like mathematics, operates on a principle, and anyone can apply the principle to any purpose. The power of focused confidence can achieve any goal, no matter whether we judge it to be good or bad. Electricity can be used to light up a city or electrocute someone. God has given us the power to create by belief, and our element of free will determines the end toward which we will apply it. Hitler believed in himself, and in the process he amassed a great deal of power. The same power that he mobilized for warfare and destruction can be used by us now to bring about healing and constructive social change. God's gifts are given freely to anyone who wishes to tap into cosmic principles. Our role is to discover the law of success, which is based upon belief in ourself and our purpose, and live it.

"Hot and Cold"

If you don't believe in yourself, you will find yourself doing things that contradict your purpose. Don't ever take a job selling something you wouldn't buy yourself. If you don't believe in your product, you don't stand a chance of bringing satisfaction to your customers or yourself. Customers don't listen to your words; they read your aura. Even thick-headed people can sense a sham. If you are selling something you don't believe in, you may be able to fool a number of people (who are willing to be fooled) but in the long run you will have fooled no one but yourself. You will not be successful and you may not be able to sleep at night. You will wonder why your life isn't working, and feel like you are living a lie. And you are. When you deny your sense of conviction about what you are doing, you have a hole in your bucket and you will not feel filled.

If you are in such a situation now, or ever have been, don't despair. Your discomfort is actually a gift from God. The universe is reminding you that there is something you believe in more than what you are currently doing, and it is steering you to your right place. Like the children's game of "Hot and Cold," your higher self is giving you clues toward the prize that awaits you when you remember your worth. There is something that you believe in, and that is the direction in which you need to move to find real happiness. In contrast to the sense of struggle that you experience when you deny your gifts, you will be amazed at how effortlessly and joyfully success comes to you when you step toward your heart's chosen field. We never have to deny our self in order to win.

Your Way

Each of us has a personal path we must follow. This is the road to our success and satisfaction in life. It is only to the extent that we find the courage to walk our own path that we will be truly effective and at peace with our purpose.

Ricky Nelson had a hit song entitled, *Garden Party*. The song arose from a painful experience Ricky had when he attempted to stage a comeback after many years of being out of the limelight. Ricky publicized his appearance at New York City's Madison Square Garden as a gala comeback, during which he attempted to resurrect a number of songs that made him popular in the sixties. To Ricky's dismay, his performance was very poorly received. The critics panned him and he felt like a failure.

Ricky Nelson's pain moved him to write a new song which

was a true expression of where he was at his present stage of life. Unlike his performance which flopped, this song was about the real and current Ricky Nelson, and it became a hit. The lyrics went,

It's all right now, I learned my lesson well.
You can't please everybody; you've got to please yourself.

My friend Eleanor learned her lesson well when she set out to fulfill a bold mission to become a minister. Although she arose from an unglamorous alcoholic past, Eleanor had a dream and she wanted to achieve it. After her first year of training in the ministry, Eleanor received an evaluation from the ministerial licensing committee. The evaluators told Eleanor that her grasp of spiritual concepts was good, but she needed to get rid of her thick New York accent. The committee advised her that she needed to be able to speak in a way that was more familiar to most people.

Eleanor wrestled with the directions she was given. She liked the way she spoke; she was comfortable with her style and she saw no reason to change it. "That's just the way I talk," Ellie told me. "It's who I am. I don't feel I should try to change it just because they want me to." Eleanor felt that she best expressed herself in that manner, and if other people didn't approve of it, that was their problem, not hers.

The following year I laughed when I received a letter from Eleanor in which she commended herself for not renouncing her accent for the committee. As if it was a confirmation from the universe, Eleanor's classmates selected her to deliver the commencement address. She, they felt, was the most inspiring speaker in the group.

Author William Faulkner was criticized for writing very long sentences in his books. Some of these lengthy grammatical mazes, I am told, were four pages long! Upon receiving disapproval for his unorthodox and unwieldy grammar, Faulkner recommended that his publisher print a page of periods at the end of his next book. Readers who wanted shorter sentences, Faulkner suggested, could take the periods and place them wherever they liked. Faulkner won the Pulitzer Prize for literature.

I, too, encountered a challenge which forced me to look into my beliefs about myself and decide who I am living to please. A few years ago I waxed creative with the publication of one of my newsletters. To provoke some fun and thought, I printed my return address as "Immaculate Cohenceptions." I really enjoyed the idea, and I looked forward to my readers getting a laugh out of the concept and hopefully finding some inspiration in the affiliation of Judaism and Christianity, two religious lineages that are rarely joined.

When the newsletter came out I received a few letters from indignant readers who were upset by my play on words. These readers felt that I was dishonoring the Immaculate Conception. Some of them were angry and asked that their names be removed from my mailing list. I even received a letter from a nun who told me that the sisters in her convent were offended.

I answered these letters lovingly and politely, assuring my readers that I certainly respected the Immaculate Conception and I meant no insult to the Catholic Church or Jesus. (After all, he is one of my relatives; I figured that if he did not like what I had done, he would contact me personally.) I told my readers that I believed that God has a sense of humor, and we are judged by our intentions. Since my intentions were entirely loving, I did not feel that I had offended God.

Still, I began to wrestle with this feedback. Part of my mind believed that I was supposed to make everyone happy all of the time, and if someone didn't like me or what I did, then I was doing something wrong and I needed to win their approval. This, of course, was a very naive attitude. It is impossible to get everyone to like you or everything you do.

At one of my workshops I voiced this issue I was struggling with, and I asked the people in the group for their ideas and feelings about it. Several people offered me some valuable feedback. One person asked me, "How many newsletters did you send out?" "Seven thousand," I told him. "How many complaints did you get?" was the next question. "Three," I answered. The group laughed. "I think you're doing pretty well!" several people noted.

Then one fellow gave me invaluable advice. "You know, Alan," Scott began, "one of the things I love most about you is your sense of humor, your unorthodox nature, and your willingness to be yourself. If you are concerned about people being offended by what you do, then I must tell you that I would be offended if you stopped sharing your humor. You will be hurting a lot more than three people if you cut yourself off because your are afraid of criticism from a few people."

Scott's words really hit home. I realized that I could never please everyone, so I stood my best chance by striving to please myself and the God within me. I saw that it is futile to struggle to uphold the opinions of others. It is my own opinion that I need to live with.

Crucifixion and Redemption

When we are following our path, we are bound to rub some people the wrong way. Criticism and rejection are a healthy sign that you are doing something real and alive. If no one is upset with what you are doing, you are probably not expressing yourself fully. Albert Einstein noted that "great spirits have always encountered violent resistance from mediocre minds." If you are not bumping up against some kind of reaction, reconsider your self-expression and find something to do that will bother someone. Then you will really be on your way!

If you would like a suggestion on how to start bothering people with your greatness, I would advise you to just start telling the truth more. The truth is the most threatening dynamic you could introduce into a world of guarded illusions. Many of our family interactions, careers, and politics have been founded on protecting lies and keeping things appearing to be a way other than they are. Most people on the planet have a huge investment in keeping lies of some kind going, and anyone who jabs a hole in the wall of the castle of pretense makes the fortress of fear vulnerable. If you have been in a dysfunctional family, for example, you know that protecting the sickness was more important than bringing fear to the light. The truth scares the hell out of a dysfunctional relationship or family, and the first one to tell it is usually ostracized. But that's not a bad thing at all when you consider that the alternative to telling the truth is to be alienated from yourself. So you may get crucified temporarily, but you may also get healed permanently.

Consider Jesus, for example. He brought a message of loving kindness and forgiveness, and these values were so threatening to the society in which he taught, that he was crucified. Crucifixion of some kind is an initiation on the path of greatness. No one escapes this world without being crucified in some way at some time. But it, too, is not a bad thing. Crucifixion teaches you that the real you cannot be crucified. Just keep in mind that when the storm passed, Jesus rose. Moreover, his good work continues to bless the world even unto this day. And so will yours.

The Most Powerful Gift

You are almost sure to rub some people the wrong way when you make a stand for who you are. But that's not a good enough reason to stop—it's all the more reason to continue. As much as people want to hide in the darkness, there is a place in their heart that wants to live in the light. If you confront people with your honest self, they may grumble and protest to your face, but they will go home and think about it. Your seeds of sincerity will find a patch of fertile soil in a barren heart, and given even a little sunlight and moisture, will sprout and grow. Do not be fooled by appearances. Behind our culture's obsession with fear and hiding, there is a massive call for authentic self-expression. The most powerful gift of redemption you can offer a world that is sick with deception is to live in the dignity of your truth.

When you believe in yourself, you bring a dynamic presence to all of your activities that seeds great inspiration and healing in the hearts of all who look upon you. Whether people acknowledge you, ignore you, or crucify you, you will make a contribution to their lives that will ruminate far beyond the time you and they walk here. Never underestimate the power that you release on this planet when you choose to walk the way appointed by your guiding spirit. If you follow your heart, you will never fail and you will never be sorry. Your heart is the voice through which God speaks to you of your worth and your strength. To believe in the goodness of your visions is to keep the channel open. Each day practice trusting your goodness more. Deny any voices that tell you that you can't, you don't deserve, or you won't. You can, you do deserve, and you will. Prove by your life that God is real and lives through you. Change the world with your acts of confidence. Make liars out of fear and doubt. Demonstrate that love is the most powerful force in the universe as it finds expression through your belief in your life and yourself.

Dare to Believe in Yourself

1) What are you doing now that you don't fully believe in?

2) What do you believe in more, that you would rather be doing?

3) What is the greater truth that you need to tell about what you want to do? To whom would you tell it? Write a letter to the person(s) to whom you need to express your greater truth. (You may or may not send it.)

4) Have you, or do you, make a stand for your truth when you may be criticized or rejected because of it? If not, what do you fear?

5) Read the biography of a great person you admire who had to believe in him/herself to acheive his/her goals.

DARE TO
RESPECT YOURSELF

A young woman sheepishly approached me after a workshop. "I just don't know what to do about my husband," Gerri confided in me. "He has been drinking steadily; sometimes he hits me and he is very nasty to our little daughter. I've tried being patient with him, we've gone to counseling, and nothing seems to work. What else can I do?"

"Why don't you tell him that you'll leave if he continues?" I asked.

"I've thought about that, but I would feel too guilty."

I leveled with her. "Gerri, this is a big lesson in self-respect for you. You don't deserve to be abused emotionally or physically. In your heart, do you really believe that this is the way a relationship is meant to be?"

"No, my heart tells me it's not right. But our pattern has become so entrenched that I don't seem to be able to get out of it."

"Know your own worth," I told her. "Respect yourself enough to refuse to put up with abuse. Don't settle for less than the honor you deserve."

A peace came over Gerri's face. She thanked me profusely. "That was exactly what I needed to hear," she told me. "For a long time I have felt that leaving or threatening to leave was a cowardly thing to do. But now, after talking to you, I can see that it may be the only way to create the kind of change I am seeking. If it came to that, I think I could live with myself now."

I did not see Gerri until a year later, when she showed up at one of my workshops. She looked radiant. "Our marriage is like new," she happily told me. "I told Tim that neither I nor our daughter deserved to be treated like we were. I told him that I would leave unless he changed. There was something about the conviction in my voice that made him realize I wasn't kidding. He started going to Alcoholics Anonymous, he has stopped drinking, and he is becoming a new person. I am certainly glad that I found the self-respect to refuse to continue in a situation that was hurting me." Then Gerri introduced me to Tim and their new baby. They all looked very happy.

Gerri's turning point came when she shifted her focus from the problem as her husband's alcoholism, and began to see the dilemma as a critical lesson in self-respect. Somewhere inside herself Gerri recognized that she neither needed nor deserved to live in such an abusive relationship. The entire process, she later explained to me, was a major life lesson in learning to love and honor herself more fully.

The Choice for Self-Respect

Statistics show that 80% of women who are beaten by their husbands or boyfriends subsequently choose partners who also beat them. If you are a woman or man who has had a life script similar to this, it is time for you to look at how much—or how little—you are loving yourself. No one deserves to live in hell on earth. Earth was given as a heaven, but we have not believed we are worthy of paradise. So we have made hell by our thoughts that our nature is evil. But our nature is good. We are born of God, and nothing less suits us. No one needs to go through life in a state of disrespect. Make a choice to love yourself more, and God will support you in living in accord with your choice.

No one needs to put up with abuse of any kind. The only reason we accept dishonor is that on some level we do not believe we are worthy of something better. We "hire" other people to play out our life scripts with us, until or unless we change the movie. Every doormat says "Welcome." If you have been walked on repetitiously, there is a part of your mind that is accepting it. *The most direct way to stop someone from hurting you is to remove their permission from your own mind.* No one can hurt you unless you are willing to accept pain. Realize the truth in this principle. I am not just explaining psychology here; I am giving you the key to your release. Use it and be free.

There is no law or power in the universe that requires you to violate yourself. God does not ask you to sacrifice your well-being for that of another. Be vigilant against thoughts and feelings that tell you that you can buy good for another at the expense of your own. Someone else cannot truly gain if in the process you are losing. We live in a win-win universe, and we must rid our mind of the notion of self-effacement as a prerequisite for healing. The temple of healing is reached through the corridor of peace. Guilt and fear cannot buy love. Only love begets more of itself.

If you choose to do something for someone out of a true desire to make them happy and your actions stem from an attitude of loving service, you will enjoy a feeling of deep satisfaction and inner reward. You will not feel that you have lost, but gained. If, on the other hand, you come away from giving your "gift" with a sense of deprivation, loss, or resentment, you have "given" from a pool of fear. You are laboring under an old belief system that the reward of pain is peace. In such a case you would do better to give nothing than to give with a feeling of self-deprivation. Let the spirit of joy be your guide.

Integrity Over Fear

Frank was a salesman who travelled to a large city for several days of meetings to nail down a big contract. One evening while he was staying in a hotel with executives from both companies involved in the deal, the client company's manager invited him to go out with some of the "boys" to a striptease show. Immediately Frank began to feel very uncomfortable. A strip joint was not a place he would choose to be. The idea of sitting in a smokey nightclub with a lot of men drinking and watching naked women was not appealing to him. Yet he knew that spending time with the client could potentially further the sale he wanted badly to close. You can imagine the difficulty of the decision Frank had to make.

After weighing all of these thoughts and feelings in his mind and heart, Frank realized that this was not an issue of finances, but integrity. He had been considering the principle that we are not required to violate our integrity in order to be supported by the universe. Now here was a challenge for him to practice it. Frank decided that getting this account was not worth selling himself out. He did not believe that Spirit would require him to be in such a distasteful situation in order to be successful. Frank politely told the client, "No thank you, that is not something I would enjoy doing. I think I'll just relax in the hotel tonight."

After the client left, Frank lay back on the bed and wondered if he had made the right decision. He had a family to take care of, mounting bills, and here he may have thrown away one of the biggest commissions of the year. "Am I fool?" he wondered.

About 11 p.m. there was a knock on Frank's door. Wondering who could be calling on him at that hour, he got up to answer it. His visitor was the executive he had turned down for the evening's entertainment. "May I have a word with you?" the man asked.

"Sure, come on in."

The client sat down on the edge of the bed and looked Frank in the eye. "I just want to thank you for following your principles," the manager told him. Frank was stunned. The man went on. "The fact of the matter is that I did not really want to go to that show, either. But all of the guys were going, and I did not want to be a party pooper. So I went, and the whole scene was pretty gross. I sat there for about an hour, feeling more and more disgusted with the atmosphere and the conversation. That was about all I could take. I excused myself and came back here. I saw the light on in your room, and I just wanted to tell you that I admired you for doing what you had to do. That's what I wanted to do, too, and you gave me some encouragement to listen to my own intuition."

The men began to talk, and they became friends. The contract was signed the next day. But even more important, Frank learned one of the greatest lessons of his career: *You don't have to deny who you are in order to get what you want. When you respect yourself, the universe lines up in your favor.*

The Respect You Need is Your Own

Some of us have spent many years of our lives trying to get other people to respect us more. We may even have built a strong case for ourself as a victim of the abusiveness of others. (Look at Rodney Dangerfield—he's made millions of dollars complaining that he doesn't get any respect!) And yet all the striving, aching, and complaining seems only to leave us more frustrated than when we began.

At some point we start to wonder if there must be another way. And there is. The key to the healing of abuse of any kind lies in this one awareness: *It is not the respect of others that you have sought and needed—it is your own.* You cannot attract people, events, or situations that are respectful to you unless you first respect yourself. Until you respect yourself, you will create people and experiences that misuse you, abuse you, cheat you, and hide the truth from you. This will happen only because you have hidden the most important truth from your awareness: *You are respectable and you deserve love.*

When you love yourself, you do not need others to validate your worth. You know that you are important whether or not anyone else agrees with you. Your self-esteem is not founded on the approval of others; it comes from inside you. Even if no one else is applauding you at a given moment, you applaud yourself. You recognize your unique gifts and know that you have something valuable to offer the world. There is no question in your mind that you deserve to be here and that you deserve all the good you desire. You remember that you are a spiritual being, and you have an infinite Source of blessing and supply. You walk, act, and love with the dignity of one who merits the gifts of God. At that point, respect is no longer an issue. You live in world of constant respect for your Creator, and you know that your Source beholds you through the same adoring eyes.

Dare to Respect Yourself

1) In what situations in your life do you feel disrespected?

2) Do you see any repetitious patterns of abuse or disrespect for you?

3) How do you give permission for those situations to happen or continue?

4) In what ways do these situations reflect ways in which you are not respecting yourself?

5) What is your vision of how you would like to be respected more in relationships, career, and other important aspects of your life?

6) What can you say or do to transform these situations or patterns to honor yourself more?

DARE TO TRUST

Trust would settle every problem now.
— A Course in Miracles

Comedian Jimmy Durante had a weekly television show which I watched as a child. Jimmy was famous for his closing musical number, which he sang as he walked offstage. He began the song in the beam of a lone spotlight. As Jimmy finished the first verse of the song, the spotlight that was shining on him went out and another small spotlighted circle appeared a few feet before him on the otherwise darkened stage. Jimmy stepped onto that circle of light, sang the next verse, and as soon as he finished the stanza, that spotlight went out. But then another light appeared a few feet ahead of him. Step by step, Jimmy Durante followed the trail of light, each ray shining only as long as he needed to stand on it and sing his tune.

The spiritual path is very much like Jimmy Durante's journey. Often we feel as if we are in the dark, not quite sure which direction to take to our goal. Sometimes we are not even clear about what our goal is. Then, just at the moment we need it, our next step is illuminated. We step onto our next square in the game of life, sing our next verse, and the current spotlight is withdrawn. But then another one somehow appears. So we find our way home, one light and one step at a time, receiving exactly what we need just as we need it.

Infinite Patience, Immediate Results

If we expect or demand to be shown all the steps at once, we are likely to become frustrated and confused. It is rare that any of us can see much more than one or two steps ahead of us. Ram Dass explains that we move ahead in life "one body length at a time." We take a step, fall on our face, and then pick ourself up to continue on our way. But this time we begin from where our head came to rest. *A Course in Miracles* reminds us that "only infinite patience begets immediate results."

We must be humble enough to admit that we do not see very far down the road, and confident enough to acknowledge that there is One within us who does see the right direction for us. If we are willing to trust the Divine Lighting Technician to show us our way, one step at a time, we are apt to appreciate our journey more and enjoy the adventure of following the path set before us—one light at a time.

Problems Solved When You Face Them

Sometimes we cannot see the next step at all, and we find ourself up against a seemingly insurmountable obstacle. As the Israelites fled from tyranny in ancient Egypt, they found themselves up against the Red Sea, with Pharaoh's army behind them in hot pursuit. Many of the Jewish people were tempted by fear and tried to rally the others to turn back. Slavery, they argued, was better than death. But there were those among them who felt that there would somehow be a way to move ahead. Talmudic scholars tell us that some of the Israelites were in the water up to their necks before the sea parted. (A fitting analogy for those times when we feel we are up to our neck and about to drown unless a miracle happens!) The rest, as they say, is history. Somehow the waters dispersed and the way was cleared for the Israelites to go ahead to a new life. (There is a debate as to whether the sea parted down the middle, as portrayed by Cecil B. De Mille, or whether the Israelites showed up at low tide. Personally, I don't think it matters. Being in the right place at the right time is just as much a miracle.) The Jewish nation did not need to give in and return to the old and painful way. They had a right to freedom, and so do we.

We might also consider a more modern metaphor. You have most likely walked through an electronic doorway at your local supermarket. The sliding glass door is controlled by an electric eye which senses your approach and signals the door to open as you reach it. When you are at a distance, the door is closed fast. Observation would show that there is no knob, handle, or means by which you could open the door manually, even if you tried with all your might. But then an amazing thing happens. As you approach the door, just as it seems you will bump into it, it opens for you—without the least effort on your part. All you have to do is keep walking and don't stop. If you stop even a few feet before the door, it will remain shut tight. But step right up to it, and the barrier disappears.

The doors of life that seem closed to us remain shut until we approach them. There is something about facing a problem that reveals the next step toward solving it. (It is said that the first step to solving a problem is to tell someone about it.) Difficulties cannot be overcome from a distance, and healing is not accomplished by brute force. Challenges are met right up close and in the light.

Just as you cannot open the supermarket door with your bare hands, your problems cannot be solved at the same level of consciousness at which you perceive them. *The answer is always on a higher level than the problem.* That is why the problem exists in the first place—to draw you to a higher awareness. If you approach the difficulty from the same level at which you have been struggling, you will find yourself going in circles. If you are in such a dilemma, you must stop and ask, "What is the higher way of looking at this? What will love show me that fear has disallowed? What is the blessing in this?" Your answer will follow on the trail of one of these questions.

Problems are not punishments; they are invitations to a higher way of thinking. The solution to the closed supermarket door is electronic, not physical. The solution to life's challenges is spiritual, not material. Remember that we are *spiritual* beings. Our purpose here is to identify with our divine nature. Everything in the physical world exists in the service of this noble quest.

The Bridge Over the Abyss

Let us consider one more example of the power of trust. In the Indiana Jones movie, *The Quest for the Holy Grail*, Indy finds himself standing at the precipice of a bottomless chasm. On the other side of the abyss stands the sacred temple in which the cup of Christ awaits him. Indy has searched the entire world for the Holy Grail, defied all kinds of rats, skeletons, and villains, nearly lost his father, and risked death many times to come to this point. Now he is so close, and yet so far. Standing alone, looking down into this endless gorge, he remembers the instruction that was foretold to help him when he reached this point in his journey: *Faith*. Indy takes a deep breath and steps out over the chasm. He sees nothing to stand on, but he decides to follow the advice to trust. As soon as he leans out over the abyss, a bridge appears and he finds himself fully supported on a solid mass. The entire chasm, which seemed quite impassible to mortal eyes, was but a test of faith. The bridge was there all along, but it could only be seen by those who stepped onto it. Faith is the vision of things unseen. Only those who see the invisible can do the impossible. Jesus instructed, "Blessed are those who see and believe, and even more blessed are those who have not seen and yet believe."

Your Destiny Will Find You

At a workshop I presented in San Diego, I asked the participants how they had found out about the event. A woman raised her hand and told this story:

"I had been reading your book and feeling my life change with each chapter. I felt deeply attuned to you and your visions, and I wanted very much to meet you and attend one of your programs. But I had no idea how to get in touch with you. Then one day last week I was driving on the freeway and I heard these words in my mind: "Christ Church Unity." I had no idea what these words meant. When I got home I looked in the telephone book and there, sure enough, was a listing for Christ Church Unity in San Diego. I called the number and asked what this church was about. The receptionist gave me a brief overview of the church's philosophy, and asked me about myself. I told her that I had just been profoundly influenced by Alan Cohen's book. 'Oh,' she interrupted me, 'he's going to be presenting a workshop here next week!' So here I am. I have no idea how that voice came to me, but I believe that I have a purpose here, and I have certainly been guided to fulfill it.''

Stories like this, amazing as this one sounds, are not unusual for me to hear. I often come upon similar accounts of people who are connected with their destiny in extraordinary ways. One fellow was walking out of a restaurant when the wind blew a piece of paper to lodge against his leg. He picked it up and read it, to find that it was an announcement of a retreat that I was about to conduct in his area. Although this man knew nothing about me, my writing, or my teachings, something inside him told him to come. Ultimately, the retreat changed his life.

I have received numerous letters from people who tell me that my book literally fell off a bookstore shelf into their hands or at their feet. One man wrote that he had sworn he would never buy another book. Then one of my books dropped off a shelf before him. He picked it up, looked through some of the pages, and found inspiration to deal with some of the challenges with which he had been struggling.

Other people report that they are attracted to one of my books or workshops as a result of seeing my photo. They describe enjoying a welcoming and peaceful feeling that draws them to me and my work. Once a blind man attended my class because as he passed his hand over my photo in a conference brochure, he felt a pleasant warmth.

I do not claim that my photo or books have any magical or supernatural powers. Neither am I asserting that I am unusual; these kinds of wonderfully synchronistic events occur for many students and teachers on many paths. I am affirming that there are some super natural powers that guide us to our destiny. Spirit will use any and all means to get through to us to bring us our good. If we are sensitive and willing to listen to the subtle thoughts that inspire us (like the woman driving on the freeway in San Diego), we will respond to God's whisper and follow our inner promptings. If we need a little more tangible communication to get our attention, we might have a flyer blow up against our leg, a book fall off a shelf at our feet, or a friend invite us to a seminar. If we are really dense and God is having a hard time getting our attention, we might carry our self-destructive patterns to a painful jolt in our life. A dramatic experience may be required to wake us up to the fact that we have been living in a way that is inconsistent with our heart's desire. Used wisely, such a jolt will teach us to choose a new and more satisfying way. No matter at what level we hear the message, one principle is certain: *There is a force of love that is always working in our best interest to guide our way home.*

Reverse Paranoia

Many people in this world are somewhat paranoid, afraid that the world is out to get them. Actually, the world *is* out to get us, but not in the way we believe. There is a conspiracy (conspiracy means "to breathe together") working behind the scenes of our life. But this conspiracy is not to hurt us; it is one of great love. God is out to do everything She can to make us happy. This conspiracy is always working, even in spite of our insane efforts to deny love's presence. Amazing as it might sound, we have unknowingly been involved in a counter-conspiracy to love. Many of us have been actively engaged in doing everything we can to avoid peace, shield healing from our hearts, and convince ourselves that hell is heaven. We are expert at finding fault with our gifts, sabotaging our success, and seeing the empty tenth of the glass instead of the nine parts that are full. But there is hope. The outcome is guaranteed: the conspiracy to love will succeed, basically because God is playing on that team (and He wrote the plot). Although the timing of our surrender to love is up to us, the final scene is certain: we will realize that the universe is a manifestation of love, and we are in God's graceful keeping.

Dare to Trust Yourself

The essential requirement for all spiritual advancement is trust. Because the universe is created by a loving God, everything in it that God created is good. Our task as students on the path of awakening is not to try to *make* things good, but to find, acknowledge, and celebrate the good that already exists. The path to healing begins with the choice to see benevolence.

One morning I was casting a banana peel into a compost bucket. As I removed the lid of the basket, my nose was assaulted by the unpleasant odor of decomposing food. "How disgusting!" I thought as I recoiled and quickly replaced the lid. Then it occurred to me that it is really helpful that rotten food smells repulsive. If it weren't, we might mistake garbage for good food, eat it, get sick, and perhaps die. The great wisdom of the universe has built this safeguard into the system of our well-being: what is not good for us is repulsive to our senses and our nature.

Taking this important principle one step further, we bear within our heart an innate recognition of the kinds of relationships, work, and living situations that nourish us, and those which will hurt us. The spirit within us is always telling us what will bring us happiness and what will bring us pain. Our responsibility is to listen and act. Otherwise we will be eating garbage, physically and spiritually—and that is certainly not in God's plan for our well-being.

I have heard the accounts of scores of women who have remained in abusive relationships while their alcoholic husbands beat them regularly. I have spoken with many men who have worked themselves to oblivion under the subconscious whip of neurotic competition. And I have borne witness to the agonized confessions of Vietnam soldiers who engaged in heinous acts of murder and torture, while working feverishly to deny, drown out, or escape from the voice within them that kept telling them that there was no reason for this.

There is no reason for any of us to stay in a situation that is repulsive or damaging to us. Perhaps in our sense of guilt or unworthiness we believe that we must endure a painful predicament because we are not worthy of better, or because we are paying off some old karma or sins. We must cast such thoughts from our mind without hesitation and reclaim our right to be happy and treat ourself and others with dignity and respect.

I reiterate that no one deserves to be abused. The first time you are abused, it is the other person's fault; the second time it is your own. You have a responsibility to listen to the still small voice within you that prompts, "This is not right. I must do something to change this." At such a time, remember that being repulsed by something that is potentially harmful is a very helpful experience. It gives you the motivation to remove yourself from pain and be at peace in your right place elsewhere. In such a case you are not running away. You are coming home.

There is a good purpose and a right place for garbage. If you keep it around you, you will get sick and think that the whole world is a toilet. But take the manure of your experience, put it out in a field, turn it into the soil, and you have a nicely fertilized plot. Then one day some beautiful flowers and food will grow to nourish you in a very healthy way. It's all good—you just have to know where everything belongs.

Dare to Be Patient

Sometimes we are faced with a problem that we can't seem to do anything about. We feel stuck and do not see which direction to turn. All angles seem to be darkened or blocked. This is a very good time to do nothing. Do not act out of fear or panic. Do not do something just because you think you have to do something. The Buddha advised, "Don't just do something—stand there."

Such a moment calls for patience and trust. Just because you don't see the answer from where you are standing does not mean that there is no answer. It just means that you do not see it. There is always an answer, and it will come. Relax. Ask for guidance. Pray. Turn the problem over to God. Use the time to do something that you feel more clear about. The answer will appear in its own right way and timing. If you have prayed and invited Spirit's help, you can release it and let the universe handle the details.

Galen Rowell is a world-famous mountain climber and photographer. His stunning nature photos have appeared in some of the most prominent magazines of our time, including a cover story for *National Geographic*. In scaling high peaks, Galen has learned a lot about faith and courage.

Once while Galen and a friend were making an ascent up the sheer face of Half Dome in Yosemite National Park, an unexpected storm blew up. The two climbers were a thousand feet high when the rain and fog became so thick that they could neither go up nor down. The face was too slippery, and the men could barely see in front of them. The visibility and weather conditions were so poor that rescue helicopters were unable to get off the ground. So what did the two fellows do? They just hung out. There they were in their mummy bags dangling over a thousand foot abyss—for *three days*. Can you imagine what might have gone through their minds? But there was nothing else to do. So they just hung out. When the storm finally cleared, they climbed down easily.

When we feel stuck, we might do well to remember the patience that was required of these climbers. Sometimes there is just no moving forward or back, and in such a case we might as well relax. If we flail and panic and follow the voice of fear, we only thicken the mire. In such a situation we need to breathe and remember peace. The storm over Yosemite passed, and so will the storms that keep us from moving ahead as quickly as we would like. Challenges that immobilize us bring us rich opportunities to delve into ourself and find the source of our strength within. Remember the inscription on a ring worn by King Solomon, a motto which helped him through trying times: "This, too, shall pass." We can bless challenges as opportunities to choose peace. The purpose of our life is to dismantle illusions and find love and safety where we once saw fear and danger. Although these situations seem difficult in the moment, used wisely they truly bring us closer to fulfilling our life's purpose.

All is Well

A Course in Miracles tells us that every encounter, relationship, and experience is helpful. The understanding of this truth is the critical shift in awareness that transforms a threatening world into a wealth of endless opportunities for healing. It is very useful to proceed from the assumption that love is present in every aspect of our life, even when we are not aware of it. This attitude recreates everyone and everything we encounter, and reforms our consciousness to receive blessings where we once saw only adversity. Trust is the bedrock of the belief system of one who truly seeks peace. Fear has no value in God's Kingdom, and a sense of safety—especially when appearances indicate otherwise—is a sign of advanced spiritual evolution.

We must believe that God is guiding us from within and without. We must have faith in our inclinations, our intuitions, and the magnetism of the heart that draws us in one direction and away from another. It is only our mind that keeps us from trusting. Jesus spoke of the lilies of the field, which are here one day and gone the next, and in the meantime are arrayed in splendor. How much more, as Jesus invited us to consider, are we cared for and blessed? Lift up your eyes to see the great good that God has poured to you throughout your life. Your life is no accident. You are here by your choice and God's, and the universe has a big investment in your well-being and mine. We need but to cooperate and let love take care of us.

Dare to Trust

1) In what areas or situations could you be more patient? When you are feeling impatient, what is it that you are not trusting?

2) Consider a problem that has bothered you for a while. How have you been avoiding facing it? What step could you take to face it?

3) Describe an experience which demonstrated to you that you were being guided and cared for, even though you didn't realize it at the time.

4) Describe an experience that seemed to be a curse at the time, but turned out to be a blessing.

5) What do you customarily do when you feel stuck? Are you able to relax and refrain from acting until you see a clear path?

DARE TO
ASK FOR WHAT YOU WANT

*It's a funny thing about life—those who are willing
to settle for less than the best usually get it.*
— W. Somerset Maugham

"Could I please have a word with you?" The voice accompanied a hand on my shoulder. Standing in the dining room at a weekend retreat, I was in the midst of a conversation with another participant. "Perhaps we could get together when I complete my talk with Jim," I suggested.

But he didn't listen. He wanted my attention, and he just kept on talking. "I need help making a decision," Chad explained. "My girlfriend wants me to do one thing; my kids have another idea of how I should be with them; my ex-wife is making demands on me; and my boss is asking me to do a special project that I'm not sure is right for me. I just don't know who to try and please."

"What about *yourself?*"

Chad was stunned. "Say what?"

"What would *you* like to do? You've told me what everyone else in your life would like you to do to make them happy. What would make you happy?"

Chad stood there in awe for a minute. "I don't know—I never thought about that!"

"Well, here's your chance."

Chad walked away slightly dazed, as if I had just revealed to him the location of the treasure of the Sierra Madre. I went back to my conversation with Jim.

The next morning at the final session of the retreat, I invited participants to come forth and share what they had received from the workshop. Chad dashed up onto the stage.

"Alan Cohen healed me last night!" he exclaimed.

"What is he talking about?" I wondered. My memory of our conversation was dim. Let's hear what he has to say, I thought.

"Last night Alan asked me the most important question anyone has ever asked me: *'What do I want to do?'* As I began to think about it, I saw that my quandary arose from my trying to please everyone else in my life. As I considered my frustration, I realized that I could never please everyone unless I took care of myself in the process. I have become such a people pleaser that I have lost touch with my own dreams. Now here's the miracle: as I began to focus on what I truly wanted, I discovered a solution that could work for everyone!"

Sweating, Settling, and Succeeding

Life is set up to be a win/win game. If you are sweating to get everyone around you to win, but you are not, then you are settling for less than you deserve. At such a point you must stop, see what it would take for you to feel rewarded, and ask for it. Others cannot truly win if you are not winning along with them.

Human relations are like sex. Giving and receiving are both sides of the same coin. If you are doing only one and not the other, you have a counterfeit relationship. Most of us know how unfulfilling sex can be when one person is enjoying her- or himself, but the other partner is not. Why, then, would we participate in a relationship, a career, or a life in which all parties are not finding satisfaction in their path? The game is set up so you can make yourself happy and bring others blessings at the same time. Do not stop your quest for fulfillment until you feel rewarded along with those around you.

The Fridge's Question

I met an author who knew that he had a right to be happy. Someone had asked him if there was one event in his life that he would have changed if he could. He answered, "I would go back to the age of seventeen, where I would be sitting in my high school locker room. There 'the Fridge' (a 300-pound football player) would come up to me, lift me up by the collar, and shove me against the locker. Then the Fridge would look me right in the eye and demand of me, 'Either you tell me exactly what you want in your life, or I'll bite your head off!' " The author went on to explain, "You see, it took me until the age of forty-seven to learn to ask for what I wanted. I wish I had known how to do that at seventeen—but now, look out!"

Your Right to be Healed

Sometimes we need to stand up and declare what we want in a bold way. The universe does not need you to tell it what you need, but you need to believe in yourself enough to ask for it with conviction.

I discovered the power of claiming our right to be healed when I was facilitating a session at a workshop. I had worked intensively with several people and I was feeling it was time for a break. I announced to the group that we would take a short breather.

"No!" A shriek pierced the group from the back of the room. "I won't let you!" Everyone was startled, and all heads turned in the direction of the outcry. A woman who had been lying down in the back of the room was sitting up, her face contorted and tears rolling down her cheeks.

"I need the group's help," she told us through her tears. "I've been sitting here wrestling with the most painful issue of my life, and I refuse to let you go on without giving me some attention. I need help too much to wait any longer."

A cry like that can hardly be ignored. Of course we had time for her. I invited her to continue.

Sandy told the group that she had recently become aware of an experience of sexual abuse that had occurred when she was a child. This was a very painful memory for her to deal with, and she had not told anyone about it. Now, in the atmosphere of acceptance and support in the workshop, she felt ready to look at her psychic wound and move toward releasing it.

We spent the remainder of the morning with Sandy, listening

to her story, feeling her cry for love, and supporting her as she began to come to terms with a very difficult experience. By the end of the session she had released a great deal of her grief and accepted love and support from many of the participants. The experience was a major breakthrough for Sandy. When she finished, she looked liked a different person.

"I just want to thank you all for giving me the time and space to work on this. And I must acknowledge myself for having the courage to claim my right to be healed."

I learned a valuable lesson from the way Sandy demanded time and attention. I realized that if we have a true need for healing, we have not just a right, but a responsibility to stand up and call—even shout—for help. Sometimes this is the only way we will get it, and moreover we go through a process of recognizing that we deserve help enough to ask for it.

Stake Your Claim

A friend of mine won six million dollars in the Oregon State Lottery. Before she could collect the money she won, there were three things she had to do:

First, Brenda had to buy a ticket. Many of us wonder why God won't give us what we want. God *will* give us what we want, but we have to put in a requisition, or throw our hat into the ring. When you buy a lottery ticket you are making several important symbolic statements. You are acknowledging that there is a gift out there for you, you have a right to it, and you are willing to do something to draw it to you. You make a small investment that could potentially multiply itself many times over. One billboard advertising the state lottery reminded potential players, "You've gotta be in it to win it."

Second, my friend had to watch the newspapers and television to see if her number was drawn. We must be vigilant for our good. We must look for every little sign that our desired goal is coming our way, and then capitalize on the good by acknowledging and blessing it. No sign of success is too small to praise and celebrate.

A Course in Miracles tells us that we are continuously dispatching messengers which bring us back news of what we want to hear. If we value peace, joy, and healing, then we shall find abundant signs of those conditions. If, on the other hand, we have an attraction to tragedy and terror, we shall find confirmation of those circumstances. The world we experience depends on the messengers we send out and to which we pay heed.

Finally, Brenda had to show up at the lottery office and claim her prize. *We must claim our good.* To claim is to state that you have a lawful license to something, and ask for it with authority. To sheepishly or apologetically ask for our good does not honor our divine nature. As Children of God we have a right to happiness, and we have a right—and responsibility—to say, "I deserve this—please give it to me."

We do not need to fight for our good. Fighting for something means that there is a part of you that does not believe you deserve it. In such a case you are really fighting against yourself. It may seem that the outer world is withholding your good from you, but it is actually you who are withholding gifts from yourself. To help you learn that you deserve more than you have been allowing yourself, you "hire" other people to manifest your thoughts of unworthiness. The moment you recognize that you deserve your good, the fight will be over. You will receive your blessings in peace as you know that you deserve to be happy.

How Big is Your Basket?

God can give us only as much as we are willing to accept. One evening I had a fascinating vision. In a class that I was teaching I saw each student sitting in meditation with a straw or wooden basket on her or his lap. Each basket was a different size, according to the willingness of the meditator to accept blessings. Over the heads of the entire group was a huge storehouse of energy, the infinite abundance of God. A great waterfall of blessings was pouring down upon the entire group without restriction. Each student was, however, able to receive only the amount of blessings their basket could hold. Those who had tiny baskets received only a little bit, while those who came with large containers received a great deal. The baskets were created by their thoughts, and they were limited only by their beliefs. Those who believed they deserved a great deal were receiving it, and those who thought they deserved less got just that. The universe was just and lawful with each person: the Source gave all, and each student received according to the capacity established by their mind.

Loving and Deserving

Our ability to manifest what we want is a function of our thoughts about what we deserve. If we love ourself, we know that we deserve to be healthy, happy, and materially prosperous. We are children of a God of infinite wealth and resources, and as such we have total access to our Father's wealth and entire Kingdom. We are the heirs of Heaven not by our labor, but by our birthright.

Jesus said, "It is the Father's good pleasure to give you the Kingdom." He was, of course, referring to the Kingdom of Heaven. That Kingdom includes all of our needs being met, even while we are here on earth. Jesus also said, "On earth, as it is in Heaven." This world was not intended to be a rival to Heaven, but the reflection of it. Everything on earth has the potential to remind us of God. The question is not, "Is God present in this world?" but, "Do we choose to behold Him here?" God is not playing hide and seek with us. It is we who are hiding, and God who is seeking us.

The most powerful key to the Kingdom is to remember our worthiness. To love is to behold worth. When we honor our right to be at peace, the conditions of peace immediately enfold us.

Dare to Tell the Truth About What You Want

If you want to get what you want, you have to tell the truth about what you want. We reach a certain point on our path where we cannot compromise, minimize, or deny our heart's desire. It is not humble to ask for less than you believe you deserve; it is arrogance. False humility is a ploy of the ego; when we act smaller than God created us to be, we deny the grandeur with which we are imbued. True humility is to become an open vessel into which the riches of the universe may be poured, and then overflowed to a waiting world. The riches to which I refer are not just the material ones; the forms of this world at best remind us of our spiritual wealth. The real riches of life are love, joy, exuberance, delight, vision, and a life with heart. If you are not receiving all of these, as well as the material things you desire, you must stretch to tell a bigger truth about what you really want. Then turn your request over to the universe. If your request is right for you, you shall have it. If it is not right for you, believe me, you don't want it. In such a case you can thank God for giving you what you really want instead of what you thought you wanted. Our job is to ask and then allow God to answer in the way that is in harmony with our best interests. "Seek, and you shall find. Ask, and you shall receive. Knock, and the door shall be opened to you."

Dare to Ask for What You Want

1) If you could live your life over, what would you ask for that you didn't ask for?

2) What do you want now that you are not asking for?

3) What is the hardest thing for you to ask for?

4) Do you believe you deserve the things you want? If not, why not?

5) Make a list of the things you are now willing to accept. Stretch to include things you were previously unwilling to allow. Include both material goods and spiritual qualities.

6) What will you do to claim these gifts?

DARE TO BE HAPPY

Most people are about as happy as
they make up their mind to be.

— Abraham Lincoln

A group of psychologists was studying the relationship between attitude and happiness in children. The researchers invited two children to their laboratory to undergo observation. One child was described as a joyful, playful, and positive little boy. The other boy was reported to be a negative, poorly adapted, and unhappy child.

The scientists began their experiment by placing the child with the negative attitude in a room filled with popular toys. The boy went from toy to toy, playing with each one for a few minutes. After fifteen minutes he was bored. "These are yukky toys," he complained, "Get me some fun ones."

Then the experimenters put the positive child in a room with a large pile of horse manure. From the other side of a two-way mirror the scientists watched to see the child's reaction. "Oh, boy!" they saw him exclaim, "There must be a pony somewhere!"

In this little parable lies the secret of happiness in life:

See the good.

Find the gift.

Keep your mind and heart on the brightest possibilities.

Dare to be happy.

The Happy Heretic

It takes a certain amount of courage and independence to be a happy person. The world as we have created it thrives on misery. Happy stories do not sell newspapers; they lack titillation

83

by fear, the potential for gossip, and they fall dismally outside the belief system that we are powerless. News stories that speak of terror, disaster, and widespread victimization are, however, the biggest sellers. We cannot blame newswriters for perpetrating darkness. It is the readers' desire to believe in hell that keeps these headlines thriving.

To be happy in the midst of a world that worships sorrow is tantamount to heresy. People who are bent on misery are often irritated by people who are happy. I remember once entering an office, whistling. I was greeted by a receptionist scowling, "What are you so happy about?"

Let's face it: happiness is downright threatening to a world founded on fear. Joy is not the norm of this world—but the norm of this world is not natural. Pain and separation are not the way God intended for us to live. We have gotten used to it, but we will never be satisfied with it. Our destiny is to live in contentment, and we will not stop until we do. Perhaps we can even begin now.

The Blessing Extractor

I have invented a fantastic machine called "the blessing extractor." This miraculous device operates something like a vegetable juicer. When using a juicer, you place a carrot in a funnel at the top of the machine, and the juicer deftly grinds the carrot up. Then it spits the pulp out of a little door, and sends a golden stream of tasty juice out another chute.

The blessing extractor utilizes the same principle: you take any experience (painful ones actually work the best), and insert the whole thing into the blessing extractor. Press the right button (a willingness to have your life be a success), the blessing extractor whirs for a few seconds, and then shoots the tasteless unusable pulp (made of the drama, facts, figures, loss, and sorrow) out into a refuse basket. Simultaneously, out of another door pours the blessings the experience has given you. Typical blessings include deeper strength, greater aliveness, fresh insights, a more open heart, new direction, the dissolution of long-standing self-destructive patterns, richer appreciation for your gifts, and on and on.

The most amazing feature of the blessing extractor is that long after the pulp is thrown away, the blessings keep flowing. It seems that each blessing the machine produces leads to many others. The only problem with the blessing extractor is that it has no built-in obsolescence; the more you use it, the more use you can get out of it. (We're putting this dilemma into the extractor.)

The God in Chocolate

Once on my way to a retreat I bought some chocolate chip cookies. I rarely buy these delicacies, but as I found myself in a grocery store passing the Pepperidge Farm treats, I heard a voice say, "Buy me." (Who am I to argue with God?)

Later that day I met a very enthusiastic fellow. Instantly I recognized Mike to be a delightful soul. He found *everything* exciting. He went wild over the accommodations at the retreat (which were fairly simple), he was in ecstacy about the program, and he discovered something miraculous in just about everything.

One evening I was relaxing in the lounge with Mike and some friends. Someone gave Mike the last chocolate chip cookie in their bag. Mike took one bite and nearly went through the ceiling. His eyes opened like saucers and his hair seemed to stand on end. "Wow!" he exclaimed. "This is so excellent! These chocolate chips are loaded with God!"

That was the first time I had ever heard chocolate chips linked with the divine so authoritatively. Most of the time when I have seen people eat chocolate, they do it with almost ritualistic apology ("Well, just one," or "I'll jog tomorrow," or, "I'll have to wash my face extra carefully tonight so I don't get zits.") But Mike did not sprinkle his chocolate with guilt—he blessed it as a sacrament!

Immediately my mind flashed on the package of cookies in my room. Hmmm. If Mike got such a thrill out of one cookie, a whole package would probably send him to the moon! I got the cookies and gave them to Mike. He practically fell onto his knees. He thanked me as if I had just given him a lifetime pass to Disneyland. It was clear that the world was a happier place that evening.

Later that night when I was alone, I began to reflect on my process of giving Mike the cookies. The element that stimulated me to do so was his vociferous expression of appreciation for the one cookie he had received. He made a clear and joyful public pronouncement of his delight in that one little favor. If he had just politely smiled or made an apologetic statement, I would never have thought about offering him some more. His appreciation invited the universe to increase his supply of the object of his delight, and I was honored to be the delivery boy.

Here we have a fascinating example of the highest element of human nature reflecting the divine. There is something within each of us that gives us a thrill when we can make each other happy. As children of a loving God who is constantly striving to bring us happiness, our nature is to do the same for one another. Our soul is keen to recognize opportunities to do so (unless it is heavily overlaid with fear). George Eliot noted, "What do we live for, if not to make life less difficult for each other?"

God created the universe as a wish-fulfillment machine. We, as co-creators, have the power to bring anything we desire into manifestation. We accomplish manifestation through thought and feeling. Action is the last stage of demonstration. The most powerful way to create any result is to think and feel about it; see it in your mind and then let your emotions ride high on the visions of receiving it. Remember how Mike created more cookies simply by enjoying the one he had.

Mike's story beautifully illustrates an all-powerful law of mind that most people do not understand or use. Once we grasp this principle and make it work for us, our life is entirely different forever. Make it yours now, and you will wonder how you ever survived without using it. The law of mind is this:

Whatever we concentrate on, expands and increases.

Whatever we think about, we will get more of. This principle can work for us or against us. If we concentrate on something we love, we will draw more and more good into our life. If we focus on what we fear or do not like, we will experience more of that. Therefore it behooves us, if we ever plan to be successful and happy, to fertilize the flowers in the garden of our thoughts and quit watering the weeds. The first step to getting more of what you want is to bless what you already have.

Happiness is a Magnet for Good

Happy people are more successful in getting what they want than unhappy people. When I have hired people for various positions, at least fifty percent of my decision to hire them was based on their attitude. I want people answering my telephone who make the caller feel welcome and important. Nothing is a bigger turn-off than calling someone to do business with them, and hearing them sound bored, impatient, or annoyed. Productivity is important, but attitude is equally important. A positive attitude is not just a fringe benefit; it is a prime component of success of any kind.

Imagine that every thought you think, every word you utter, and every feeling you experience will automatically magnetize more of the same. Metaphysical teachers urge us to speak of only those conditions we want to see manifested, and to avoid declaring anything that we do not wish to bring into our life. Our words have power. ("In the beginning was the Word.") Speak loving words and attract love. Speak of success and attract prosperity. Speak of healing and lift the world out of sorrow and into the light.

Imagine that you can create the kind of life you want to live by putting yourself into the frame of mind as if you are already living it. As a co-creator with God, you have the tools and the opportunity to make of your life what you wish. The power is in your hands. Do with it as you will. Be a force for love, and you will be empowered by every noble thought in the universe.

Attitude Before Behavior

While happiness in this world seems to be consistently elusive, there is a principle which makes inner peace consistently attainable. It is the awareness that our satisfaction in living is not a result of what happens to us; *it is a direct result of the thoughts we think.*

A Course in Miracles explains that healing is not simply a result of behavior; it is based more deeply on attitude. Life does not make of us what it wants; we make of life what we want. Real change comes not through militaristically forcing ourself to change—very few people are successful at such a regimen. But many people are successful at learning to love themselves. When we stop hating and berating ourselves, we unplug the mental and emotional magnet that draws to us experiences of ill health, broken relationships, and failure. Self-love, our natural and most powerful state, is then free to attract to us the optimum conditions for our well-being. Enlightenment is an inside job.

I heard a radio interview with a famous teacher of weight control. This woman has lost a great deal of weight and has since helped many other people do so. Her method is one of attitudinal change. She referred to a joke that some of her clients tell her, "If I just see food, I gain weight." She said that there is actually some truth to this statement. She explained that the emotion of fear sets up a chemical reaction in the body which activates the self-protection process. One of the offshoots of this reaction is to build fat, which is a food reserve. Fat is something your body can live on if it does not have another source of nutrition. People who are worried about gaining weight often become anxious in the presence of tantalizing food, as they feel guilt about breaking their diet and fear failing or looking unattractive. So they walk into a room, see a colorful smorgasbord, and go into anxiety. The anxiety mimics the fight-or-flight process, which stimulates the body chemistry that builds fat. That is why it seems that some people can never lose weight—worrying about losing weight is exactly the factor that keeps the weight on!

The answer, of course, is self-love. When we know that we

are lovable and beautiful as the person we are, we understand that we have a right to look good, feel good, and enjoy the food we eat. In our natural state of self-appreciation, we will not see food as a threat or, if we have been on many diets that have not worked, as a symbol of temptation, testing, and failure. There are many people who eat plenty of enjoyable food, including an occasional rich delicacy, and are in fine health and look good. The trick is to not let food become a bugaboo, a dark monster that runs our life. Food can be our taskmaster when we make it a god by overindulging in it, but it hurts us equally if we are afraid of it. Let food be your friend. See it as a gift from God. God wants us to enjoy eating. If food weren't supposed to be attractive and enjoyable to us, we would not survive. God's logic is simple.

The spiritual guide Ramtha made a fantastic observation about nourishment. He noted that "the thing that nourishes you when you eat is not the physical vitamins and minerals in the food—it is the joy you feel in eating it." So here we have a radical yet profound instruction—you will be happiest and healthiest by eating the food you enjoy!

My friend Dr. David Singer is a world-famous chiropractor. When I first met David, he gave a series of three lectures on good health. The first was on care of the spine; the second, proper nutrition; and the third—which he described as the most important—was on positive thinking. During that seminar Dr. Singer recounted that as an intern he was assigned to a clinic in a ghetto of New York City. There he treated patients who had some of the poorest health habits you could imagine—diets consisting of heavy intake of meat, highly processed foods with much sugar, regular use of alcohol, caffeine, and nicotine, and so on. Dr. Singer was astounded to find that despite these poor habits, some of his patients were in fantastic condition. Why? Because, as Dr. Singer explained, "they had a marvelous attitude about living. They were easy going and playful, they laughed a lot, and they enjoyed people." Through that internship, Dr. Singer learned that *the most important component of good health is attitude.* His career is a strong example of the power of a positive attitude. In just a few years Dr. Singer built a small suburban practice up to a huge volume, and went on to be a nationally-respected consultant in the field of chiropractic. He, like "Chocolate Chip" Mike, *A Course in Miracles*, and Ramtha, stands very clearly for a bottom-line principle of happiness: *it's not so much what you do that counts; it's what you think about what you do.*

The Boldest Dare

While happiness is criticized by skeptics as being unreasonable, it is actually the most logical investment you can make in your life. It costs nothing to be happy, except the release of the pain and sorrow that you have been hypnotized into believing are your friends. Rather than allies, fear and attack are like deceptive houseguests who smile and convince you that they are helping you during the day, and then rob you blind at night. You would lose nothing to dismiss attack thoughts summarily and welcome joy back into your household. Even one day of happiness would reveal the utter uselessness of the doubt and fear that may have held power over you for years.

To be happy in a world of sorrow is indeed a bold dare. It is also the only way out of the darkness. Thousands of years ago Plato spoke of a cave in which many people were chained to the walls, and believed that bondage in darkness was the only way of life. Then, as the philosopher described, one man broke loose of his chains and found his way to the opening of the cave, where he discovered light. When he went back to tell his captive friends that they, too, could be free to live in a newer and brighter world, they doubted and criticized him. They had become so acclimated to the darkness that their belief system could not allow for a greater possibility. But one by one, they did venture forth to find the light. At first the light hurt their eyes because they had been living in darkness for so many years. But their desire for freedom was so great that they pursued what made them happy, and ultimately they were able to live in a world totally unlike the one they had known.

We, too, have the capacity to live in a new and brighter world. Our potential for joy is not limited by what we have done; our happiness is as grand as the doorway we give it to flow into our heart. If you want to be happy and invite the world to join you, you must become a radical lover. Dare to break the chains that have bound you to the wall of the cave of limited thinking, and venture toward the light. Your eyes may hurt a bit to behold the day, but you will never return to the darkness.

Dare to Be Happy

1) List three experiences or situations you could put in the blessing extractor. What blessings can you extract?

2) What problems or pet peeves would you have to give up if you chose to be happy right now?

3) List three of your behaviors or habits that you judge against. Imagine that the behavior is not as important as your attitude about it. How could you look at each behavior so you see its helpfulness?

4) Make a similar list of behaviors or habits that you judge in someone else. With a shift in attitude, how could these be seen as good?

5) Describe three things you love that you will increase by blessing them more.

DARE TO ACCEPT LOVE

How Much Can You Take?

How are you at accepting compliments? Most people have a great deal of difficulty receiving praise or acclaim. Many of us become very uncomfortable and want to wriggle out of the spotlight. Most of us do not know what to do with genuine compliments when they are given.

What we do with compliments is a marvelous metaphor for our ability to receive love. There is a part of our mind that believes that we are not worthy of compliments or love. It is strange that beings who are good by nature would flee from the acknowledgement of their beauty. But there are many things about this world that are strange.

In some of my workshops I offer a demonstration of the ways we deal with compliments. I ask each participant to stand before the group, one at a time, and receive compliments from the others. At that point a wave of fear rolls through the group, so large that you could surf on it. You would think that I was asking them to stand before a firing squad! But it is not a firing squad—it is an inspiring squad. It is an exercise in giving and receiving love. But part of our mind is so afraid of being exposed as a bad person, that when someone seeks to expose us to honor our goodness, we run like the dickens.

Here are some of the ways I have seen people handle compliments:

A. "That's a lovely shirt you're wearing."
B. "It's a nice print, but I don't think it fits quite well."

C. "Congratulations on losing twenty pounds."
D. "I still have ten to go."

E. "I really enjoyed the class you taught this morning."
F. "I can do better—my presentation was nothing compared with some of the teachers I've seen."

G. "Thank you for counseling me yesterday."
H. "Don't thank me. Thank God."

If people keep giving us gifts and we continually toss them into the trash in their presence, it will not be long before our friends will become frustrated and find another place to share their valuable offerings. The greatest gift you can give someone who is complimenting you is to receive their love with an open heart. They want to bless you, and in your receiving their tribute they are also blessed. Accepting a compliment gracefully is one of the most powerful ways to expand love in the world and bring Heaven to earth.

No Excuses

I learned an important lesson in accepting love when my first book, *The Dragon Doesn't Live Here Anymore*, was published. Readers told me that the book had changed their life, and as a result of putting its principles into action they experienced powerful healings in their body, relationships, and spiritual path.

I did not know what to do with such powerful acknowledgements. My reaction was to toss them off. I did not feel worthy of those compliments, and so I found ways to deny their offerings. I would tell them, "Well, God really wrote the book"; or, "The book is simply a reflection of you"; or, "I'll bet you could do the same"; or some other self-effacing spiritual platitude which I thought was appropriately humble, but which was actually a cover for my terror in receiving acknowledgement for my achievements.

As I became more sensitive to these interactions, I noticed that many of these people walked away somewhat disappointed. They were giving me a precious gift, and I was throwing it back at them. They wanted the satisfaction of thanking me and letting me know that I had helped them, and I was not receiving their blessing. It can be very frustrating to try to give someone a gift when they are not willing to accept it.

My turnabout came when I had a house guest who kindly went out one morning and weeded my garden, which was long overdue for a cleanup. I was delighted to come home and find the garden freshly manicured and lovingly cared for.

"Thank you so much!" I told her. "I really appreciate you weeding the garden so beautifully."

A stark and rather programmed look came over my guest's face. She responded, "Don't thank me. Thank God."

I felt stunned. Here I was feeling a tremendous gratitude for a gift she had given me, and I wanted to let her know it. I felt thwarted when she was unwilling to accept my thanks. If I had woken up one morning and found the garden magically cleared of weeds by the Absolute Invisible Lord, I would have thanked Him directly. But in this case, God had worked through this loving woman, and I figured that if He did the work through her, then I could thank Him through her.

The deeper lesson, of course, was for me to learn how to accept compliments, which I had a hard time doing. I realized that when people thanked me for the book I wrote, I could receive their gifts more graciously, rather than paddle their words back to them. From that time on I have made it a practice to consciously receive, appreciate, and celebrate the kind words that come to me. And I notice that those who offer their praise feel fulfilled to have their gift accepted.

The Master's Way

My teacher Hilda was a fantastic model of how to handle compliments. She would always give the complimenter another chance to give more. Someone would tell her, "That was a wonderful class, Hilda," and she would answer, "I'm so glad; did you really like it?" Then the other person would go on about what they had received.

At first I wondered if Hilda was just milking compliments, but later I saw that she was really giving a gift to the giver. They needed to express their feelings, give support, and celebrate the good they had received. Hilda served them most powerfully by opening the door for them to do so. In one class, during a time of prayer, Hilda instructed us to mentally give her thanks. "I don't need your thanks," she explained, "but you need to give it."

In a way, all of life is a compliment. Being alive is God's way of telling us how much She loves us, how beautiful we are in Her eyes, and how precious are the gifts that we have been entrusted to express. We do not make God greater by making ourselves smaller. We glorify God most fittingly when we let our lives be reflections of God's magnificent attributes. God is wondrous not in contrast to us, but *through* us. As St. Ignatius declared, "the glory of God is humankind fully alive."

Don't Bite the Hand that Feeds You

My parrots teach me some fantastic lessons. These delightful, intelligent, and sometimes zany creatures are a source of inspiration and education for me. One day I went into my aviary to feed the birds. As I lifted my hand up to put seeds into Yogi's feeding bowl, he scampered over and began to nip at my hand. Although I was giving him what he needs and loves, an element of his genetic conditioning told him that my hand in his bowl was an invasion, and he must defend it. The irony was that I was actually giving him something that would make him happy. But his programming did not allow him to see the whole picture, and so he saw my offering as an attack.

Perhaps we humans are not so different than Yogi. How often do we mistake a gift for an attack? Sometimes people try to love us and we perceive them as attempting to take our good from us. We feel threatened, when all the while they are actually in the process of delivering our good to us.

Love's Invitation

I have a friend who I have had a hard time being with. Often when I spent time with Sam, many of his mannerisms irritated me. Sam reminded me of some people in my past by whom I felt threatened. For a long time I resisted Sam's attempts to be my friend. On numerous occasions he invited me to share in social activities, and I turned him down. And Sam, being a sensitive person, felt rejected and hurt. From his perspective he could not understand why I would shun his loving gifts.

Then one day while I was meditating, Sam's face came to me. In my relaxed state of mind I saw him through the eyes of love, not fear. Suddenly I realized that Sam had shown me only kindness. He reached out to be my friend and I did not allow him into my heart. Because I was seeing Sam through the filter of my past programming, I was not seeing him as he is. I recognized that my problem with Sam was not something in him, but in my own mind. I had been defending myself against my own good and denying love's invitation. As my heart opened I gained a real appreciation for Sam and his presence in my life.

I telephoned Sam and told him how much I loved and appreciated him. He was very touched. We enjoyed a beautiful healing and a deepening of our friendship. *A Course in Miracles* tells us that "the holiest place on earth is where an ancient hatred has become a present love."

The Key to the Kingdom

The key to receiving the riches of the Kingdom lies in our willingness to accept them. God can give us all the blessings in the universe, but if we are not willing to accept them, they go unknown and unappreciated. We live in the midst of an ocean of good. It is up to us to let love support us. Arrogance is not believing that we are better than anyone else; it is believing that we are less than ourself. It is denying the good that wants to pour to us and through us. Blasphemy is not attempting to make ourself bigger than we are; its tragedy lies in our attempt to make ourself smaller than God created us to be.

It is time for us to accept the good that is offered us. We do not need to seek for it, create it, or try to earn it. We cannot earn God's favor, because we already have it. Now we need but to express it. Let the love of God flow into your heart like a mountain stream, and then send forth healing waters to the dry and dusty plains below. The world has fearfully built bulwarks against healing, and there is an urgent cry for souls like yourself to let celebration be the new guide for this planet. We have seen the pits of depravity, and now it is time for us to behold the majesty of love. Together we will awaken from the long sleep of fear, and establish kindness as the crowning virtue of our passage here.

Dare to Accept Love

1) Make a list of five things (physical items, positions or symbols of success, or spiritual attributes) you would like to receive.

2. Close your eyes and imagine that each thing you desire has been given you free of charge and without sacrifice. Are you be able to accept each one graciously and whole-heartedly? If not, what feelings arise within you?

3. Write a list of compliments to yourself. Include all of your positive attributes that you can think of. Be generous.

4. Write a list of compliments to those with whom you are closest. Focus on anyone you may not be getting along with. Be generous.

5. Note any compliments you've given in the past that were not totally sincere. Why did you offer them?

Dare of the Week:

Whenever you feel an appreciation, voice it to the person that you are appreciating. Do not give any compliments that are not honest or completely sincere.

Dare to
Live Now

DARE TO LIVE NOW

"Lionel, if you don't watch out, you're going to go from being a 'has been' to a 'would be' without ever being an 'is.' "

— Mrs. Jefferson

An intriguing sign alongside a highway in Texas caught my eye. The billboard, posted at the entrance of a new housing development outside Houston, announced, "If you lived here, you'd be home now."

Many road signs offer succinct metaphors for the lessons we must learn on the journey of life. *Yield, Maintain Speed on Hill,* and *Do Not Pass* remind us of actions and qualities we need to master. This sign, however, offered a shining lesson in the power of the moment: *If you lived here, you'd be home now.*

So much of our life is spent trying to get somewhere, striving for the next reward, conquering the upcoming hurdles, protecting ourself from future danger. Happiness always seems to be just around the next bend, slightly beyond our reach. The dramatic character Shirley Valentine, a middle-aged London housewife who finds herself withering from boredom and routine, explains, "I always said I'd leave when the kids grew up, but when they grew up there was nowhere to go."

How much time, by contrast, do we spend in the wonder of the present moment? How often do we seize the day rather than assume that there will be a tomorrow to which we can postpone our joy? What if happiness were not miles, years, or lifetimes away, but here in the simple recognition that wherever we are, God is? And what if the most direct way to find fulfillment were to do the thing that would make us happy now?

The Way to Go is the Way to Be Here

Recently I went into a local restaurant where I enjoy talking with the owner, who is a friend of mine. While I usually bask in Lucy's delightful upbeat presence, this day I found her sullen. "What's the matter? "I asked her.

"Oh, Alan, my husband just passed away suddenly."

I was startled to hear this news. I reached out and held Lucy, and she wept in my arms.

"What happened?" I inquired.

"It was a scuba diving accident. Lenny went down and didn't come up alive. He's had a heart condition for eleven years. When he first found out about the illness, the doctor told him that he shouldn't dive anymore. But diving was what he loved to do the most. So he didn't listen; he went out every week and enjoyed himself. Luckily, nothing happened for all that time. But this time he didn't make it."

I thought about Lucy's account. Actually, I admired Lenny. I pondered what his life might have been like for those eleven years if he had listened to the doctor. Lenny probably would have been miserable, yearning to participate in his favorite pastime, but feeling unable to do it. He probably would have gotten old, stiff, and mean, like many people who are not living their heart's desire.

Instead Lenny chose to take his chances and live for today. Every Sunday he woke up excitedly and went out to enjoy scuba diving—and he was a happy man for it. I knew Lenny. He was the principal of a local elementary school. He was a gentle, joyful, and amiable man. All the students and teachers loved and admired him. Perhaps Lenny was so popular because he was true to himself. He honored himself enough to keep doing what he loved, even if there was a risk involved. Personally, I believe that he was the winner on his gamble. He enjoyed eleven more rewarding years of scuba diving, and he died doing the thing he loved most. Perhaps it would be more truthful to say that he *lived* doing the thing he loved most.

Jack London declared, "I would rather be a superb meteor,

every atom of me in magnificent glow, than a sleepy and permanent planet. I'd rather be ashes than dust. The proper function of man is to live, not to exist. I shall not waste my days in trying to prolong them. I shall use my time."

When award-winning aerial photographer Bob Cameron was asked why, at the age of seventy, he continues to hang out of helicopters to get pictures, he answered, "Because nothing makes me happier. And when my time comes, I guess falling out of a helicopter would be as good a way to go as any."

I saw a film on rock climbing. I was astounded to watch two young women scale a thousand-foot sheer rock wall. It was amazing to me that they could make their way up that cliff! Upon their return a reporter asked one of the women if she was afraid of being killed in the process. She answered, "I can't be preoccupied with fear of dying. Otherwise I wouldn't do anything. And if I do die, it would be doing something I love."

Lovers Make a Fool of Time

When we are in love or loving what we are doing, time disappears. When you are making love, who cares what time it is? What a perfect metaphor for all of life: *Do what you love so much that you escape from time by forgetting about it.* Instead of losing yourself in the face of a clock, you will recognize your own.

Buckminster Fuller noted that "human beings are the only creatures on the planet who tell time and think we have to earn a living." We cannot earn happiness by doing something that makes us unhappy. You cannot get apples from an orange tree, and you cannot find healing through fear. Misery is the longest road to joy, and the most unnecessary. Happiness is not the reward of struggle—it is the fruit of living for what we truly believe in. We do not need to earn our good. Our good comes to us naturally when we let go of our struggle for it.

Time is an invention of the mind which was created to help us focus. Time was meant to serve us, not for us to bow down to it. When used unconsciously, the numbers on the face of a clock become prison bars. Time cannot imprison us, but our mind can. The way out of the prison of time is not to hurry up, but to wake up.

Swami Satchidananda, a wise Indian sage, makes a delightful observation about time: "When I began to learn the English language, I noticed that everything related to time was tense. 'Past—*tense*...future—*tense*...present—*tense*.' It made me wonder if I wanted to be on time—it seems that every time in your culture is tense!"

The only purpose of time is to learn to use it wisely. Time is here for us to make the most of it. We always have enough time to do what we love.

Living Without Fences

In that marvelous film *Lost Horizon*, spiritual seeker Robert Conway is engaged in a conversation with Chiang, one of the lamas in the temple of Shangri-La. Chiang has just explained to Conway that many of the residents of Shangri-La are hundreds of years old. These vital people are healthy and active, and they retain the vibrancy of people many years younger than they are. "That's remarkable!" Conway responds. "If I may ask, how old are you, Chiang?"

"Oh," Chiang laughs, "age is a concept that means nothing to me. Every time we mark a birthday, we put another fence around our mind. As for me, I prefer to live without fences."

I have a friend who has jumped her fences. At the age of seventy-eight, Tensie has more energy, spunk, and zeal than just about anyone I know. When I first met her a few years ago, Tensie had just returned from an underwater wedding. She showed me a video of her parading as "Ms. Outrageous" at the Lahaina Yacht Club's annual beauty contest. Amidst a bevy of curvy beauties in slinky bikinis, Tensie made a show-stopping entrance in leotards, snorkel gear, and a parasol. The Jewish word for that kind of display is *chutzpa*.

Tensie has been married five times, probably because no man could keep up with her. I'm sure she tuckered them all out! When a friend of mine, age forty, took a walk on the beach with Tensie,

Ms. Outrageous left my friend in the dust. Age has nothing at all to do with the body; it is entirely an attitude of the mind. When we live in the now, age is meaningless and disappears.

Tensie attended one of my workshops, during which I asked the participants to make a list of all the things they would love to do if they could. Tensie announced that she was planning to meet a man who could keep up with her, take dance lessons, travel to Africa, open up a bookstore/espresso cafe, and the list went on. Of all the people in the room, Tensie had the longest list of dreams she planned to fulfill. Although she was the oldest person at the workshop, physically speaking, she was actually the youngest. Tensie's vision of what she planned to do with her life was even brighter than it was as a child. I have no doubt that is why she is so vital and healthy.

If anyone has made fool of time, it is Tensie. Perhaps she has lived so long because she has lived so well. She has kept her joy light burning, and she is not about to curtail it because most of the people in the world have allowed theirs to flicker. Tensie's heart has gathered power with time.

Author James Michener, who is about Tensie's age, was asked if he had any more books in the works. "Oh, yes!" he answered. "I have about thirty. Let's see...at about three years a book, I'll be a hundred and seventy-three when I'm done."

Mind Your Business

While we may have told other people that our age is none of their business, it is none of our business, either. It would only empower, enliven, and strengthen us to completely forget the notion of age. Our business is to live in the moment, do the things we love, and keep our heart open. Most other pursuits are trivial by comparison.

Each night as I lie in bed before going to sleep, I review my day. I feel the feeling in my chest around my heart, and I consider if today I lived the life I want to be living. I notice that when I have given or received love, enjoyed quality time with friends, or spent time in nature, I feel very satisfied. "Thank you, God—a day well spent," I say to myself, and I rest content.

Sometimes I do not feel that I have used my time well. Sometimes I have spent the day in the office and gotten caught up in business, money, deadlines, and fear. When I lie in bed on those nights, I feel as if I have wasted a day on earth. I experience a hollow empty feeling in my stomach and heart. And with that feeling I realize that this is not what I want to be doing with my life. I ask God to help me stay on purpose in accord with my soul's calling. I want my time here to be well used.

Home Now

Time can be a sticky web, but it can also be a doorway. There is a great purpose for time, and that is to help us learn to use it wisely. Every moment is an invitation to love, a hand held out to support our walk to richer beauty. We already have everything we need within us; we just need to know it and live it. *"If you lived here, you'd be home now."* We *do* live here, and we *are* home. We carry Heaven within our heart, and we bring it to earth by remembering it even as we walk here.

No heaven can come to us unless our hearts find rest in today.

— Fra. Giovanni

Dare to Live Now

1) Name three things that you would love to do, that you have been putting off for a later time.

2. Write one step that you could take toward each desire that would allow you to do it now, or sooner rather than later.

3. Imagine that today is your last day on earth. What do you wish you had done sooner? What will you do today? Who will you spend your time with?

DARE TO LET GO

Whatever I have to let go of, I leave claw marks on!" a woman reported to our workshop group. Everyone in the room laughed at her vivid depiction of her need to learn to release her past more easily. All of us could identify with the need to trust more in letting go of what does not serve us any longer.

It seems that it is only when we are up against the wall that we are willing to let go of what the universe is calling for us to release. We try to engineer life into a little box called, "I know what's going on, and I will struggle with all my energy to keep everything the way I think it should be." Stubbornly we hold out in painful resistance until it is clear that our way is not working. Then we let the universe have its way, and we see that there was a bigger design than we understood when we looked through the eyes of fear.

Life is a journey to greater love and freedom. There really is a plan for our good. As our faith and vision expand, we become more willing to let God handle the show. Instead of struggling to maintain the way it has been—even if that way is not working—we find peace in turning troubling situations over to God. There is a higher power which guides us through rough waters. When we allow Spirit to be our beacon, a tremendous burden is lifted off our shoulders. We find the freedom that we could not know while trying to do it all ourself.

Cut the Sack

The movie *The Mission* depicts the plight of a man who feels tremendous guilt and remorse about a murder he committed. Moreover, he was a slave trader who spent years selling Amazonian Indians into bondage. Upon realizing his errors, he seeks to atone for his sins by suffering, and devises a scheme to amplify his pain. He throws a huge sack of heavy weaponry over his shoulder and sets out to climb a mountain of rocks beside a towering waterfall. Torturously he ascends, sweating and struggling, feeling that he is paying off his sins with every agonizing step.

When he arrives at the top of the waterfall, he finds waiting for him a band of ferocious-looking Indians—the very tribe from which he had extracted slaves. The chief, recognizing the man, approaches him with a huge gleaming sharp knife. Certain that this is the moment of his death, the ultimate recompense for his iniquities, the man falls to his knees and awaits the final blow. The Indian steps toward him, raises the knife, and briskly cuts the bag of penance from his shoulders. Together they watch the sack hurtle into the abyss. He is free.

We are sometimes like that man, bearing a sack of sorrow on our weary shoulders, laboring under a heavy burden of self-inflicted penance. We believe we have sinned or been victimized, and we labor under the bleakness of our thought for hours, days, weeks, years, or lifetimes. Yet all the while it is not a real sin or loss that weighs heavily on our soul, but our thoughts about it. We believe pain will buy us atonement, when all it really brings us is more pain. Then we blame God or life for being cruel, when it is but our own mind that has kept us in chains.

We do not need to exact payment from ourself or others for past errors; we just need to let them go. How many times can we relive a personal horror movie before we realize that it is not bringing us peace? There is a way to release yourself from the torment of guilt or sorrow: *Walk out of the theatre*. Forget about it. Cast your past into the stream of life, and allow the healing waters to carry your sorrow to God's infinite ocean of forgiving love. There the heart of compassion will take your illusions, touch them with the grace of forgiveness, and return your memories to you transformed with clarity for your healing. Give it all back to God, and be free.

What's My Line?

If we carry a sense of sadness or victimization long enough, we begin to identify with it. If we receive enough attention or pity for a drama we continually glamorize, we may be tempted to use it as a suit of armor behind which we can hide from true intimacy. We develop a personality or even a mission around our pain, and we feel justified in exacting vengeance from ourself or others for a past crime. Yet the sad irony of such a morbid quest is that every time we glorify the crime by repeating its horrid details, we recreate it in our experience and hold the movie over for many repeated engagements in the theatre of our mind. Thus we miss the beauty of the current moment, which is where all the glory of life lies.

There was a marvelous character who illustrated this pattern in that wonderful comedic epic, *The Princess Bride*. Rodrigo Montoya is on a lifelong mission of vengeance to find and slay the man who killed his father. This crusade is all he thinks about, and all he talks about to everyone he meets. For years and years Rodrigo practices the statement of revenge that he will declare to his father's assassin: "My name is Rodrigo Montoya. You killed my father. Prepare to die!" Rodrigo has rehearsed this line so often that he has it down to a science, and he delights in practicing different intonations and emphases.

Finally Rodrigo finds the assassin and they engage in a long swashbuckling swordfight. During the entire duel, Rodrigo keeps shouting his statement of vengeance at the criminal: "My name is Rodrigo Montoya. You killed my father. Prepare to die!" over and over and over again. Finally his foe can stand it no more. He interrupts the duel long enough to cry out, "Would you please stop repeating that ridiculous line—it's driving me crazy!"

Rodrigo eventually does the assailant in. Afterwards, as he

exits the castle, Rodrigo's companion asks him, "So now that you've finished off your foe, what will you be doing?"

Rodrigo stops in his tracks. A startled look befalls his face. He turns toward his friend and tells him, "I don't know—I've been in the revenge business for so long that I have no idea what I will do without it!"

And so it is with those of us, or the part of us, that is identified with our drama. We have become so entrenched in our story line and gotten so many perceived benefits from our problem that we are reluctant to let it go. We may have to get a new identity. We may have to venture into the vulnerable world of the open heart. We might even have to be happy—and then what would we do?

To be a professional victim may be lucrative, but it certainly is not rewarding. While our personality may find a seeming safety in milking our problems, our soul yearns to live in power, not weakness. Our true strength is in joy, not sorrow. We came here to express greatness, not frailty.

Pain is to be used as a steppingstone, not a campground. We can bless our challenges, but we cannot afford to become addicted to them. We can learn from our trials, for each hurt points us to a deeper truth that we are needing to understand. But the true master extracts the lesson as quickly as possible, and then moves on. Why hang out in the swamp longer than we need to? The meadows are just on the other side of the muck, and there the sun awaits us, ready to dry the mud that is caked on our boots.

Check Your Drama Meter

As I have found increasing joy and harmony in my life, I find myself having less and less tolerance for hiding behind a drama or a story line. I have noticed what I call my "rap." There is a part of me that enjoys repeating the same story, drama, or line over and over again to different people.

I first became sensitive to my "rap" when I watched a film called *The Heartbreak Kid*, a poignant and humorous tale of a young man trying to win the hand of an attractive woman. When Charles met Cybil he told her, "I feel it's time we stopped taking from the earth, and started putting back into it." A very good philosophy, to be sure. But was he in it?

Our hero wrangles his way to Cybil's home for dinner with her parents. "You know, sir," he tells the girl's father, "I believe it's time we stopped taking from the earth, and started putting back into it." Cybil's dad, an astute businessman, sees through Charles' charade immediately, and just about throws him out on his ear.

Charles is, however, persistent, and he ultimately convinces Cybil to marry him. The final scene of the movie shows their wedding reception. The bride wants to introduce her new husband to some friends, but she can't find him. The camera locates Charles sitting on a couch in the parlor with a few ten-year-old children. As the camera pans in on the groom's face, we hear him explaining to the kids, "You know, I think it's time we stopped taking from the earth, and start putting back into it." The kids, bored to tears, look at their watches. Finally they tell Charles, "Excuse us. We have to go find our parents." Then they get up and leave.

No one is impressed by words in which we are not present. There is no life in them, and no true communication. Our soul wants to be in communion with our friends. When we play out a story in which we are not fully alive, there is no spirit in our voice. And where there is no spirit we must stop and ask ourself, "What am I missing and what do I need to do to reclaim aliveness?"

If I find myself recounting a personal drama more than two or three times, and not feeling a sense of movement or healing in my sharing it, a little "rap alarm" goes off in my brain. It notifies me that I am not fully present and I have more of an investment in the drama than in healing. I ask myself why I am using this story. What do I truly want to receive? Do I want the spotlight, or the Light? Do I want sympathy, or empowerment? Do I want to be right, or happy?

I want to be on the cutting edge of my destiny. If I am missing the experience of love by hiding behind a story, then I do not want it. I cannot afford to make statements that affirm my smallness. To belittle is to be little. I want peace more than attention for something I don't want to be identified with. When I realize this, I can let go of the masquerade and move on to accept the gift of what's happening now.

Dare to Support Others in Letting Go

We can help others to be strong by inviting them into the moment with us. If someone else is playing on their rap, we do not serve them or ourself to sit through it politely. It is not polite to let someone hurt themself by living in a fantasy that is disempowering them. It is polite to give them strength by remaining in our own truth and calling them to theirs.

There was a time when I thought I would be rude not to listen to a long tale of woe or an impassioned victim diatribe. I remember regularly sitting at my desk, listening on the telephone to someone's "rap," feeling bored, annoyed, and impatient, waiting for the moment I could get off the phone. I believed I was being kind to listen. But they really weren't saying anything, and I really wasn't listening. I would look at the clock, shuffle papers around on my desk, put paper clips in the drawer, read articles, and make notes about things I had to do that day, all the while appearing to listen. This was not listening, and we were not communicating. Precious moments of life were being wasted out of insecurity to tell the truth, couched in the guise of politeness.

Now I realize that I was not helping them or myself. What I was doing was tantamount to buying an alcoholic a drink. I was enabling rapaholics. When I began to have less and less patience for my own rap, I found more confidence in drawing other rappers into a more powerful communication. One man called me almost daily and went on about problem after problem. I listened, felt with him, and offered much constructive support. For every response or suggestion I gave him, he quickly found a reason why this would not work. After a time I realized that this man had more of an investment in the problem than in finding a solution. I explained to him that I could not truly offer him my presence or my assistance until he was willing to do something other than complain about his problem. At that level of interaction we were going in circles, and we were both wasting our time. My desire to empower both of us was greater than my fear of hurting his feelings. I had to trust that there was a part of him that wanted to hear the truth, even though his ego was vociferously orchestrating his presentation. Sometimes tough love is required. I served him most powerfully by inviting him to change rather than stay in prison. Real compassion is to behold a brother's strength and call him to it.

Reframe

"Is it possible to change the past?" a teacher asked a class I attended. Almost unanimously, the group answered, "No."

"Then what *can* we change?" the teacher questioned.

An astute student responded, "The way we look at the past." It is possible for all the events of the past to remain as they were, but to see them in a way that makes our history a blessing. It is not so much the things we did that hurt us, but our interpretations and judgments about them. What we believe were our sins were honest errors. We and those around us have always done the best we could with the knowledge, experience, and understanding we had at the time. If we could have done better, we would have. Remember that if we were totally perfect in expression, we probably would not be here in the first place. But we are here, we are learning, and compassion frees us to walk our path as we acquire wisdom. We can liberate ourselves from years of pain or heartache by taking another look at past experiences and reframing them in a bigger picture, one which reveals them to be blessings.

Seen through God's eyes, we are innocent and everything is helpful. Norman Lear, the gifted and successful television producer of many of the most popular comedies of the seventies and eighties, grew up in a house where he was shouted at and criticized constantly. At first he took the verbal abuse personally, but then he learned to laugh at it. He discovered how to use humor as a safety valve for his sense of frustration. As a result of mastering that coping mechanism he developed the classic *All in the Family*, his most successful series about a family in which judgment and bigotry are taken to a laughable extreme. *All in the Family* and Norman Lear's other situation comedies were milestones in television programming, as they brought many sensitive ethnic issues to humorous light in the consciousness of millions of viewers. His programs, in addition to being extremely entertaining (because we could identify with the foibles of his characters), made powerful social statements and major contributions to the awakening of the masses. When we consider that these shows were direct results of Norman Lear's challenging childhood experiences, we see that all of our experiences can ultimately be used for our own healing and success, as well as the service of others.

God is always present, even in situations that seem to be hopeless. God's presence does not depend on our awareness of it. In fact, the hand of love often works most powerfully in situations where we do not see it at first. In the remembrance of God's presence lies our power to release what we believe to be our past abuses and misdeeds, and open the door to see them in a new light and become new ourself in the process.

The Gift of Release

Sometimes the greatest gift we can bestow on a friend is to let them go. When the universe is calling for them to move to the next stage of their good, we empower them most meaningfully by supporting them in their move. If we are attached to them being with us, releasing them can be a very difficult and painful experience. But what is the use of fighting against the tide of life? If someone or something has a destiny elsewhere, we hurt ourself by attempting to keep them tied to us.

At such a time we need to remember that there is only love. This person or thing came into our life by the hand of love, and it is by the same hand they leave. We fear to let go only when we do not trust that we will be taken care of without the person or thing we want to hold onto. But we will. Spirit needs to make a space for something new and more wonderful. We must turn our life over to God and trust that His vision of our good is broader than ours. And it is.

Sometimes our dear ones simply need space to go through an important experience that we may not understand at first glance. We must honor their need. Caterpillars become butterflies one by one, and they need to enter the cocoon by themselves. Can you imagine the caterpillar's girlfriend knocking frantically on the door of the cocoon, crying, "Please take me with you!"? Such a request denies the all-important truth that she, too, has the capacity to fly, and she does not need her beloved to do it for her. Her beloved cannot do it for her. But she can do it for herself. If she is just patient, her day of flight will come. She would be wisest to see her beloved's experience not as a sign of her loss, but as a promise of great things to come for herself. True love takes delight in allowing our fellow caterpillars to become butterflies rather than attempting to keep them earthbound. (There is a cartoon depicting two caterpillars on the ground looking up at a butterfly. One caterpillar turns to the other and resolutely tells him, "You'll never get me up in one of those things!") The miracle is that one day all of the caterpillars will join those who have learned to fly, and together they will meet fluttering around the flowers instead of creeping along the road. To give our beloved ones space to grow and change is one of the most precious blessings we can offer them.

When my mother underwent surgery and did not appear to be recovering, I became very anxious. I was very attached to my mom, and I could hardly accept the possibility of her passing. Following her surgery she did not eat, she remained very weak, and the doctors did not know if or how she would regain her strength. My reaction to this frightening situation was to cling to her even more adamantly. Daily I spent hours at her bedside in the hospital, anxiously attending to her and hoping she would recover. My attitude was filled with worry. I sat and tried to pray for her healing, but most of my thoughts were morbid.

After about a week of this maudlin routine, I became sick myself. I contracted a staph infection and I soon found myself at home in bed, unable to find the strength to do hardly anything, let alone take care of my mom. I had worn my batteries down, and now the universe was presenting me with a poignant message: quit worrying and take care of yourself. Life was giving me a big clue that I was on the wrong track. I had no choice but to release my mom as the object of my distress and turn my attention inward for renewal.

After several days in bed I called my mom in the hospital. To my amazement, she reported that she was much better! Her comeback began the day I had stopped visiting her. By the time I spoke to her, she was eating, up and around, and well on the road to recovery.

Surveying that entire experience in retrospect, I believe that my attitude was standing in the way of my mother's healing. Thoughts and feelings are powerful, and my anxious fears in her presence were covering her like a blanket of doubt; I was actually unconsciously working *against* her recovery. It was only when I removed myself from her psychic space and released her that she began to heal. In such a case the best gift I could give her was to let go. And since I wasn't willing to do that myself, the universe gave me a blunt nudge in that direction. While it seemed that my illness was a problem at the time, it was actually a helping hand that served both of us.

The Window of Light

There is a phenomenon in the psychology of transition (dying) that demonstrates the power that we have to hold others to us or release them. Many hospitalized people on the verge of death pass on when their relatives are absent. Often such people leave this world in the middle of the night, or make their transition when their relatives leave the room for a few minutes. The attending family steps out for a little while, and when they return grandma has gone on. This is a very common phenomenon.

I believe that in such cases the patient is longing and ready to make their transition, but the presence and fearful thoughts of their family tend to tie them to earth. Like me sitting at my mother's bedside, anxiously wanting her to recover and physically remain in my life, the family's clinging tends to magnetize the patient to this world. It's harder to leave if your loved ones are pulling you to stay. When the family leaves the room or when the psychic space is still in the middle of the night and the veil between this world and the next one is very thin, it is easier to cut the cord. Once again we see that we must honor our loved ones' free will.

Honor Their Request

If someone asks you to leave them alone, then do it. Assume that they know what they need to do. Even—or especially—if they are upset, they may need time and space to take care of themself. Why is it, I wonder, that so often we believe that our will for another person or for our relationship with them is more important than what they tell us they are needing? Are we so insecure that we need to impose our own fears and needs onto their well-being? I think it would be a fantastic experiment to just believe someone when they tell us they are needing something, without interposing our judgments about it, and do our best to give them what they are asking for. Perhaps then, in such an atmosphere of unconditional support, our friend would feel so loved and understood that the issues that stood before them or between us would dissipate like mist in the morning sunlight.

If someone tells you they need space, then take their word for it. Someone who is feeling pressured or attacked does not become more willing by further pressure. Even if your intentions are honorable, their perception of intrusion is enough of a reason to let them be. You will be amazed at the results of releasing them and giving them the space they need. If they truly belong to you, they will return, and if they do not belong to you, there is no reason to try to coerce them to stay; in the long run you will not find the happiness you desire with them. But you will find peace by placing them and your relationship in the hands of God, and trusting that love is at work no matter what the outer appearances indicate. Outer appearances are notably deceptive, but the truth of the heart is consistently clear and rewarding.

Forget It

In a world that believes the way to get what we want is to struggle for it, we may accomplish a lot more by simply releasing. When we know that God is always working for our best interests, the wisest thing to do may be to simply stand aside and let God take over. If we believe that we have to run the universe (an ambitious undertaking indeed!) then we may have a hard time allowing God to handle the job. But the truth is that we cannot run the universe; our vision is simply not broad enough to fill the post of universal CEO. When we cannot find the wisdom or love to handle a challenging situation, we can summon the resources to do so by sincerely inviting God to take over and bring the situation to peace for the highest interests of all concerned.

It is impossible to hold onto the past and find our way through the present. When we cling to old losses or accolades, we deny welcome to the angel of the now. Now is an excellent moment to loosen your grip on old hurts. Nearly everyone in your past has forgotten the deeds that you still remember with pain, and sooner or later everyone, including you, will forget them entirely. Your darkest memories will be as if they never occurred. With but a little more openness of mind, we can forget it all now and move ahead with our life.

Picture a life in which the past has no power to cast its shadow on the fullness of the moment. Picture a world in which we are guided not by guilt or regret, but by courage and enthusiasm. We cannot blame the past or romanticize the future and still enjoy the blessing of today. Today is brimming with the richest blessings, and our vision and enjoyment of our good depends on our willingness to cut the sack. We don't have to struggle up any more mountains with a load of ancient weaponry on our shoulders. Punishment is not God's will, and neither is it ours. Neither do we need any of the Indians from our past to cut the sack for us. We can do it ourself, and we can do it now. Hurt yourself no longer by clinging to loss. It is not your savior. Your savior is love.

Dare to Let Go

1) What is in the sack you carry up the waterfall?

2) List three past misdeeds for which you are still punishing yourself.

3) List three past abuses under which you still labor as a victim.

4) Next to each "sin" or abuse, write down a way you could look at it differently. Find the purpose that bestows a blessing.

5) What specific steps (telling more truth to someone you want to release; forgiving or paying a debt; discarding relics) could you take to make your release complete?

DARE TO FORGIVE

The quality of mercy is not strained.
It droppeth as the gentle rain from Heaven.
— Shakespeare, *The Merchant of Venice*

Word came to Father Bernardo about a woman in his town who was said to be talking with Jesus. Many people were praising Maria's gift, reporting that she had interceded for them in their prayers and brought them great help. The townspeople believed that she was indeed communicating with God.

Father Bernardo, however, was a rather cynical man. He had begun his vocation with hope and enthusiasm, but over the years his vision had become obstructed by a dark cloud of doubt. Although he was a man of the cloth, Father Bernardo had allowed guilt and fear to undermine his belief in his own innocence and that of others. Suspecting this woman to be a fraud, the priest decided he would put her to a test. Father Bernardo went to see Maria and asked her, "Is it true that you talk to Jesus?"

"It is so," she answered.

"Then would you ask him a question for me?"

"Certainly."

"The next time you talk to Jesus," Father Bernardo requested, "ask him what was the sin I committed when I was in the seminary." He smiled politely and bowed his head, feeling smug that he had cornered the alleged oracle.

"Very well," Maria responded, "I will ask Jesus this question. Come back next week and I will have an answer for you."

The week passed, and Father Bernardo returned. "Did you talk to Jesus this week?" he asked.

"I did."

"Did you ask him what was my sin in the seminary?"

"Yes, Father, I did."

125

"And what did he say?"

"He said, 'I forgot.' "

Real forgiveness, *A Course in Miracles* tells us, is *selective forgetting*. To find healing we must remember the blessings and let all else go. We cannot afford to cling to grudges and feelings of betrayal. God does not punish us for holding onto insults against us; we punish ourself instantly with the pain and torment we cause ourself when we see ourself as a powerless victim.

God has already forgiven us. It is our own forgiveness we need to activate. Our supplication to God to win His forgiveness is really our search for our own higher understanding. It is useless to attempt to gain God's forgiveness, for He has already granted it. But it is very useful to find the place in our soul that recognizes our innocence. Our goal is not to pay off our sins. It is to bring our vision into alignment with God's sight of our purity.

The *Course* likens our holding judgments to being a guard in a prison. Imagine that your job is to keep someone in jail. In order to keep them incarcerated, you must sit at the door of their cell and watch them constantly to make sure they don't escape. The net effect of this responsibility is that you must stay in prison with them for as long as you would keep them there.

The sad irony of holding condemnation over another is that the other person is never in jail at all; it is we who keep ourself bound by our fears and judgments. Truly when we release others, we release ourself.

Instant Release

Caroline was a massage therapist in a hospital. One day she was assigned to massage a woman with an advanced case of cancer. Mrs. Hansen, Caroline was told, had just a few weeks to live.

As Caroline began to treat Mrs. Hansen, she asked the patient about her life. The therapist knew that there is always a connection between what is happening in our inner world and the symptoms we manifest. Knowing that there is a relationship between cancer and resentment, Caroline asked Mrs. Hansen if there was anyone in her life against whom she was holding a grudge.

"My sister and I haven't spoken in twenty years," Mrs. Hansen told her. "We had a fight at a wedding, and we have been at odds ever since."

"Tell me more," Caroline invited.

Given the opening, Mrs. Hansen began to tell Caroline of the pain she had been carrying for so long. She really didn't want to be mad at her sister. She really loved her, but she had a hard time letting go of the hurt she felt. As the older woman continued to speak, her voice became shaky and soon tears began to flow. The tears, which were a manifestation of the pent-up grief over the loss of love in Mrs. Hansen's life, led to a torrent, and she sobbed heavily on Caroline's shoulder. Caroline knew how important it was for this woman to release her sorrow and bitterness, and so she gladly gave Mrs. Hansen the time and support she so badly needed. After a while Mrs. Hansen stopped crying and she thanked Caroline for her caring.

It was just then that the x-ray technician came to take Mrs. Hansen for some tests. The women bade each other a fond good-bye. Caroline noticed that her patient looked significantly more peaceful than she had upon their meeting.

A few days later Caroline was on the floor where she had treated Mrs. Hansen, and she decided to pay her a visit. To Caroline's surprise, Mrs. Hansen was dressed, wearing make-up, and packing her suitcase.

"Well, what's happened to you?" Caroline asked.

"Oh, darling, it's like a miracle!" Mrs. Hansen responded brightly. "When they took me down for x-rays, they found *no trace of cancer* in my body. The doctors were baffled, since just a day earlier my body was riddled with the disease. They've repeated the tests, and they tell me I look fine inside. They're sending me home!"

Caroline smiled, embraced Mrs. Hansen, and shed a few tears herself. Inwardly she thanked God. Caroline knew that love and bitterness cannot share the same house. With Mrs. Hansen's release of her resentment, so went her disease.

Who's Counting?

The Apostle Paul is best known for his poetic tribute to love in his letter to the Corinthians. Paul said that "the greatest is love," and so it is.

In that moving epistle Paul declares that "love does not keep a record of wrongs." It is the ego, the voice of fear that pettily counts the errors of others (to distract our attention from our own) and holds sins against the "wrongdoer" in self-righteous judgment and "justified" cause for attack. I had a marvelous opportunity to observe this dynamic in my own mind. While waiting in line at the express checkout counter at a supermarket, I noticed that the woman in front of me had more than the allotted number of items. Feeling impatient, I counted the number of items in her shopping cart, and became further incensed as I observed each additional item over the limit. The vindictive part of my mind counseled me to call this transgression to her attention, or even better yet to report this scofflaw to the checkout girl. Here was a case where I was clearly right, with "just cause" for my indignation. But I was not clearly happy. I remembered the *Course in Miracles* question, "Do you want to be right, or happy?" It became apparent to me that I had more of an investment in self-righteousness than peace. I had sold my soul for a few paltry items on a conveyer belt. The Apostle Paul, I realized, was not teaching an esoteric lesson. He was speaking to me in the checkout line at the supermarket. "*Love does not keep a record of wrongs.*" There I was, counting my sister's wrongs by the item, and I was definitely out of love.

Here was my opportunity to put Paul's grand truth into practice. I decided to relax, leave the counting of the items to the cashier, and refocus my mind to love this woman whom I had considered my enemy. Quietly I beheld her in the light of innocence and sent her kind thoughts. That felt better, for sure.

Then the miracle happened. At that very moment she turned around, saw that I had just a few items in my hands, and offered, "Would you like to go ahead of me?" I was delightfully amazed. "Why, thank you!" I smiled brightly. "How kind of you!" And it was. She had no idea how richly she had served me.

One Moment of Light

Forgiveness is a miracle in every form that it appears. It goes beyond the laws of this world and undoes fear in a moment of awakening. Forgiveness is the crowning attribute of those who reflect the love of God even while living in this world. There is nothing that is beyond the ability of forgiveness to restore to its full worth and make new.

I spoke to a computer programmer who explained to me how a microchip is manufactured. A microchip is a miniature electronic brain which contains the programmed information that runs a computer. The program, my friend explained, is imbedded in the memory of the microchip by electronically pounding in the information, over and over and over again. After many focused repetitions, electronic grooves are cut into the mechanism so that it will perform according to its manufacturer's purpose.

This process, I intuited, is similar to the way our minds are programmed with fear and doubt. Through the continuous bombardment of the laws this world believes to be true, we absorb the beliefs of our parents, teachers, and the media. It does not matter if most or all of these beliefs are untrue. (The computer world calls this principle "G.I.G.O."—"Garbage in, garbage out," indicating that a faulty program will keep producing faulty results.) If we live in the presence of lies long enough, eventually we will believe them and act as if they are true.

The process of erasing a microchip is perhaps even more fascinating. To get rid of all the programming on a microchip, you simply subject the device to ultraviolet light. One pass of the light is sufficient to undo all the memory that has been pounded into the unit. Here we have an excellent metaphor for forgiveness: *One moment of true forgiveness can erase a lifetime of guilt or fear*. Even if we have harbored or pounded into ourselves years of anger, negativity, or separation, one moment in the right light is sufficient to release us from it all.

Do not underestimate the power of a forgiving thought. If you turn on a light in a dark room, it does not matter how long the room has been dark. With the introduction of light, the dark disappears, no matter whether it has been dark for twenty minutes or twenty years. Such is the power of the light. The light, of course, is the same as love. Forgiveness is the light in which all of our past, no matter how dark or encrusted we have become, is dissipated forever. *Forgive now, and be released from all of your past.*

A Higher Law

Jesus said, "You have been told, 'an eye for an eye and a tooth for a tooth,' but I tell you to forgive." Sin is always in the past, and forgiveness is always in the now. Guilt feeds on old mistakes, and absolution is in the present moment. Fear of the future is also in the past, for such fear is based only on past experience; what evidence do you have that your future will be anything like your past? As you release yourself from your past misdeeds, you discover that God has already released you.

The law of karma would bind you to time, limitation, and debt, telling you that you must pay off your sins with suffering. You can live under this law and verify this code in your experience—if you believe it to be so. But there is a Higher Law to which you are truly subject—the Law of Grace. Under this compassionate principle, you are free of all past mistakes the moment you forgive yourself for them. If something you have done has caused pain to yourself or another, and you have grown in awareness to the point that you would not hurt yourself or the other person in the same way, then I assure you that God has released you from the effects of your act. God is a God of forgiveness; His interest is not in punishment, but awakening. If you have indeed awakened through your experience, then you are free.

It cannot be overemphasized that God does not punish. We look upon a punishing God only if we believe that we are punishable. To see yourself as guilty is to forget that you are innocent. There is no end to guilt, except through innocence. If you expect to pay off past wrongdoing through present or future pain, your sentence will extend itself unto eternity. If you are in jail now, you will be there forever, for there is only the now. The moment you choose innocence you release yourself forever. Vision through the eyes of forgiveness reveals that guilt has never existed in the mind of God, and as His perfect child such a dark verdict has no place in your mind.

Together let us make a vow. Together let us join in seeing only the blessings that Spirit has given us. Together let us place all of our past on the altar of peace and release all that is not worthy of love to be consumed in the flame of divine compassion. From the ashes rises the phoenix of transformation, the symbol of hope where there once seemed only tragedy. The flowers of springtime blossom in the presence of the warmth we welcome. The spring rain that momentarily blocked our view of sun, was but a blessing in a form we did not understand. But now our compassion has opened a way for clearer vision. There is nothing beyond God's capacity to overlook, and nothing in us unlike our Father.

Dare to Forgive

1) Make a list of the grudges and resentments you carry. Next to each item record the length of time you have been carrying it.

2) What is the price you pay for each withholding of love?

3) Are you willing to release some or all of these grudges? If so, write down a statement of forgiveness next to each one you want to release.

DARE TO FEEL

Before we can become fully divine,
we must become fully human.

— St. Ignatius

I was sharing a quiet evening with my friend Corri, who was going through a very difficult time in her life. "Everything seems to be changing so quickly!" she told me. "I am in the midst of a divorce; the man with whom I expected to spend my life is not speaking to me; and the kids are in the middle of our differences, growing up faster than I wanted. I don't know why all of this is happening. I feel so overwhelmed—I've never felt so alone in all my life." A few tears rolled down Corri's tender cheeks.

Quick to be helpful, I took out a tissue and started to wipe her tears away. I tried to reassure her, "Don't worry. It will turn out O.K.—this is just a time of change you're going through."

Corri did not turn her head, but spoke straight to me.

"I know that may be so," she responded, "but can't you let me be touched by life? These are important transitions for me. I need to feel them in the deepest way; I can't just gloss over these feelings and try to distract myself from the pain. Even though these experiences hurt, they are connected to important lessons for me. Please allow me to feel what I'm going through."

There was nothing for me to say. Corri was claiming her right to gain the understandings she needed to master. It was not for me to try to rob her of her meaningful experience just because I was uncomfortable watching her weep. Her need to feel her pain was more important than my need to take it away.

"Let me be touched by life." Corri was not asking to be a victim or a loser. To the contrary, she was seeking to become stronger and more powerful through absorbing and integrating

the messages her feelings were bringing to her. The tears came and went, but the awareness that the tears uncovered gave Corri wisdom that would last a lifetime.

The Invitation to Greater Harmony

It takes courage, self-confidence, and trust to go through hurtful feelings and stay with them until you come out on the other side. Pain is not a punishment, but a call for deeper awareness, an invitation to wake up and find greater harmony in living. Pain is a warning flag, a helpful signal that we need to look at a situation differently or find a more honest way to respond to a challenge. Thus we can understand the advice to "love your disease—it's keeping you healthy."

If we hearken unto the lesson that pain or disease brings us, we can make a course correction that will enhance our quality of living. How good can our life be if we are harboring subconscious patterns that defeat joy? We are not here simply to survive; we are here to live. Any block that prevents us from expressing our highest nature must be discovered and transformed. Pain and disease are the universe's way of getting our attention so we can begin the necessary process of transformation.

Birth Pangs of the Soul

Sometimes we have a tendency to gloss over, deny, or push down pain when it arises. We may choose a non-confrontive path in which we can hide. We latch onto a belief system that protects our presentation and we justify our fear with a dogma. Then we attract people around us who agree with our masquerade, which hurts us even more. No one has ever found peace by manipulating colleagues to agree on an illusion. Our best friends are not those who protect our fantasies; our true friends are those who love us enough to invite us to move ahead. We are blessed by agreement on integrity, not doctrine.

Our greatest need on the spiritual path is truth, even if it does not seem comfortable according to the niche we've cozied ourself in. Our ego wants to hang out in comfortland, but our soul calls us to our purpose. Our spirit wants to grow and come closer to real happiness, even if that means cracking the shells in which we've become encrusted.

When such a breakthrough comes, the immediate effects may seem chaotic, but the more enduring result is greater freedom. The artist makes a mess in the process of creating, but eventually the clutter disappears and a work of beauty is delivered to the world. You are in the process of bringing your soul to birth. While you may experience sharp pangs in the delivery, when you hold your child in your arms you will forget the pain and bless the entire experience as helpful.

Experience, Not Opinions

Because your feelings are so important to your personal path of awakening, you must honor them above the opinions of the outer world. The quickest way to avoid arguments, or end ones which arise, is to talk about your experience rather than your opinions. *Anyone can argue with your opinions, but no one can argue with your experience.* If you know that something is right for you, then you must act on it. If you are walking true to your spirit, you do not need to defend, explain, or justify your actions to anyone. Those who do not wish to believe you will not listen to your explanations, and those who believe in you do not need any. Never minimize the value of the forces which move you to self-expression. Be sure not to judge yourself by your friends' opinions. Most people in this world do not have a handle on their own lives; how, then, do you expect them to see yours clearly? Everyone sees you through their own emotional filters; it is rare that someone will advise you without a personal investment on their part. Especially if someone is angry at you, you can be sure that they are not seeing you clearly. Any sense of attack, resentment, or judgment on their part is a sure sign that they are operating from fear, the one voice that is always a lie. Country wisdom advises us, "Never wrestle with a pig; both of you will get dirty—and the pig likes it." Be careful what consciousness you step into. Ask yourself, "Is this worthy of the kind of life I want to live?" In your answer lies your guide to action.

The good news is that we are blessed with some people in our life who love us enough to see us clearly and tell us truth that is very helpful if we are open to hearing it. These people are our true friends, for they value our strength and well-being more than our drama, and they want nothing more than for us to be happy. If you have such friends, cherish them, thank God for their gifts, and listen to them with your heart when they speak to you. They see you through the eyes of love, and that is what you will become when you see yourself with the same vision and act on it. Pray to be such a friend to others.

Truly Helpful

If we attempt to dispose of our pain or that of another before we have grasped the lesson calling for attention, we may block or delay the gift the discomfort is knocking on our door to deliver.

I attended a psychology workshop focused on releasing and healing emotional blocks. Our class did an exercise in which we lay down on the floor with our heads together and our legs fanning outward like the spokes of a wheel. One person began the process by saying, "Love me." The next person in the circle was to answer, "I love you." The next person called out, "Love me," and so on, until we created an ongoing succession of "love me's" and "I love you's." At first the game seemed contrived and many people said the words mechanically. After several rounds, however, the words we were saying became attached to feelings, and many of us felt deep emotions welling up. The "love me's" and "I love you's" increased in dramatic power with each round. I began to feel the parts of me that were calling for love, along with the parts that were giving it.

At one point I became aware of a few people in my life whose love I very much wanted, but did not feel I was receiving. As I said the words, "Love me!" I saw how deeply I had been desiring their attention and approval. I became aware of a tremendous, almost aching frustration and pain of rejection over the love that I didn't feel I was getting. My feelings became stronger until I burst into tears. I had no idea how deeply those feelings had resided within me without my being aware of them. Although I was touching a deep-seated sorrow, I felt healed to find it, feel it, and begin to release it. I had uncovered a pocket of sadness that could now be defused. I lay there weeping and appreciating my release.

At that moment a woman next to me leaned over and began to hug and stroke me in a kind and motherly effort to comfort me. When she did that, however, I felt as if I was being robbed of an important feeling that I needed to experience. She was telling me, "Now, now, that's OK." But that is not what I wanted or needed to hear at that moment. For those few minutes I needed to lie there and cry. I needed to discover the years of feelings of abandonment and seeking approval that I had stuffed away into a dark and painful pocket that seemed to be out of sight, but which controlled me more than I realized. I did not want a band-aid—I wanted to change my life so I could get out of pain. I continued to let myself feel the hurt, and after a while a great deal of the sorrow had dissipated. I felt relaxed, released, and much lighter and freer.

Since that time I have not experienced that issue of seeking approval or validation from a teacher. That healing was facilitated by my getting in touch with those feelings, letting them come up, experiencing them fully, and letting them go. Those four elements are very important in emotional healing.

To Value Realness

Some people believe that spiritual growth is demonstrated by looking happy all the time. But appearances are not the same as reality, and acting joyful is not the same thing as being joyful. Touching life with our feelings will bring us more joy than living up to an image. The sad irony of living to look good is that we usually don't fool anyone but ourself. Moreover, we cut ourself off from real intimacy in relationships. Remember that real friends value us as we truly are rather than who we would have them think we are. They want to touch our soul rather than bow to our presentation.

My partner Karren and I were visited by Joyce and Barry Vissell, the dear authors of *The Shared Heart* and several other excellent books on relationships and parenting. All of us had made plans to go to the beach together one afternoon, and the time came for us to leave the house. But Karren and I were going through a very difficult time, and we were in the midst of a tearful and emotional conversation. Joyce and Barry sensed that we were in no condition to enjoy a beach day with them, and they thoughtfully asked us if we would rather spend the time alone. We acknowledged that we did want to go on with our unfolding dialogue, and began to apologize for breaking our appointment with them. "Oh, no, that's perfectly alright," they reassured us. "We value realness—this is what you need to do, and so we want you to take care of yourselves." This was a true gift from their heart, and Karren and I appreciated the valuable time we went on to share with each other that afternoon.

We value realness. Those strong kind words still ring in my mind. How precious are friends and teachers who encourage us to feel what we are feeling, and respect our process as we go through emotionally sensitive times. There is no greater gift we can offer our friends than to stand beside them as they explore the frightening yet exhilarating regions of the heart.

Humble Mastery

One evening my teacher Hilda was feeling troubled about a painful decision she had to make. "What shall I do, kids?" she asked our class of three hundred students. I admired Hilda for her humility. She dropped her head into her hands and wept openly. We students just sat quietly and allowed her to go through her process. After a few moments of tears, she lifted her head, sat up, and spoke strongly, "Thank you, my friends—I needed to feel that deeply; now I can more easily see my next step."

Release the Hidden Splendor

A Course in Miracles reminds us that we are not here to seek and find love, for that is what we already are. We are here to discover the blocks to our awareness of love's presence, so we can release them and let our true loving nature shine forth in full splendor.

If we fear that we will be destroyed by our emotions, we will never look at them long enough to receive the messages they are bringing us. Our emotions are not given to destroy us; channeled wisely, they empower us. True mastery of living does not mean squelching our feelings. To the contrary, it means bringing our life into harmony with all the forces that move within us, and coming to peace with who we are. We cannot discover and express who we are as long as we are denying a part of ourself. Emotions are not dissipated by denying them; they are amplified. What you run away from, runs you. What you face, you master. This is the path to enlightenment.

Do not seek for pain, but neither seek to run from it. Seek to wake up. Seek to use everything that comes into your world for your transformation. Then pain will no longer be your enemy; it will become your ally. Every person and experience we meet on the path of truth can and will become our ally. The world of feelings is a fertile arena for self-discovery, psychic transformation, and the healing of fear. To feel deeply is one of the great gifts of life. Welcome the riches that God has bestowed upon your soul.

Dare to Feel

1) How do you usually deal with your feelings?

2) How do you respond when you see another person in pain?

3) What feelings are calling to you for attention or expression? What fears have held you from acknowledging these feelings?

4) How much weight do you place on the opinions of others? Do you have the strength to follow your heart if it guides you to a different path?

5) Make a list of the friends you value the most. What makes these friendships meaningful?

DARE TO LIGHTEN UP

There are only two things to remember in life:
1. Don't sweat the small stuff.
2. It's all small stuff.

Johnny was a precocious eight-year-old who had a knack for asking his mother all the questions she didn't want to answer. "How old are you?" "How much do you weigh?" and "Why did you and daddy get divorced?" were three unwelcome queries at which he persisted. The more he pursued, the more his mom refused to answer.

One day Johnny came to his mom with a smug smile and reported, "Guess what, mom—I know how old you are!"

"Yes?"

"You're thirty-eight!"

"That's right," mom conceded.

"And I know how much you weigh!" the boy proudly announced.

"How much?"

"A hundred and thirty-five."

"That's very good, Johnny," mom had to admit. "How did you know?"

"When you were taking a nap I looked in your purse and I found your driver's license. And I found out why you and dad got divorced."

"Why's that?" mom had to ask.

"Because you got an 'F' in sex!"

Hopefully you enjoyed a chuckle and perhaps a good laugh by way of this cute story. There is no great meaning or cosmic truth behind this tale. It has one intention—to make our heart light and laugh a bit. And that is a very good purpose indeed. Laughter is very high on God's list of ingredients that make life worth living. To laugh deeply is to know God.

The Test of Sanity

There is one criterion by which you can ascertain if you are looking at a situation with a clear mind: Can you laugh about it? If you cannot, you can be sure fear has gotten a foothold on your consciousness and clouded your ability to see the bigger picture.

There is nothing in this world that is beyond laughter. In fact, the heavier a situation seems, the more we need to laugh about it. An inability to see the humor in a situation means you are stuck somewhere and you need to look at it from a higher perspective.

You might make a list of things you feel you cannot laugh about and use those situations as focal points for your healing. Open up your mind and heart and see life anew. Nothing is so bad that you cannot rise above it. Look back for a moment on the things you thought were so horrible at the time. You can probably laugh about most of those experiences now. In high school whenever I had a big date, I would get a huge pimple on the end of my nose. I invested great amounts of money in Clearasil, but that zit just parked itself there until the date. Then it went away the next day. At the time I believed this was the most horrible thing that could happen to anyone. Now I can laugh about it. New problems are not worse than the old ones; they are just different— this year's model of a familiar drama. In a few days, weeks or years you will be laughing about the things that seem so heavy now. Why bother waiting to laugh? Perhaps if we moved these somber challenges into a space in our heart where we can make light of them, they would disappear more quickly.

A Course in Miracles tells us that "all sin ends in laughter." This means that you know you are healed and complete with a situation when you can laugh about it. It further means that when we release our judgments about ourself and others, we can laugh about them. Forgiveness and laughter walk side by side; where you find one, you will always find the other.

No Excuses Necessary

One Sunday I was delivering the message at a growing church in the northeast. Just after my talk the children of the congregation came onstage for their customary blessing. This morning the kids were an especially motley gang. The little boys clumsily bumped one another as they stepped forward, and the girls lifted up the hems of their dresses to chew on them. A delightful childlike energy filled the meeting hall.

As everyone quieted down in preparation for the blessing, one boy began to giggle. The little freckle-faced guy kept giggling until he burst into unrestrained laughter. Soon the child next to him began to laugh, and before long all the kids on the stage were having a laughing party. Their laughter was so infectious that the congregation caught on quickly, and in less than a minute the entire church was rollicking.

The minister asked the boy who started it all, "What's so funny, Jay?"

"I don't know," the youngster responded "—I just feel like laughing!"

As I sat back in my chair and enjoyed laughing with everyone, it occurred to me that in that one statement the child had given a better sermon than I had in half an hour of talking. He did not need an excuse to be happy. He didn't blame the world for his sorrows, and he didn't need something to entertain him to make him happy. He just felt like laughing, and that was a good enough reason. And in his joy he brought delight to hundreds of people.

There is a bumper sticker which affirms, "*I do not need an excuse to experience joy!*" That day in church Jay gave a group of serious adults a living demonstration that real happiness proceeds from inside out.

The God of Delight

Somewhere in our cultural psyche we have developed an image of a very serious God, and this notion has hurt us greatly. We believe that God is an old man with a white beard who sits on a cloud and judges us, ready and eager to cast us into the ovens of hell for the slightest transgression. This is not the God that I know, nor is it the God that is. It is a picture of fear that we have projected onto the only figure in life who loves us consistently

143

without condition or clause. We would do well to let this picture go forever; it is a portrait of pain.

God is a God of delight. Remember that gravity is the thing that keeps us bound to earth. Celebration is the energy that brings us true release. The lighter we are, the closer we rise to Heaven.

I appreciate clergymen and women who remind me of God's delight. Of all the religious people I have met, there is one group that I have found to be consistently joyful—Tibetan Buddhist monks. I have known a number of these priests, and if there is one thing I can say about them, they know how to laugh. Some of them wear ear-to-ear grins and shake with mirth readily and heartily. These monks are very light souls. They have no possessions, they do not worship money, they are not busy building glamorous institutions, and they pretty much go where God tells them. Perhaps they are onto something.

By contrast, many of the clergymen and women I have met and seen in the Judeo-Christian traditions are rather heavy of spirit. Their sermons are fraught with fear, laden with guilt, riddled with threats of punishment and damnation, and some of them spend great amounts of time attacking practices which they do not condone, such as homosexuality and abortion. Such preachers are not bringing their listeners to healing; instead they are tightening the shackles that have kept the world in pain. Who could learn to love a God of revenge? God does not participate in wrathful judgment. Teachers of vengeance are entrapped by fear and invite others into their circle of terror. They dramatically laugh, cry, pound the pulpit, and spend half their television time raising funds for the new sanctuary. If there is one message that a naive viewer may absorb from such a model, it is that God is a punishing father who wants our blood and our money.

This is not so. God wants nothing more—or less—from us than to be happy. To find God does not require punishment, just awakening. Fear is not the route home. We have all tried being afraid for many years. Has it brought us any results we value? Certainly not. But joy brings instantaneous reward. In a moment of lightheartedness we unveil the beauty of God's creation and the freedom of our spirit. There is nothing to fear, and much to laugh about.

Perhaps the harbingers of doom would do better to put aside fund-raising and replace it with fun-raising. There is nothing wrong with collecting money to build a sanctuary; a beautiful sanctuary is a praiseworthy altar to Spirit. The question is, "With what will we fill the sanctuary?" If you're going to make more room to scare people, that is not at all necessary. We can just sit at home and watch the news if we want to find things to worry about. But if we build an edifice to honor the God of light, we have a worthy purpose indeed! Such a temple will be filled with people who want to come because their hearts draw them there. The hall will be overflowing with souls who are eager to put aside the gods of loss and sorrow, and come to celebrate the glory of a happy heart.

Instead of membership drives at our churches, we need campaigns to awaken. If you are driving for membership only, you are on the wrong road and you will drive your church over a cliff. Unfortunately, most churches have the cart before the horse in building programs. They believe that if they get more people, they will get more spirit. But that is exactly the opposite of the way success really works. If you have the spirit, the people will be attracted. As Jesus aptly advised us, "Seek ye first the Kingdom and all shall be added." And in a more modern metaphor, "If you build it—(the spirit)—they will come."

A friend of mine was being interviewed by a board of directors in her application to become the minister of a church at which attendance was sagging. One of the first questions she was asked was whether or not she would spearhead a new church building program. She told them, "I can't promise that I will build a new building, but I will build consciousness." Perhaps their focus on the form of the temple rather than its essence was the reason they were losing members in the first place. If you have a building but no consciousness, you have nothing. If you have consciousness, everything you need will be attracted. We have too many churches that are full of people, but empty of spirit. We need to build new churches—with our hearts.

Don't You Realize?

Jesus explained that the way to get into Heaven is to become like a little child. Children have their priorities in order. Happiness and play are at the top of the list. Perhaps as adults we may not be able to play all the time, but we can certainly adopt an attitude of ease that we may bring to all of our endeavors.

On the eve of the war in the Persian Gulf I gathered with a group of about thirty people around a campfire on a mountain to pray for peace. The mood was very somber. Many of us sensed that war was imminent, and most people were experiencing some kind of fear. Some participants were physically ill.

Our ceremony consisted of each person offering a prayer. As we went around the circle, each of us voiced our wishes for peace. At the gathering there were three little children who had come with their parents. While we adults were offering our prayers, the children were playing at the fireside. At one point the kids began to giggle loudly. This disturbed some of the adults, especially the mother of one of the children. Feeling embarrassed, she reprimanded them, "Quiet—Don't you realize what we're doing?" The children complied and returned to their play in more subdued tones. I imagined hearing a child's voice returning, "Don't you realize what *we're* doing?"

The children were happy. They were not beset by fears, anxious anticipation of the worst, or quandaries about morality and political strategy. They were laughing. They were not living in the foreboding peril of January fifteenth; they were living in the glory of now. That evening there were at least three people on that hillside who were making a significant contribution to world peace by not living in the consciousness of war. When I realized that the children were living in a different reality than us adults, my first thought was that they were too young to be afraid. Then I realized that they were too smart to be afraid.

The Bible foretells, "A child shall lead them." Perhaps if we want to find the way out of war we should pay less attention to military strategists and more attention to our children. And if we wish to escape the war of psychic conflict that rages within us, we need to bypass our weighty reasoning mind and consult the child within us.

The Way Out

Sometimes when we are getting too serious we need someone with a light heart to remind us that we don't need to be afraid. Fear and love cannot share the same room. When the two meet, one has to go. Love will never flee from fear, but terror will make a hasty exit (or rebellion) in the face of peace.

When my mother's doctor told me that she had but six months to live, I became very anxious. As I mentioned in an earlier chapter, I was very attached to my mom and I had a great deal of resistance to her leaving this world.

During the last year of her life, I went to visit my mom regularly at her apartment. We would sit on the couch and watch TV together, but much of the time my thoughts were morbid. I probably wasn't much fun to be with.

One evening my mother turned to me and saw a morose expression in my eyes. She took me by the hands, looked me in the eye, and began to sing, "Feelings...Whoh-oh-oh...Feelings," *à la* Barry Manilow. Then she burst into laughter. She was making fun of me. While I was quite fearful about her death, she was not very worried about it at all. She had done everything she wanted in this life, there was nothing left for her here, and she was ready to go. If I wasn't ready for her to go, that was my problem. And her answer to that was comedy.

It worked. Seeing my mom make light of her own death, even as I was unable to do so, created a major shift in my attitude. On an emotional level I realized that if she wasn't worried about it, then I didn't need to worry either.

My mom's sense of humor was one of her greatest gifts. She had had a hard life. Growing up during the Depression, she left school at the age of thirteen to work in a pocketbook factory, had her first husband die in her arms at a young age, and went through four miscarriages before I was born when she was forty-two years old. She could have had a lot to complain about, but she didn't. My mom's humor was her saving grace. She had a winning ability to laugh about anything. Nothing was beyond her making fun of it. She was living proof that a light heart is the best antidote to life's troubles.

Take Care of Your Heart

I saw an after-school special on television showing two ten-year-old boys walking home from school. One boy turned to the other and told his friend, "You know, Joey, I don't think I want to grow up."

"Why not?" Joey asks.

"Because when you grow up, your heart dies."

The child's statement really got to me. I realized that what he was saying is true. Most people allow their heart to close down with age. Not because we have to. Not because God set life up that way. Because we let it be so.

It doesn't have to be that way. If we choose, we can keep our heart alive and be fully in life at any age. Lived correctly, the curtains of our heart continue to open like the petals of a flower as our life progresses. In his ninety-fourth year Charles Fillmore, the co-founder of Unity, declared, "I fairly sizzle with zeal and enthusiasm, and I go forth to do the things that ought to be done by me!"

No, our heart doesn't have to die. We just have to remember to keep our light shining as brightly as possible. We are like lighthouse keepers. The light is quite present and powerful, and it will do its job just by being what it is. Our role is to keep the mirrors polished so it can radiate far and strong.

Stay Light

To stay light in the presence of other joyful souls is easy. But to be a light in the midst of darkness is a gift among gifts. Adrian Cronauer, portrayed by Robin Williams in *Good Morning, Vietnam*, was one who delivered such a gift.

My favorite scene of the movie is the one in which Cronauer has just been fired from his position as a disk jockey broadcasting over the army radio to the troops in Vietnam. Although his outrageous humor is universally loved by the G.I.'s who listen to him faithfully, Cronauer's superiors have no patience for his irreverent levity, and he is summarily ousted. Adrian has given a lot, and his dismissal is very painful and disappointing to him.

On his way out of the city Cronauer encounters a convoy of troops en route to the combat zone. The soldiers recognize Cronauer and beg him to do a few of his routines. Although he is feeling angry and hurt, he complies. Instantly his comedy brings a welcome release to these tense young men on the eve of battle.

The scene really touched my heart. Here were hundreds of young soldiers facing possible death, and for a moment Cronauer gave them some joy. He made them laugh and lightened their hearts. For a moment they forgot that they were headed for the battlefield, and they relaxed and breathed. That scene allowed me to appreciate the gift of humor more than ever. Laughter is God's antidote for the tension that comes with living in a world of painful illusions. It is a blessing unique among the graces God bestows.

Life is Too Important to be Taken Seriously

Bobby McFerrin sang, "In every life we have some trouble; when you worry, you make it double—Don't worry, be happy." The Jamaicans' motto is "No problem." And the Hawaiians remind each other, "Hang loose."

We can all lighten up. We live in extraordinary times. Our age is tense, challenging, alive, and exciting. There has never been a transformational time on earth like this before. We are seeing more changes more quickly than ever. And the process is good.

Perhaps lightening up is our best defense against the fear that seems to plague our world. I often remind myself that life is not so much about what I do, but about how I hold it; not my accomplishments, but my attitude. In many cases a positive attitude is a more significant accomplishment than a physical feat. Many people can sell a car or build a house, but how many can keep their spirits high in the process? I believe that the world remembers us not so much for what we do, but for who we are as we do it.

People who laugh a lot live longer, but more important they live better. What is the use of living if you can't enjoy yourself while you're here?

Laughter is a gift from God. I know that God has a great sense of humor. I'll bet He laughs at most of the renditions of his son as a painfully serious teacher. One who knows God knows laughter. Some people criticize humor as irreverent. Humor is very reverent; it is, in fact, a very high form of prayer. If there were more laughter in churches, there would be more people in churches. I know several ministers who are very humorous teachers, and their congregations are among the largest. People do not want to be taught that life is a downer. Many of us have been taught that lesson for most of our life, and the ensuing burden has worked against our enlightenment. Perhaps we are ready now for a new lesson. Perhaps we are ready to learn that gaiety is an intrinsic ingredient of health and success. Perhaps we are ready to let go of the heaviness with which we have associated the spiritual path, and see it through new eyes.

Wouldn't it be a riot if we got to Heaven and there we found God laughing? I can just see us serious people being ushered into God's anteroom with our knees shaking and our breath bated for the final verdict, anxious and fearful. Then I imagine God coming to greet us on roller skates, with a Sony Walkman on His head, a surfboard under one arm, and a chocolate chip cookie in the other hand. "What happened to the angry old man with a white beard?" we ask, confused. "Lighten up," the Creator invites us, "and be sure you don't get an 'F' in sex."

Dare to Lighten Up

1) Name something you don't think is funny. Imagine a way you could look at it so you find some humor in it.

2) Think of a time in your life when you were the happiest. What can you say about your sense of humor at that time?

3) Apply the truth that "all sin ends in laughter" to something you have judged against yourself for doing.

4) List the attributes of an angry vengeful God, and those of a forgiving, light-hearted God. What do you really believe about God? How do your attitude and actions reflect your beliefs?

5) Name the three happiest people you know. What can you say about their sense of humor?

6) Who helps you the most with their light-hearted attitude? Whom do you help in the same way?

DARE TO BE WRONG

Would you rather be right, or happy?
— A Course in Miracles

Jumping from Conclusions

The 747 pulled to an astonishingly quiet halt at the Los Angeles terminal. I gathered my belongings and moved with the masses through the jetway and then through the maze of sheetrocked halls. I felt like a corpuscle pulsating through an artery in a body that was eternally under construction. Life, I surmised, is like an airport; you just have to trust that your baggage will meet you when you arrive.

I was looking forward to getting together with Jakki. It had been a while since we had seen each other, and it would be good to have some time together.

When I arrived at the baggage claim, however, Jakki was not there. I was surprised and disappointed. She was usually prompt, and I wondered what had happened. Was she upset over something I had said? Our last meeting was distressing for both of us, and perhaps it had bothered her more than I had known.

I looked around the terminal. A little boy was giving himself a ride on the conveyer belt. When his mom noticed his escapade, she pulled him off. Actually, I was rooting for the kid. Riding on the belt looked like more fun than just waiting for your luggage. The child seemed happier than the mom—maybe he was on to something.

Fifteen minutes passed. Still no Jakki. "Where is she?" I began to wonder. She knew the arrival time. I started to feel impatient. Was she trying to get back at me by not showing up?

The clock ticked on. Nearly everyone who had been on my plane had found their luggage, and they were off to their destinations. But not me. I stood there trying to be peaceful, but feeling pretty irked.

The last passenger lifted his suitcase from the belt and the airline agent emerged from the office to pick off the unclaimed luggage. Now this was getting serious. Nearly forty-five minutes had passed. If this was Jakki's idea of a joke, it had gone far enough. I was really getting bugged. I began to consider all the things I would say to her if and when she arrived. All the complaints I could justifiably lodge. All the ways I could make her feel guilty for making me wait. All the ways I could be right because she was wrong.

I looked at the clock. This had gone far enough—it was time to take action, I thought. I found some change in my pocket and headed toward the outside pay phone to call Jakki's house.

As I opened the door I bumped into a woman frantically running in. "Excuse . . ." My apology was interrupted when I saw it was Jakki. My first impulse was to blurt out all my complaints and my sense of righteous indignation about her keeping me waiting. Should I unload?

Then I remembered a lesson taught to me by my teacher Hilda. During a class Hilda prescribed a long Hindu mantra guaranteed to bring peace to those who chanted it. After she demonstrated several repetitions of the mantra in sanskrit, Hilda announced that it would be sufficient to simply repeat the initial letter of each word: "*K.Y.B.M.S.*" Grateful for any technique which would bring us closer to happiness, our class complied. "*K.Y.B.M.S...K.Y.B.M.S...K.Y.B.M.S...*" The chanting echoed through the halls of the great cathedral. "Now," Hilda explained, "if you would like to know the translation of this most important mantra, I will tell you: '*Keep Your Big Mouth Shut.*' "

Now here I was facing a wall of smog and foggy thinking, recalling a maxim taught to me ten years earlier. Perhaps it was no accident that of all the lessons in my memory bank, that one should rise to the surface. I decided to take a gamble and K.Y.B.M.S.

Jakki and I gave each other a quick hug and I told her it was good to see her. It was. Still I had to fight off an urge to caustically ask her why she was so late.

We exited the terminal and walked toward the parking lot.

Right outside the door we began to pass a huge gleaming white stretch limousine at the curb. Joking, I asked Jakki, "Is this our car?"

Giggling, she answered, "Yes!"

I smiled as if to note, "that's a cute idea," and continued on to the crosswalk and waited for the light to change.

But Jakki didn't follow me. When I turned to see what had happened to her, she was standing by the limousine with the door open. "Why don't you believe me when I tell you something, sir?"

A tall young man in a chauffeur's outfit stood at the open trunk of the car, motioning me to bring my bags back.

I could hardly believe it! She was not kidding. The lady had hired an elegant limousine to pick me up from the airport! If this was a joke, now I wanted to be in on it! I stepped into the rear seat and we stretched out and relaxed.

And what a cushy ride it was! We kicked off our shoes and Jakki poured us some cold sparkling cider from the bar. "I'm so sorry we were late—the limo got caught in traffic on the way to the airport. Thanks for being so patient." She stretched her arms around me.

I gulped. Was I glad I had kept my B.M.S! If there was ever a time that I was happy I listened to that inner voice, that was it. We put our feet up on the cushions, leaned back, turned the radio on, and watched the traffic fade into the background. I was happy to be wrong.

Pray to Be Wrong

Sometimes we are better off wrong than right. Usually we are better off wrong than right. Whenever we are angry, upset, or feeling like a victim in any way, we are better off wrong than right.

I have discovered a most powerful prayer: I pray to be wrong. Whenever I perceive myself as losing, hurt, or unjustly treated, I close my eyes, turn my mind to Spirit, and ask God to show me that I am wrong about the way I have been seeing the painful situation.

You might like to try this prayer. Take a pencil and paper and write down everything you are unhappy about. List all the areas of your life, including career, health, relationships, and finances, in which you feel powerless, unloved, or unfairly treated. Be sure to note the situations in which you perceive yourself to be a victim or loser. The more honest you can be, the wider you will open the door to real transformation. Then hold the paper between your hands in a prayerful way and ask, "God, please let me be wrong about all of this."

I am happy to promise you that your prayer will be answered because, quite frankly, you *are* wrong about all of it. We are created in the image and likeness of an omnipotent God, and as His children we are never powerless. If you are willing to release your sense of victimization, even to the slightest degree, you will see that you have painted yourself into a corner simply by erroneous perception. If you look again, or think about your situation in a different way, you will see that there is a door where you thought there was only a wall. Your first step out the door is to begin to consciously find gifts, lessons, and blessings where you once saw attack, insult, and curses. You can save yourself a great deal of time and pain by seeing that you have chosen to be right about your hurts rather than happy about your strengths. You do not realize the cost of such a choice. To be right about being a victim is to deny the truth that you are a cherished entity in a loving, supportive universe which is masterfully orchestrated by a gracious God. Either you are right about your problem, or God is right about the solution. There is no compromise, gray area, or bargaining about the untraversable gap between these two ways of seeing and being in life.

We have the right to cling painfully to our position, and we also have the power to release it and be healed. God can whisper the truth in our ear, but He cannot choose or act for us. God will heal us, but we have to take a step toward letting go of our denial of the presence of love. Thus our healing lies in our own hands. And you will ultimately choose peace, for it is the nature of God's children to return home. The only thing that is up to you now is the length of the movie.

Let Me See This Differently

Healing is not a matter of setting things right, but *seeing* things rightly. In truth, all is already healed and whole. The only gap between the problem and the solution is in our consciousness, and that is exactly where the critical shift to healing takes place.

Several years ago I received a letter from my aunt, who lives in a retirement community in Florida. I opened the letter to read a depressing account of her life:

> *Dear Alan,*
> *Life here is pretty much the same every day. I get up, have a few eggs for breakfast, then I watch the game shows on TV. For lunch I go down to the local deli, where I have a grilled cheese sandwich and gossip with some of my friends. Then I come home, watch some soap operas, sit on the balcony, read a while, and go to sleep. People are getting on in years here, and it seems that each day another one of my friends passes on. Hope to see you before long.*
> *Love,*
> *Aunt Rose*

I put the letter down. "How dreary!" I shuddered. "The same lunch every day...game shows, gossip, and soap operas...friends passing on like subway passengers going through a turnstile—yuk! What a terrible existence—this plot sounds like the antithesis to *It's a Wonderful Life.*" My body began to contract in a dark cloud of despair.

Then I remembered a lesson from *A Course in Miracles:* "*Beware the temptation to perceive yourself as unfairly treated.*" I knew that the lesson applied not only to me, but to my vision of any person or circumstance I perceived as less than whole. Was it possible that I could see my aunt's situation in a different light?

I decided to read the letter again, but this time I would look for joy and beauty in her words. I picked up the paper and began: *Dear Alan.* I was dear to her. How wonderful that she cared about me! I felt loved. *Life is pretty much the same here every day.*

Thank God that she is no longer going through the turbulent upheavals that agitate so many lives. Her life has finally come to a sense of calm and stability. *The same lunch and game shows.* It sounds like she enjoys that! Just because this is not something I would like, it does not mean that it is a bad thing. I cannot judge what makes someone else happy. (My mom used to love to sit and watch TV just about all day long—she asked me not to call her while *Perry Mason* was on.) *Hanging out at the deli with her friends.* That is exactly what I have done for a lot of my life. First in the college cafeteria, then at the health food bar, and now at the local fruit stand. On second thought, Aunt Rose and I had a lot in common! *Friends passing on.* She didn't say "dying;" passing on means going somewhere, entering a new life—maybe even a better one than the retirement community. (Visions of *Cocoon* splashed through my brain.) Good for them! *Hope to see you soon.* How I appreciated the thought of our getting together! What a blessing to have a heartful relationship with my dear aunt!

By the time I put the letter down after the second reading, my soul was smiling. Not only did I discover that my Aunt Rose was doing much better than I had originally thought, but I was a little jealous that she was doing so well with issues that I was still working on! But most important of all, I learned a personal lesson about healing and happiness: *To find peace and healing, we need but to look at the situation differently.*

The words on the paper of my aunt's letter did not change, nor did the activities in her life. The pivotal difference was in the lens through which I read the letter. I changed my mind about what I was willing to see, and my heart followed.

Right or Happy

In college I used to irritate my roommate by always having to be right. I did this in a most insidious way: even if I agreed with him, I would find some way to have an opinion that was more correct than his. One day he asked me, "Alan, how come I say something, and then you say the same thing in different words, and then you tell me you think you are correct?'' There was not much I could say to that one. His question stimulated me to consider for the first time that having to be right was actually a way of losing, and it was costing me happiness and friendship.

The world's view of victory dictates that one person's winning must be at the expense of another person losing. Through Spirit's eyes, however, one person's win must bring a blessing to everyone.

The key to real winning is to discover how we are the same and see that we all gain when we join as a team. When we shift our focus from how we are different to what we share (as I did with my aunt's letter), we can see the way to let go of fear and make way for success.

Dare To Look Silly

One of the greatest opportunities for healing is to make an embarrassing mistake in the presence of a group of people whom we want to like us. The ego would advise us that we must look good at all times and all costs. The name of fear's game is, ''protect the image.'' Blowing your image occasionally is a wonderful way to step out of the cage of self-protection and join with other people in the safety of the heart.

Charley Thweatt and I were presenting a program for *The Inside Edge*, a professional support group which met at a posh restaurant in Beverly Hills, the very nightclub featured in *Beverly Hills Cop II*. We were offering a workshop for a large sophisticated audience which included many people in the entertainment world.

Charley began the program with his original song, ''You Are Light.'' When he reached the second verse, Charley kept playing the guitar but no words came out of his mouth. After a few more chords he stopped playing altogether and laughingly announced, ''I forgot the words!'' There was a moment's silence, followed by peals of laughter from the audience—and then a strong wave of applause. The listeners enjoyed Charley's lighthearted handling of his error. They let him know they were with him and they wanted him to continue. Charley took a deep breath, began the song again, and this time sang to the end without missing a word.

I learned a valuable lesson that day. Audiences are made of people, not judges. We don't have to neurotically worry about always performing perfectly. We can relax and enjoy sharing our presentation with people like ourself. This audience was a particularly appropriate one to goof in front of, as many of the listeners were entertainers themselves, and they had plenty of compassion for *faux-pas* on stage. Every single one of them had forgotten lines, sang sour notes, or told jokes that fell flat more times then they cared to remember. Their response to Charley was not condemnation, but understanding. They knew from experience that we need to give and receive encouragement from our peers. Charley's error gave everyone a marvelous opportunity to break out of judgment and into support.

Black, White, and Color

I was reading an issue of *Life* Magazine featuring a tribute to Martin Luther King, Jr. on the twentieth anniversary of his assassination. I was inspired by many touching articles, photos, and thoughtful testimonials honoring the noble virtues for which Dr. King lived. The tribute which impressed me the most was a statement by a large company which bought a full page ad, printed with white lettering on a black background. On the center of the page there were blazed these bold words: *In honor of Dr. Martin Luther King, Jr.—a man who did not see the world in black and white*.

Of course he didn't. If he did, he could not have brought about the great changes he set in motion. The power of Dr. King's message was not in attacking the white world or seeking black supremacy; his strength lay in finding a way for all people to join as one, children of the same God. Many white people marched with Dr. King, and many more do today. Those who are truly interested in healing see beyond the skin, the words, the shape of the eyes, or the political beliefs. Those who are dedicated to healing look beyond differences right into the heart.

It's the only way to restore wholeness in the face of the separations that have caused us so much pain.

It's a blessing to be wrong—wrong about the things we have been afraid of, about our judgments against ourselves and others, about the differences we have allowed to divide us. We may have different ways of expressing ourselves, but they are cause not for judgment—they are a reason for celebration. What a boring world it would be if we all expressed ourself in the same way! What a clever God there is who has created an infinite number of ways of saying, "I love you."

Dare to Be Wrong About Who You Thought You Were

Ultimately we must let go of our erroneous perceptions about our identity. All of our problems stem from our loss of the memory of our true nature, which is love. We are lovable and we are loving. But we may have forgotten this great truth and become hypnotized by the doubts that sap the creative life force from our lifestream. We may believe that we are dark, selfish, and evil. None of this is true. We are the light.

Now you must face the greatest dare of all: the dare to grow beyond your illusions about who you are. You are challenged to release all notions of yourself as lost, hurt, or lacking in any way. You are called to step out of the circle of doom inscribed by the world's naysayers and walk freely in the light. All other dares are in the service of this one.

Be glad you are wrong about what you thought you were. If you were right about your guilt, there would be no God, love would be meaningless, and the world would be doomed to oblivion. But none of that is so. We are here not to suffer, but to remember. This world brings us a thousand opportunities a day to recall our divinity and let it shine into fuller expression. Every interaction invites us to change our mind about who we thought we were and step into our own noble shoes. We are on a miraculous journey of self-discovery, and we shall not rest satisfied until our full golden nature is revealed in all its splendor.

Dare to Be Wrong

In what areas of your life have you chosen to be right rather than happy? Fill in the chart below (Repeat for several situations):

Situation	
The way I have chosen to be right	
The "benefits" I seem to receive from being right	
What I lose by staying right	
What I could gain by finding a way to join with the other person	
A way to look at the situation which would promote joining	
How I would like the situation to be transformed	
A step I could take to bring about the results I desire	

DARE TO
CHANGE YOUR MIND

I am committed to truth, not consistency.
— Mahatma Gandhi

It may seem odd that a book containing a chapter entitled, "Dare to Commit" would also include a chapter inviting you to dare to change your mind. But changing your mind is a very real element of a commitment to truth.

If we observe the natural world as God created it, we see constant change, evolution, and transformation. Nothing in nature stays the same. The majesty and fascination of the physical world lies in its movement, both graceful and dramatic. Clouds delicately form before our eyes, swell to great dark and porous masses, deliver torrents of rain to thirsty plains, and disappear as magically as they formed. The Morning Glory emerges as the sun rises, offers her splendid show of burgundy blossoms, and shyly retreats when the sun takes leave, with no hint that she will return for another performance the next day. Great volcanoes even to this day issue massive explosions of magma that build the earth just as they did at the beginning of time. Truly change is one of God's unique gifts to a world that would wither of stagnation and boredom without it.

We, as children of a God who becomes ever more colorful in kaleidoscopic forms, must honor the changes which emerge within and around us. To be attached to a form or a plan in the face of all indications otherwise is a statement not of integrity, but resistance. Because we usually see with a very limited vision, we must be open to adapt, adjust, and accommodate along our way if and when a larger or another picture is revealed to us. Flexibility is a high sign of spiritual advancement.

163

The Power of Prerogative

As a child I heard the phrase, "a woman's prerogative." The notion behind this statement was that women, by their nature, have a right to change their mind. This, of course, is a rather limited concept, for men certainly also have the same prerogative. But there is a deeper truth to which this phrase points. Our culture suffers from an overdevelopment of our masculine nature. We are out of balance. We call God a "He," men are vastly overdominant in our politics and the decision-making echelons of our influential institutions, and more basically we are attached to making decisions with the left side of our brain, the correlate of our thinking process that is ruled by reason, logic, and rigidity. As a culture we have far less respect for and practice of the feminine, intuitive, artistic approach to life. By contrast, the oriental mind (as reflected in Taoism and Confucianism) is much more attuned with the subtler, more creative, mystical way of allowing rather than forcing.

There was a long epoch on earth during which God was acknowledged as feminine; people prayed to the Mother rather than the Father. But because that power was abused, the pendulum has swung in the masculine direction for most of the history we know. There will come a time (the seeds of it have already sprouted) when we will enjoy a more harmonious integration of the masculine and feminine energies of life.

Under right-brain guidance, decisions are not planned; they emerge. Life is not to be organized; it is experienced. In this way of being rather than doing, creativity is more important than structure and expression gleams brighter than formation. The element of space is as intrinsic as the walls. The heart is as wise as the mind. Love is present rather than sheer power.

If you are attached to approaching life through planning, the free-form way of being will at first drive you crazy. This dynamic often emerges in marriages in which the man is a serious organizer and the women is a fluent feeler. He can't understand why she doesn't think things out before she acts, and she feels frustrated because he is emotionally inexpressive. It's an old story, actually a classic paradigm. But remember that we keep playing out our lessons until we learn them. Such a disparity in approaches in a relationship—or within us—is a call for a deeper marriage; not just of two people, but in honoring both ways of approaching life. The advanced soul calls upon both reason and intuition in making decisions on the path of spiritual mastery. Both ways are important and both are appropriate, depending on the circumstances.

The Whole Picture

In our culture we need to practice and develop the use of our intuitive faculty. Our higher sensing will help is in many situations in which logic cannot show us the whole picture. I was interested to find that on the new *Star Trek* television series, the crew of the Starship *Enterprise* includes a woman called "Counselor." Her job is to psychically intuit any aspects of a challenging situation that the captain (who is a very strong male figure) cannot ascertain. I know a number of psychics who are regularly employed by police departments to assist them to decipher crimes that their investigators cannot solve. By contrast, you might remember the furor that was created when it was revealed that Nancy Reagan was consulting an astrologer. There was no end to the speculative criticism that our country's political decisions were being based on an occult science. That controversy was an excellent example of how a culture entrenched in left-brain rational decision making is threatened by the notion of subtler ways of learning. We find an even more dramatic example in the massive witch hunts in seventeenth-century New England. Many innocent people were burned at the stake because the religion in power was entirely incapable of accepting any spirituality outside of rigid dogma. Remember that the Puritans were militaristic in their approach to God. Their life was bound by regimented edicts. Their belief system had no allowance for creative thinking or the application of the intuitive faculty. It stands to reason, then, that such a regime would hunt down and destroy anyone or anything which threatened their dogmatic creed.

Fortunately we are living in an era when the pendulum is beginning to swing to a more centered position. The communist doctrine has lost its grip on European countries, and many nations around the world are moving beyond archaic dogmas and allowing space for more creative thinking. This process is slow and we have a long way to go, but the signs of a shift in mass consciousness are clearly budding. If we are going to survive on the planet as people and as nations, we will need to give greater credence to our intuitive faculty. "Survival of the fittest" does not simply mean that those with the biggest muscles will outslug weaker creatures. It means that those who learn to fit in, or adapt, are actually the strongest. The Chinese philosopher Lao Tse reminds us that "the yielding is more powerful than the resistant." Perhaps we are ready to learn that now.

Planning and Healing

A Course in Miracles tells us that "the healed mind does not plan." This radical yet illuminating teaching points out the power and importance of allowing our choices to emerge rather than conform to an earlier decision. A mind that is in communication with God trusts that the right guidance comes at the moment we need it. Sometimes that guidance is consistent with a previously laid plan and sometimes it is not. We need to have the courage and openness to revise a plan if a new one seems better.

Peter Caddy, the co-founder of the famous Findhorn Garden, stayed in the home of some friends of mine. Peter told them that he is experimenting with making decisions on intuition only. He is planning as little as possible and allowing Spirit to speak to him in the moment. Peter's idea inspired me to do the same, and I am feeling very rewarded as I practice intuiting my way through life. I am accepting invitations or declining them largely on a feeling level, and I am finding that my higher mind is willing to help me in the most mundane situations, right down to which items to order on a menu. You might like to go on Spirit's guidance system. You may be amazed at how present is the inner counselor and how willing it is to serve you if you are open to receive its gifts.

Time to Attune

There is a voice within us that knows what we need. If your body requires a certain vitamin or nutrient, you will be attracted to foods containing that ingredient. If, when presented with a menu in a restaurant, you attempt to use only your thinking mind to choose your meal, you will probably come up with a very reasonable choice that may or may not satisfy your nutritional (or joy) requirements. And you may become confused because your body is asking for one thing and your mind is telling you to get something else. In such a case you may do better to listen to your body, which knows what it wants and needs. You have to trust that there is a true voice that will speak to you if you ask.

The wisdom of the moment is a very practical guide, but its treasures remain hidden if we are living in our head. When asked if we are ready for dinner, we ask in return, "What time is it?" as if hunger depends on the position of the sun rather than the prompting of our stomach. Then we look at the clock again to see if it's time to go to sleep. The time to sleep is when we are tired. And then we try to plan our lovemaking. We think, "Saturday night at midnight is our time." But what if you both feel moved to hop in the sack at six o'clock on Monday? That would be an excellent time! It's excellent because that is what's happening.

Dr. Fritz Perls, the foremost voice of Gestalt therapy, stated that real psychotherapy consists of "losing your mind and coming to your senses." Allow yourself to be spontaneous. Spontaneity is very high on God's list of qualities of living. Let passion move you rather than simply execution of strategy. Do you fold and hang your clothing carefully when removing it for lovemaking? Personally, I think tearing clothes off and casting them asunder is great fun. If you have the time and interest to hang them up, then your passion is, shall we say, out to lunch. I've travelled many trails, and one of my favorites is the trail of clothing I find in the morning that leads from the living room couch to the bedroom.

A Society of Planaholics

Our culture is obsessed with planning, and much of it is inspired by fear. Heavy scheduling is a formidable way to avoid intimacy. If we are constantly busy, we do not have to face our feelings and deal with our issues in relationships. "Oh, I'm just too busy to be with a woman," is a clear indication that the speaker is terrified of love and is willing to erect an array of barriers to protect himself from feeling the loneliness that is actually running him. A saturated day planner is often a symptom of weighty denial, and it should be recognized immediately as a warning flag of great psychic distress that is not being acknowledged or dealt with. (The insidious twist in the planaholic's plight is that nearly our entire culture is heavily hypnotized to avoid intimacy through busy-ness. It is much more difficult to become free when most of the people around you share your form of insanity and call it reality.) Someone who is heavily overscheduled is usually seriously threatened by absence of structure or quiet alone time. Such a one realizes that given even a little bit of space, she will have to face her feelings, and that kind of intimate confrontation is to be avoided at all costs. Sorrowfully, those costs include aliveness, health, and fulfilling relationships. You cannot be intimate if you erect a calendar as a wall between you and a potential beloved. And neither will you ever get to know yourself. To discover yourself through your joy, tears, passion, and vision is the greatest adventure of life. There is no more welcome gift than to find the beauty within you. If you are busy doing, doing, doing out of fear of being, you will never release that magnificent person who is calling to live and breathe and bring unique and precious gifts to the world.

A Higher Vow

The question may reasonably be asked, "What about vows, commitments, and contracts that we make with other people? Is there integrity in changing my mind after I have made a commitment?" For the answer to this very important question, you will have to look into your heart. A vow is a sacred statement that should not be taken lightly or made indiscreetly. When we make a vow we invoke the power of the word, which is our greatest creative energy.

But there is another factor in human relations which also cannot be overlooked. Sometimes people, relationships, or conditions change to a point where an agreement we made long ago is no longer true. While we may have entered into the agreement in all sincerity and with the intention of following through on it for as long as we promised, the truth of our individual or shared life may be different now than it was then. Many of us have entered into marriages with great unconsciousness or set out on business ventures with hopes, visions, and expectations that were unrealistic. If in the course of the marriage or the venture we find that we are not the same person who made the vow, or that we cannot continue in all honesty or integrity to carry on as we had said we would, we must tell the truth about our position. The only tragedy more disastrous than breaking an agreement we made is to go on living it out when our heart is no longer in it and it does not work for us to continue. (There are some people who would rather die than get divorced—and they do.) In such a case we are violating an even deeper commitment—the vow to live in truth. This is an agreement we made with ourself and God, and it supercedes all human agreements. If we cannot keep an agreement we made, we must go to the other person and speak to them directly, clearly, and honestly. We must ask to be released from the agreement.

I am not encouraging anyone to break an agreement or leave a relationship unless you have exercised deep and sincere soul-searching before coming to such a decision. Many of us have a tendency to run away when the fire gets hot, and that is also a violation of our integrity. I believe that we should make every effort to follow through on our word. If, after we have meditated and contemplated on the situation, discussed it with a counselor or someone of integrity whom we trust and respect, and most important, taken the situation to the God within us, we feel a true need to undo our vow, then and only then should we act on it. And if we do, we must trust that in the long run the other person or people will be served by our decision. Remember that your good cannot be at the expense of another's, and if you are truly acting under Spirit's guidance there is a blessing for everyone involved. Trust the truth of the heart.

The Art of Living

Creating a life is like forming a vase on a potter's wheel. We start out with an amorphous chunk of material and we continually mold and remold it. The clay goes through many revolutions; each time it passes through your hands you have another opportunity to bring your work of art closer to life. No great artist forms his masterpiece on the first attempt. The hands are constantly pushing, pulling, pressing, releasing, refining. Art, like life, is a process of continuous revising, updating and improving.

Remember this basic principle as you recreate your life anew each day. A life without change is not a life; it is a stagnant pool. To change your mind frivolously is a cop-out. To change your mind under the direction of the wisdom of the heart is a brush stroke on the masterpiece you are delivering to the world. If Spirit guides you to change your mind, you have a responsibility to do it. Remember that you see but a small tile of a great mosaic. A step under Spirit's guidance can lead to much more good than you can see or imagine now.

Courage is required to stop doing something you have been doing for a long time and start something new. But consider the alternative. If you are not true to yourself, you miss the loftiest and most satisfying reward of living. If you do follow your heart, you will bless your time here. No one in the outer world can tell you what to do. But there is One within you who is an infallible guide. Dare to change your mind. Or dare to continue on your present path. No matter what path you take, there is one torch that will light your way—the honesty of a loving heart. Walk in the dignity of the highest truth you know, and your journey will be well worth the walking.

Dare to Change Your Mind

1) How easily can you act spontaneously? List three acts you have done recently on the spur of the moment.

2) Are you able to release a previous plan if a new and better one comes to the fore?

3) On a scale of 1 (lightest) to 10 (heaviest) indicate how much your life is planned. How would you feel if you had a lot of time on your hands and no plans?

4) Does your scheduling substitute for intimacy?

5) List three things you would like to change your mind about, but have not done so. What would it take for you to act on these changes?

DARE TO TURN YOUR SCARS INTO STARS

What is a weed?
A plant whose virtues have not yet been discovered.

— Ralph Waldo Emerson

A re you afraid of heights?" the cowboy asked me. I looked up at the hill before us.

"Nope" I answered.

"Want to go up there?"

"Sure."

I gave Smokey a gentle nudge in the side of his belly, and off we went. It was only my second horseback ride in years, and I seemed to be doing quite well. It was a perfect day. A strong wind massaged the south coast of Maui while the sun respectfully warmed my arms. It was good to be with the elements again.

As we made the ascent I found myself getting a little queazy. This hill did not look very formidable from a distance, but as we approached the top it was beginning to feel like a mountain. I began to sense that I was in for more than I had bargained for. The *paniolo* (Hawaiian cowboy) brought our party to a plateau overlooking the ocean. I looked down over the edge of the precipice and felt myself stiffen up. It was a long drop to the beach. "Breathe," I told myself. I forced myself to gulp some lungfuls of oxygen. I made some comments about how beautiful the view was, but I was not enjoying it at all; I just wanted to get down from there as soon as possible. I did not feel safe. I would rather have been on my own two feet.

"You guys ready to go?" the *paniolo* finally asked. I thought we'd never leave. It seemed like an eternity on that cliff.

"Yeah, alright," I tried to sound nonchalant. (I don't think I fooled anyone.)

173

"Let's take the back way around."

Back way? Did he say, "Back way?" I was not particularly thrilled with the front way. The back way sounded even less appealing.

So around the back way we went. I am glad I teach people how to deal with fear, or else I would have turned around then. (Actually, that's a lie. There *was* no place to turn around.) The back way consisted of a tiny sliver of a trail not much wider than the horse's girth. This slim footpath wound its way on an earthen ledge over the ocean. I leaned over to see how far up we actually were, and I quickly stopped looking. Below me was a sheer fifty foot drop to the ocean, where the surf pounded brutally on jagged lava rocks. "How did I get myself into this?" I wondered. The question soon became, "How can I get myself out?"

But there was no way out but through. My horse did not have a reverse gear, and I had no choice but to endure this terrifying trial. Step by step Smokey lumbered along, and (believe me) I watched his footing carefully. I thought to myself, "I'll just trust the horse," but that did not really quell my malaise. "Forget about the horse," a louder voice advised "—Pray to the Lord!"

And so I did. I asked God to somehow bring me peace. I could not remember the last time I felt so frightened.

Then another voice spoke. This one, by contrast, was gentle and clear. It asked me, "How would you be feeling if you were guaranteed that this horse would not fall into the ocean with you on it?" Hmmmm. "Imagine that you knew you would not be hurt," this guide suggested. "What would you be experiencing if you were not afraid?"

I tried the idea on for size. It felt a lot more comfortable then my current train of terror. Then a more exciting feeling followed. I felt the wind blowing through my hair. I looked up at the graceful verdant slopes of Mt. Haleakala. I peered into the crystal blue waters sparkling offshore. The colors, the power, the moment reached inside me and grabbed me by the heart. I felt a tremendous wave of exhilaration charge through my being. What a rush! So this was why people enjoyed horseback riding!

And I had been missing out on all of these magnificent feelings because I was afraid!

I began to breathe more deeply. Then I remembered a statement by Fritz Perls, who defined fear as "excitement without breath." Sure I was afraid, but behind the fear was a tremendous excitement. Was that all there was to fear?

Then I remembered that the word "terrified" comes from the same root word as "terrific." There is a core connection between the two experiences. It's the same river of life that wants to move through us. If we block the energy with fear (like crimping a garden hose), we become terrified. If we let the current course through our system, it's terrific. That's the only difference between something that's terrifying and something that's terrific. In one case we resist and shut down; in the other, we move it with breath and enjoy. The same principle applies to events that are "awful" or "awesome." Fight it and it's awful. Go with it, let it be, and it's awesome. Here before me was the fine line between suffocation and joy, living and dying, denying and loving.

Then I actually began to enjoy the ride. Whereas just a few minutes earlier I had been gripped by a nearly overwhelming angst, now I felt more alive than I had in a long time. I relaxed and decided to appreciate the moment. And what a fantastic moment it was!

By the time we finished the outing I was high as a kite. I had pierced through the membrane of fear that had been suffocating me like an invisible plastic bag. I had a glimpse into the inner dynamics of terror and realized there was nothing to fear. It was not a horse, a cliff, or a cowboy that kept me captive; *it was my own mind*. That frightening experience was one of the most helpful lessons I have ever learned, and now I think of it as a gift.

Wouldn't it be wonderful if we could see all of our life as a gift? Sometimes it seems as if we are on a perilous ride over which we have no control. But if you can find a moment to take a breath and ask, "What is the gift here?" *you will see the way out*. And in that opening is the key to your healing. You will see exactly why the situation is happening and what you need to do to attain mastery over it. That is how you turn your scars into stars.

Mistake Salad

Some of the best things in life happen "by accident." In truth, there are no accidents. When things seem to be going wrong, we have a great opportunity to remember that there is a divine plan, even if we don't see it in the moment. We actually see very little.

A friend of mine looks forward to her family's Thanksgiving gatherings, where the traditional first course of their meal is "mistake salad." She laughed as she explained how her family found the recipe and chose that name. "It was entirely by mistake!" she told me. "One Thanksgiving my mom had the recipe book open while she was making a new salad, and when her back was turned the wind blew the pages to another recipe. She just kept on preparing the dish, but unbeknownst to the chef, the first half of the salad was from one recipe and the second from another. When we sat down to eat, everyone enjoyed the new salad more than anything else at the meal. When we asked for the recipe, she discovered that she had made a big mistake— but she had also made a big hit! Since that year we recreate the 'mistake' as a tradition, and it is one of the favorite courses of our meal!"

I had a "mistake salad" of my own when I was preparing the cover for my book *The Peace That You Seek*. When I needed a photo of myself for the book jacket, my friend Mark Tucker and I went out onto the sand dunes of Asilomar to shoot some pictures of me in a meditative pose. When we examined the developed slides, there were two that I liked, but neither one seemed attractive enough to be used by itself. I took both slides to my graphic artist, who agreed that we needed something better than either one of the shots. She handed me the slides and as I began to put them back in the envelope she exclaimed, "Wait a minute—let me see that!" "See what?" I asked, wondering what more she could be seeing than the slides we had just viewed. "Don't move your hand," she cautioned me. When I looked into my hand I saw that the two slides sandwiched together created a fascinating double exposure effect. We held the sandwich up to the light and instantly agreed that this was the image we were looking for. While neither of the pictures worked by themselves, they worked perfectly together—proving that the whole is greater than the sum of the parts.

Sometimes we have all the elements in hand and we just don't know it. It takes another view of what is already there to see that we have what we need. It was no mistake that the individual photos didn't please us and neither was it an accident that I was holding them in the position that caught the artist's eye. There are no mistakes in the universe; only opportunities for broader vision.

Problems and Potential

Perhaps Steve Martin elucidated the "scars into stars" principle most astutely in his movie, *My Blue Heaven*. In this film Steve plays a successful gangster who is trying to go straight. Although he is still running with the mob, his heart opens to a group of little leaguers who need a new ball field.

One night Steve's gang sets out to hijack a shipment of stereo components, but by mistake they end up with a truckload of empty five-gallon water bottles. When the other mobsters complain, "We really botched this job!" Steve gets a glimmer in his eye. He realizes that he can use the jars as fund-raising receptacles for the new little league field. Smiling, he informs his cronies, "That's the difference between you and me—you see problems, and I see potential."

Mr. Destiny

Michael Caine and James Belushi starred in another enlightening movie called *Mr. Destiny*. This film depicts Belushi as a thirty-five-year-old man who is unhappy with his life. His basic dilemma is that he wishes it were all different. Years ago in high school he was a star baseball player who had a potentially bright future as a pro. That dream was foiled on the last day of the season when he struck out on a pitch that could have won the game if he had hit it. That was the end of his baseball career, and from that time on his life was forever different. Now he is bored with his girlfriend, his job is unstimulating, and he lusts after his boss's wife. You might say he turned out to be a regular kind of guy.

Enter stage left one Mr. Destiny, played by Michael Caine. Mr. Destiny has the mystical ability to alter the past so that the present is different. At Belushi's request, Mr. Destiny rearranges things so that Belushi had hit the home run ball and become a baseball star. This, of course, set into motion a series of circumstances through which Belushi became incredibly wealthy, heads his own company, and—you guessed it—is married to the woman who would have otherwise been the boss's wife.

All of this is fine and dandy—for a while. But there is one basic problem: Belushi is entirely out of place. Wealth, glamour, and sleeping with the object of his fantasies, it turns out, are not as great as he imagined them to be. They are, in fact, not what he really wants after all. He wants his old buddies; he cannot be bothered with high finance; and most of all, he misses his girlfriend.

There is a classic scene in which Belushi as the rich man escapes from a fashionable yet pretentious restaurant and takes his former girlfriend (whom he is trying to woo) to Pizza Hut. As he sits down at his familiar fast food haven, a great smile of relief eases its way across his face. Ah, now he is at home. This is the real him. His nature is not to live in a fancy palace or to be fending off labor disputes. His real joy is to hang out in Pizza Hut and listen to the jukebox with his girlfriend. They order his favorite pizza and a Coke, and we see a picture of man at peace with himself and his life.

The moral of the story is, of course, that we have a right place in life—the one we choose—and it will not help us to try to be something we are not. Nor will it serve us to deny our current good because we believe we made a mistake that might have brought us better. Neither shall we find satisfaction in trying to fit into a mold that seems glamorous from the outside, but is terribly stifling from the inside. The question below the title on the advertisement outside the theatre asks, "Would you give up everything you have for everything you want?" Perhaps in this case the answer is that everything you have *is* everything you want.

Disappointments are the Hooks
Upon Which God Hangs His Victories

There is a way to deal with disappointment that can make you a winner. Remove the "D" with which disappointment begins, and replace it with "H." Thus "disappointment" becomes "Hisappointment." In other words, remove the incident from the projections of your expectations and imagine that God has caused the situation to turn out this way because He has a bigger and better plan than the one you formulated. Our idea of the way things should be pales in the face of God's vision for how good it can and will be.

One day I was dictating a stack of letters to my secretary, who typed them into a computer as I spoke. We spent about three hours catching up on correspondence that had accumulated over a long period of time, and I felt relieved to have handled these outstanding communications.

Then she turned to me sheepishly and told me, "I think I made a mistake—I accidentally erased all the letters." I could hardly believe my ears! Here we had spent a great deal of time and energy on this project, and she lost it all with one erroneous keystroke! We made a number of attempts to recover the lost material, but the results soon became painfully apparent: we would have to do it all over. I did my best to overcome my upset, but I was very disappointed and somewhat annoyed that she had made this blunder.

So we set out to redo the letters. Then a miracle of a lesson came forth: we finished the same work in about forty-five minutes. Both of us were amazed at how little time our job actually required. In the process I realized that a pile of work that I had originally believed required three hours to accomplish could take as little as forty-five minutes if I set my mind to it. By "accident" we had unveiled a new paradigm for how quickly and easily such a project could be completed. Since that time I do my letters much more quickly because now I know that it is possible. So my secretary's error was not a curse—it was a gift.

As God Thinks

Jesus was about to perform the miracle of the fishes and the loaves. The disciple Peter realized Jesus' intention and questioned him, "Master, how can you possibly feed all of these people with this little bit of food?"

Jesus turned to Peter, looked him in the eye and answered, "Peter, you're thinking as men think, not as God thinks."

As God thinks. God thinks in an entirely different way than most people, for God sees only possibilities. The mind of God is not limited by the past, insufficiency, or fear. God sees only the good, and when we see with God we become one with the Force for Healing.

In a more modern metaphor Dr. Emmet Brown, the outrageous scientist in *Back to the Future*, was confronted by Marty McFly who, like Peter, questioned the master about his ability to extricate both of them from a dangerous predicament. "Marty!" Dr. Brown appeals to his younger cohort, "You are not thinking four-dimensionally!" Four-dimensionally, in this case, meant that Marty needed to lift his mind above and beyond the three dimensions by which he saw himself as bound, and consider another dimension through which he and his partner could escape from a three-dimensional predicament. The real predicament we face is never the one that seems to threaten us in the outer world. Our true challenge is to meet our mind on the field of our awakening and conquer fear with love. As long as we allow fear to hold power over us, everything we see is a potential danger. Once we choose love as our guide there is nothing that can remove our good. We must relinquish our hold on the limitations we perceive and lift our vision to a broader dimension. It is said that "the winds of grace are blowing all the time. We have only to raise our sails."

180

The Only Attitude that Works

Once again we arrive at the basic question that will follow us until we come to terms with it: Are we alone, or is God present? If you have come this far on the journey of daring to be yourself, you must have at least some abiding sense that there is indeed a loving hand behind the apparent chaos that seems to encroach upon the peace we seek. Our task, then, is to develop our awareness of Spirit's presence and draws it forth as the predominant element of our consciousness. The development of faith takes practice, and that is what this life is for. Our world is but a laboratory in which we experiment with different attitudes until we learn that love is the only one that works.

As we go through times of testing, the remembrance of God is the knowledge that will see us through. Charles Weston said, "we turn to God for help when our foundation is shaking, only to recognize that it is God who is shaking it." God would never remove one foundation from us without replacing it with a firmer one. If your foundation can be shaken you can be sure there is a deeper one of which you are worthy.

It is said that "problems are the doors through which we walk to peace." We must hold the awareness that everything that comes to us can potentially work in our favor. Our thoughts are the keys that will open the door to the storehouse of blessings. Like the alchemists of old, we can transform the lead of our pain into the gold of our enlightenment. There is no sorrow beyond God's ability to transform into a blessing, and nothing we cannot do when we walk with the One whose touch delivers miracles.

> *Life is so generous a giver, but we, judging its gifts by the covering, cast them away as ugly or heavy or hard. Remove the covering and you will find beneath it a living splendor, woven of love, by wisdom, with power.*
>
> —Fra. Giovanni

Dare to Turn Your Scars into Stars

1) Describe an experience that seemed to be an accident or a mistake. Can you see a bigger plan behind the apparent error?

2) Name something that you were or are terrified of. How could this experience be looked at in another way so that it becomes terrific?

3) List three problems, and next to them the potential for good that could come out of the situation.

4) Describe a disappointment that you can transform into Hisappointment.

5) Describe a situation that you currently find challenging. How would God or an enlightened person see this situation differently?

Dare to
Be Yourself

DARE TO LOVE BOLDLY

After five hours of air travel, most of us were ready for a soft bed and a good night's rest. Eleven PM can be a bleary time at an airport. There was not much more on anyone's mind than getting home.

Except for one person. A young man behind me on the jetway wore a huge wooden sign hanging from a rope around his neck. His placard bore the shape of a heart, painted white with huge red letters boldly asking, *"Pam, will you marry me?"*

Suddenly I wasn't tired anymore. Was he really going to propose? I looked ahead toward the end of the jetway and there, sure enough, stood an attractive young woman with a darling little girl. "This is going to be rich," I thought. I positioned myself off to her side to watch the scene unfold.

Then he did it. The fellow got down on his knees and proposed to his beloved right there. It was an inspiring moment! Immediately a small crowd gathered to observe and applaud this daring demonstration of love.

To the delight of the crowd, Pam said, "Yes." Comments spontaneously emerged from the onlookers, who came to life. "I wouldn't say 'yes' to him," one observer called out, ". . . he has bow legs!" A man commented, "You sure are smart to ask her; if you didn't, I would!" I, too, had something to say. I approached the groom-to-be and told him, "Thank you for having the courage to do that. You really inspired me. I, too, would like to express my love that boldly. It was a marvelous gift. I wish both of you a wonderful life together."

As the entire group rode the escalator down to the baggage claim area, a cheerful friendliness pervaded the gathering. We had been a group of distant strangers invited to share an intimate moment which transformed us into a family. I, for one, felt privileged. I was amazed by the dramatic change in the energy of the group. A throng of weary travelers was renewed by a bold and magical act. The airport, in that moment, became a festive place where everyone put aside their tired thoughts and remembered the beauty and power of unashamed loving.

Stand Behind Your Love

An excellent motion picture called *Secret Admirer* offers a profound lesson in the importance of making a stand for our love. The tale begins with a teenage boy receiving an unsigned love letter. The note is from his best friend, who happens to be a girl, but because he is so familiar with her, he overlooks the possibility that she may have deeper feelings for him. Instead he imagines that the romantic letter came from the hottest girl in the school. Motivated by his fantasy, he sends the teenage temptress a love letter in response, and although she is something of a bubblehead, they strike up a relationship.

The original love letter accidentally finds its way into the accounting book of the boy's father, who opens it during his night school class. He assumes that it was put there by his female accounting teacher. The man is excited by her profession of affection, and although both of them are married to other people (she to one of his friends), he makes advances toward her. Although she is surprised at first, her weakness for flattery runs deeper than her integrity, and the two set out to have an affair.

The teacher's husband and the student's wife find the letter, get wind of the affair, and in retaliation they decide they will become lovers. Oh, what a tangled web we weave!

You can imagine the gnarled—and hilarious—series of complications that unfolds between all of these unlikely couples, who are acting more out of fantasy than caring. And to think that all of these convoluted courtships stemmed from one love letter that went unsigned! Each of these lonely people read their secret wishes and hopes into the letter, and instantly became enrolled in a crash course in facing fantasies.

Meanwhile the original girl who wrote the letter, who is a sweet, innocent, girl-next-door kind of soul, becomes discouraged and disgusted as her unknowing beloved keeps nagging her to write love letters for him to Miss Bubblehead, who has fallen for him because, through his passionate communiques, she thinks he is a brilliant and sensitive poet. Little does she know that these romantic renderings are being ghost written by Miss Girl-Next-Door, who is saying all the things through the boy that she would like to say to him. (If you can follow this plot, you will receive extra credit.)

Finally the girl next door gets fed up and signs up for a senior year at sea, for which she will soon set sail on a boat that travels around the world. By this time, however, our beleaguered young man has discovered that his fantasy girl is rather empty, and he realizes that it was his dear friend who penned the romantic message. Moreover, he realizes that he has loved her all along, but he was just taking her for granted.

Our hero flags down a car, bodily removes the driver, and races down to the dock in an attempt to stop his dear one before she steams off to sea. He arrives at the port to see the ship a hundred yards out into the bay, chugging toward distant lands bearing the woman of his heart, whom he may never see again because he was too busy chasing glitter. If he wants to get her attention, he is going to have to do something radical—and quickly. He leaps onto a stack of crates and shouts to her, "I know you wrote the letter!"

"So what?" she yells back.

"I love you!" he answers.

"What?" we hear from the bay.

"I love you!!"

"I can't hear you!" (Right.)

Finally our young man is forced to muster all of his breath, strength, and intention. *"I love you!!!"* he screams, his voice echoing through the harbor. There, he said it. After all those crazy escapades, he voiced his deepest feelings. *"Do you love me?"*

There is silence from the ship. This gnarly mess began

because she was afraid to declare her heart's desire. Now she must own it in full public. But she doesn't have time to delay anymore. Within seconds she will be out of earshot and her ship will be out to sea—perhaps forever.

She can wait no longer. *"I love you!"* she answers.

Simultaneously the two lovers dive into the water and meet in the center of the harbor, where everyone can behold their unabashed profession of love. The film concludes with a soggy but welcome kiss.

As I sat before the rolling credits of this very entertaining movie, I was struck by the profundity of its message: *Have the guts to declare your love and stand behind it.* This convoluted maze of affairs began because one person was not willing to be responsible for her feelings and trust her instincts enough to express her heart's desire. All the couples involved used the ambiguity of unsigned love letters to protect their secret fantasies and ultimately get minced by them. The entire mess never would have occurred if the girl who first wrote the letter was willing to be direct in her expression of caring. (But then I would have missed a marvelous movie, and all of us a pithy lesson.)

Consider as well the way the couple had to correct their errors. Two people who were afraid to admit their caring were forced by the lesson they set in motion to literally shout their love from the rooftops. Their fear created the perfect circumstance for them to practice the remedy. The story came full circle. Their shyness had been transformed to boldness, their hiding to assertion, and their protection to vulnerability. Through all of these valuable metamorphoses this couple ultimately became more powerful and got what they wanted all along.

Give Your Birthday Card

One who stands as a shining example of courageous expression is John Keating, the transformative teacher portrayed by Robin Williams in *Dead Poets Society*. In this masterful motion picture, Keating takes a group of regimented, uptight, and spiritually impotent students at a rigid boarding school and inspires them to make their lives extraordinary.

These young men, as Keating points out to them, have lost sight of their dreams and ambitions. They are mechanistically living out their parents' programs and expectations for them. They plan to become doctors, lawyers, and bankers because that is what their parents have told them they are going to do. But these dry fellows have given hardly any thought to what their hearts are calling them to express.

An early scene in the film shows Mr. Keating taking the boys down to the school lobby where a trophy case displays photos of earlier graduating classes. "Look at these pictures, boys," Keating tells the students. "The young men you behold had the same fire in their eyes that you do. They planned to take the world by storm and make something magnificent of their lives. That was fifty years ago. Now they are pushing up daisies. How many of them really lived out their dreams? Did they do what they set out to accomplish?" Then Mr. keating leans into the cluster of preppies and whispers audibly, "*Carpe diem!*—Seize the day!"

At first the students do not know what to make of this strange teacher. But soon they being to ponder the importance of his words. They come to respect and revere Mr. Keating, who has given them a new vision—or returned their original ones.

One character in the movie, Knox Overstreet, has a terminal crush on a gorgeous girl. The only problem is that she is the girlfriend of a famous jock. Knox is infatuated with this lovely creature down to a cellular level, but he lacks the confidence to approach her. Then he remembers Mr. Keating's advice: *Seize the day!* Knox realizes that he cannot just go on dreaming—if he wants her, he is going to have to do something about it. And so he does. Boldly and poetically he declares to her his most sensitive feelings for her. In the process he gets turned away by her, punched in the nose by her boyfriend, and he faces embarrassing setbacks. But Knox is unwilling to forsake his dream, and he pursues his heart's desire. Ultimately she feels the genuineness of his caring and she opens her heart to him. Although

Knox is not especially good-looking or popular, the girl is won over by the power of his sincere intention. He has made his life extraordinary.

I had a chance to practice seizing the day myself. I developed a crush on a cute girl I met in a pet store. She was younger than I, she led a very different lifestyle, and we did not have a great deal to talk about. But somehow none of this seemed to matter. I enjoyed being with her and I felt a sparkle in her presence. And it seemed to me that she enjoyed my company as well.

When I learned that her birthday was coming up, I decided to ask her out. On the threshold of calling her I sat and looked at the phone for about half an hour. Then I dialed and hung up before it rang. I felt like a high school boy bouncing between excited anticipation and fear of rejection. A fearful voice kept telling me that she would not like me and that I had a lot of nerve asking her out. But I felt too enthusiastic about being with her to let those fears stop me. Finally I got up the nerve to ask her. She thanked me for asking and told me she already had plans.

I felt shot down. The same voice that told me not to call advised me to give up before I was further embarrassed. But I was intent on seeing what this attraction was about. There was more inside of me that wanted to come to life. I had feelings for this woman, and I had to express them.

I went to the mall and got her a pretty birthday card, on which I wrote a poetic note. I walked around the corner to the pet shop where I knew she was working. As I approached the door, that same disturbing voice cautioned me, "What if she doesn't like you? What if she rejects you?" Feeling vulnerable, I stuffed the card under my shirt. I decided that if she showed me signs of affection, I would give it to her; if she was cool to me, I would leave the card hidden. This way I would not be at risk, and avoid rejection or embarrassment.

We talked for a while and I did not get any signs one way or the other from her. Feeling ill-at-ease, I began to make my exit.

As I approached the door, however, another voice spoke to me. It came in a whisper, not unlike that of Mr. Keating. It prompted me, "Remember Knox Overstreet...*Carpe Diem!*" Here

I was confronted with my aspiration to fully express my heart, and my resistance to face the insecurity of emotional nakedness. How can I go around telling other people to live their vision, I asked myself, when I am not living my own? Besides, what's the worst thing that could happen? Any woman would be delighted to receive a poetic birthday card. I decided to seize the day. As I made that choice I felt a surge of courage course through my veins. There was indeed power in intention.

I took the card out from under my shirt, turned around, walked up to the counter, and gave it to her. As I handed it to her I felt an incredible aliveness and excitement—plus fear. (Emmett Fox said, "Do it trembling if you must, but do it." I did it.

And do you know what? She was not particularly impressed. She said "thanks" and put the card aside without even opening it. My heart sank. I felt disappointed and rejected. Getting no response seemed even worse than a direct brush-off.

I offered a polite good-bye and walked out of the store. Then something amazing happened. I began to feel exhilarated. A huge rush of internal satisfaction welled up within me and surged through my whole being. I had expressed my heart, and that felt fantastic! I had stretched beyond fear and gotten out on the dance floor. Yes, I had been a little clumsy, but I did it in spite of my fears of looking foolish. I had put my heart on the line without demanding a guarantee of the results. I did not give in order to get something back. I opened my feelings to her without an attachment to a particular response. I had been true to myself.

My exhilaration deepened to a warm bliss. I felt more satisfied and at peace with myself than I had in a long time. I realized the purpose of the whole experience: I needed to learn to open my heart and give love without requiring anything in return. This experience was not about creating a relationship with this woman. It was about deepening my relationship with myself. About making way for the energy that was asking to come forth from deep inside me. And I did it. Mr. Keating would have been proud. But most of all, I was proud.

I have not seen the girl much since then, but the experience changed my life. Through that simple interaction I clearly saw the dynamics that are required to make any relationship, and perhaps the whole world, work: *Just keep putting your love out there.*

We believe that we are hurt when we don't receive love. But that is not what hurts us. Our pain comes when we do not give love. We were born to love. You might say that we are divinely created love machines: we function most powerfully when we are *giving* love. The world has led us to believe that our well-being is dependent on other people loving us. But this is the kind of upside-down thinking that has caused so many of our problems. The truth is that our well-being is dependent on our giving love. It is not about what comes back; it is about what goes out.

I have spoken of this experience at many of my workshops, and a most fascinating phenomenon has occurred. I have received many letters and telephone calls from people telling me that I inspired them to give their "birthday card." They report that they have been walking around with a gift that they, too, have very much wanted to express, but were afraid to give. Their gift was a statement of caring, or a project that they were reticent to pursue, or a difficult situation they were shying away from facing. After hearing my story about the girl at the pet shop, they went out and gave their "birthday card" to someone. The results, these people report, have been awesome. They all experienced the deep joy and release that I felt when I found the courage to express my heart's desire.

All of us are walking around with some kind of birthday card we would like to give—some personal expression of joy, creativity, or aliveness that we are hiding under our shirt, waiting to see if we will be rewarded if we give it. But the universe does not reward us before we act. Life can teach us only when we are bold enough to venture into uncharted territory. Healing always occurs outside the "safe" zone. Real learning comes when we try something we have never done before. You cannot know the result until you do it. Our ego wants guarantees, warranties, and promises of success before we even step onto the stage of life. But few great actors have been assured of acclaim for any role before they played it. They go out there, offer their talent to the best of their ability, and hope for the best. Sometimes they are rewarded and sometimes they are disappointed. But one who gives from the depth of his soul enjoys the unique reward of being able to rest his head on his pillow at night and say to himself, "Well done; I gave it all I had to give."

By contrast, I heard about a nun on whose tombstone was inscribed, "*Here lies Sister Martha—No hits, no runs, no errors.*" Sister Martha led such a "safe" life that she made no errors. But she also did not make any hits or runs. If everyone sits on the bench in fear of making a mistake, there can be no ball game. The very way we learn to make hits is by making errors. No one has ever gotten up to bat for the first time and started hitting consistently. The biggest home run hitters are also the biggest strike-out artists. They swing for the fences, and they often do not make contact. But when they do, watch out!

You might like to take a moment now to consider what birthday card you are carrying around with you. What is the worst thing that could happen if you give it? What is the best? Remember that your job is not to secure a certain outer result. It is the inner result that makes all the difference. Your job is to put your love out there and live your truth. The universe will take care of the rest.

The Most Sacred Gift

A popular maxim advises us, "It is better to have loved and lost than to never have loved at all." Good advice, to be sure. But the slogan is only half true. If you are loving, you *cannot* lose. The reward of loving lies not in the response you elicit, but in the joy of giving expression to the most sacred gift you could offer—your spirit. If you are loving, you are winning.

The only way we lose is when we withhold love. To withhold our love from a beloved or from the world is the greatest lie with which we can hurt ourself. Because our nature is love, we deny our identity when we refuse to give it. When we withhold love we miss out on the richest joy of living. And when we give it, we are fulfilling our purpose on earth.

As I observe the lives of happy people, I see that they all have one thing in common: they have chosen to keep on giving love. They do not let outer circumstances dictate whether or not they will keep their heart open. They *create* circumstances by virtue of their generosity of spirit.

You and I have the capacity to be love givers rather than loves seekers. Daily we are invited to go beyond our limits of how much love we thought we could give or receive. And daily we will find greater strength of heart as we are willing to take love's hand and let its gentle guidance illuminate our path. Never stop loving. It is our only salvation and our only hope of finding true peace.

Dare to Love Boldly

1) What is the most outrageous expression of love that you have ever given? How did you feel when you did it?

2) To whom or what would you like to express your love more than you have been? What is stopping you? What would it take for you to express it? Describe how you would like to love more boldly.

3) What is your "birthday card" that you are carrying under your shirt?

4) Describe the inner you that has more love to give than the world currently sees.

DARE TO BE ORIGINAL

Buttercup: *We'll never make it through the Fireswamp!*

Wesley: *Nonsense! You're just saying that because no one has ever done it before.*

— *The Princess Bride*

When Kevin Costner accepted his classic role in *Field of Dreams*, his advisors told him he was crazy. They called the film "a Care Bear movie" and promised him that he would ruin his image as a streetwise heartthrob. His confidants warned him that unless he was swearing, fighting, or bedding a starlet, the movie would flop badly along with his reputation.

But there was something about the story that felt good to Kevin. He decided to honor what was going on within him rather then succumb to what he was hearing around him. Against all advice, he turned down other major offers and took the part.

Kevin's faith in this venture was called to the fore when he met with the film's director, Phil Robinson. Robinson was facing coercion from his superiors to add some sex and violence in order to sell the film to the masses. Kevin believed in the film enough to say to Robinson, "You may feel a lot of pressure from the studio. I'll be your rock. I'll be behind you saying, *'Don't change it.'* "

Thankfully, the film was not changed, and for all its innocence, idealism, and vision, *Field of Dreams* went on to become a runaway hit of the year and was ultimately nominated for Best Picture of the Year at the Academy Awards. Somehow this mystically romantic film crept into the hearts of millions of viewers who wanted to be reminded of the importance of following the inner voice, healing with our families, and pursuing our dreams.

The drama behind the movie, like a Shakespearean plot, was a play within the play. On the screen as hero Ray Kinsella questioned his sanity in building a baseball diamond in the middle of his Iowan cornfield, his innocently wise little daughter promised him, "Don't worry, daddy—people will come!" Meanwhile, actor Costner and director Robinson were learning to hold fast to their vision and not bow to external urgings to make the movie more palatable to the mainstream. At any moment they could have plowed the film under and grew the kind of feed that would sell easily on the market. But they had to honor their dream and pay heed to the same voice that Ray Kinsella heard. They did, and the people did come.

It's easy to capitalize on a formula. Any screenwriter, songwriter, or advertising agent can tell you what to do to make a product saleable to the masses. But how many people have the guts to do something that has never been done, to launch a custom-built boat into uncharted waters and float their reputation with it? Risk and originality are two sides of the same shiny coin. The very excitement that makes your heart flutter to think of bringing your dream to life will scare you formidably when you consider what you are going to have to put on the line to accomplish it. But what else are we here for? Certainly not to be safe. Many of us have tried playing it safe, and we nearly died of boredom. No, hiding in the harbor is not the destiny of a seaworthy vision. Adventure is far superior to security, and life has much more to offer than the known.

Cute Like Yourself

One day I was driving to the beach with my five-year-old guru Shanera and some friends. One fellow in the car, Jorge, was teasing Shanera by mimicking her. The following conversation ensued:

"Don't copy me!"

"But you're so cute!"

"You don't get cute by copying anyone."

"Then how did you get so cute?"

"God made me that way."

"How can I get cute like you?"

"You can't get cute like me. You have to get cute like you. That's the way God works."

Out of the mouths of babes...

What Shanera was telling Jorge was absolutely true. You can only be cute like yourself. You can't get into Heaven wearing someone else's costume. The requirement to enter the kingdom is to remove the masks that have covered our innocence, and trust that our true beauty *is* worthy of God. The cosmic irony is that our true beauty is the face of God. We have been hypnotized into believing that we must make ourself more like other people to become loveable, while our greatest strength lies in expressing our unique gifts.

Dare Not to Compare

Recently I received a complimentary letter from a reader. She honored me by exclaiming that I am "Buscaglia, Dyer, and Viscott rolled into one."

I felt very flattered to be described in that way. Leo, Wayne, and David are teachers whom I admire a great deal, and her likening me to all of them was a colorful honor. I began to fantasize about how I might use her accolade for publicity purposes. I thought about printing her quote on the cover of this forthcoming book.

Then I stopped in my tracks. The flaw in my reasoning became obvious to me. Here I am writing a book entitled *Dare to be Yourself* in which I am encouraging my readers to find and express their unique gifts, and I am basing my success on being like other people! I had to laugh. No, a borrowed identity wouldn't quite do. While I appreciated my reader's compliment, I saw the trap I could fall into if I carried the train of thought further. I tossed my fantasies in the trash can and felt thankful for a strong lesson.

To evaluate our worth in terms of other people is a childish and ultimately dissatisfying endeavor. Many of us felt hurt and frustrated when parents and teachers barbed us with, "Why can't you get A's like your older brother?" and similar putdowns by comparison. To strive to be valuable because we are like someone else is an insult to our true being. Yes, we may be inspired by the examples of others and strive to develop similar qualities of character, but those qualities will be expressed by us in our own way. God made no two people exactly alike because He had a different idea for each of us. To the extent that we live that idea, we are fulfilling our purpose on earth.

Don't Walk Out of the Store

When I first began writing books I was very fortunate to not know what I was doing. I didn't think of myself as an author, and my goal was not to break into the book business and become famous. I was simply recording my ideas for the joy of self-expression, with the hope that those who read my words would be able to relate to them and find value in them. I knew nothing about the book trade, advertising, marketing, or anything in the commercial aspect of book publishing and sales. And I was better off for it.

One day after I had published several books I walked into a chain bookstore and looked over the sections of books similar to my own. I was nearly bowled over with the number of books on subject matter similar to mine! There were hundreds, perhaps thousands of books in the psychology, metaphysical, self-help, religion, spiritual, and inspirational sections! Many of these volumes were written by eloquent, famous, and well-respected authors who wrote on topics akin to mine. It occurred to me that if I had ever walked into that store before I had written, looked up and down those stacks of books and asked myself, "What do I have to say that is different or better then these successful authors?" I never would have even picked up a pen to write a word! I would have felt mercilessly intimidated and walked out of the store, believing that the market was already saturated several times over.

But fortunately I entered this work with no sense of comparison or competition. All I knew was that I had something to say and I wanted to say it. If anybody read it, that was God's business. I was bearing a child calling for birth, and I was the midwife.

Now I know Spirit's secret of success: While my subject matter is similar to that of other authors, *I have a unique way of saying it*. And so do the other authors and teachers. Let's face it; King Solomon was right—there is nothing new under the sun. The principles I teach are as old as history, and millions of people have said them in millions of ways before me. But no one has ever said them exactly like I do. No one has my fingerprints and no one will ever write exactly like me. I have a corner on the market of me! And you have the same for yourself.

Your uniqueness is the one gift that no one in this world can ever crowd you on. Don't fall prey to discouragement by comparing yourself to other people. You may look to others for inspiration, but never use them as a fulcrum for self-deprecation. Your gifts are just as valuable as anyone's, and to the extent that you are willing to bless and express your particular gifts, the world will reward you and take care of you. That's the way God gets Her kids to do what we came here to do.

First One on the Dance Floor

Someone described how they liked the way I speak intimately about my life without waiting for someone else to be honest first. They told me, "You're like the first one on the dance floor."

I love that metaphor. I remember going to high school dances at which the band played half a dozen songs before anyone got up and danced. No one wanted to be the first one on the dance floor. Everyone knew that all eyes would fall upon the first dancers and they would have to go beyond their fears of judgment and presenting themselves in public. Then a brave couple would step onto the dance floor. For a few seconds the crowd watched them, and soon twenty other people were dancing.

Life is pretty much like a high school dance: everyone would like to be out there having fun, but not many people want to do it first. Meanwhile the band is playing and the floor is open. It takes courage to be the first one to do something, but the payoff is equal to the risk. Participating is always more fun than sitting on the sidelines. Life is not a spectator sport. You have to be in it to win it. If you are the first one on the field, you take the chance of looking silly, but you also buy the right to enjoy yourself immensely, play longer than anyone else, and perhaps change the world while you're at it.

The Answer is at Hand

Originality does not mean that you create all of your ideas from thin air. There are very few completely new and original ideas. Sometimes the best inventions are combinations of existing ideas or materials put together in a fresh and more useful way.

Don't be stymied because your idea is not entirely original. Nothing is entirely original. One could say that no one has ever written anything entirely original, as all writers are using the same twenty-six letters. But ah! What new forms we can put those letters in!

When Frank Baum was writing his beloved series of *Oz* books, upon which the classic *Wizard of Oz* was based, he was sitting in his office with a friend discussing his visions for the books. At that time a title had not been chosen, and he had not yet given a name to the land that Dorothy visited. "What do you think you'll call this kingdom?" his friend asked. Baum's eyes moved around the office and lighted on his filing cabinet. He looked at the lowest drawer, which was alphabetically labeled, "O - Z." Frank stopped and pondered for a minute. "Oz," he answered, "*Adventures in the Land of Oz.*" And thus was born the name that has been etched into the hearts of millions for generations.

To consider the quality and success of that series of books and the ever-favorite movie that sprang from it, one might think that this mystical name came to the author in a vision, deep meditation, or introspection. But it did not. It came in a very simple and natural way, drawn from the elements of the author's life at hand. My teacher Hilda used to say, "Take whatcha got and make whatcha want," and that is exactly what Frank Baum did.

Trust Your Ideas

Fabulous ideas are being poured to you and all humankind constantly by the great creative mind of God. These ideas, if put into action, will bring blessing, healing, and joy to all whom they touch. Albert Einstein told his students, "I have not arrived at my understanding of the universe by means of my rational mind." He was explaining that his most important insights were born through his intuitive faculty. He also stated that "imagination is more important than knowledge."

Great innovators tell us that their inspirations come to them in intuitive flashes. Steven Spielberg describes that "once a month an idea crashes into my brain, and I get so excited that I can't eat breakfast or do anything else until I've put the idea into motion for expression."

A research scientist at the 3M company is a cogent example of the importance of following our creative promptings. He was working on an experimental project to develop a new glue that would bind papers together and then retain its adhesive nature to be reused without damaging the papers when they are separated. After a long time on the project he was unable to develop such a product. His supervisors felt that the company had put enough time and money into the experiment. Despite his protests, they summarily cut off funding and assigned him to a new project. But he wasn't ready to quit. He believed in the idea and felt that with enough focus and study he could succeed. So he continued to experiment on his own time at his own expense. Ultimately he found the formula he was searching for. In the process he invented the glue that holds "Post-It's" together, the little memo note pages that have become standard equipment in the world of office memo communications.

Another man in a more advantageous position was the president of Sony Corporation. He had an idea for a personal portable cassette player/radio with headphones which would give the listener maximum sound quality and disturb no one else as he listened. He suggested the development of this product at his research board meeting. His panel of his experts scoffed at the idea and told him it would never work. He didn't agree, and (since he was the chief honcho) he told them to research it anyway. The result was the Sony Walkman, which has sweepingly altered the stereo electronics field, brought listening pleasure to millions of music appreciators, (granted a reprieve to parents of heavy metal enthusiasts) and brought billions of dollars of revenue to Sony and other electronics corporations.

All of these successes came about because creative people were willing to listen to their intuition and act on their ideas with confidence. They refused to pay heed to outer voices of negation, the worship of the status quo, and fear. These innovators trusted the inner voice that prompted them, "This is a good idea. Go ahead and do it." They trusted that they would be shown the way, even if they didn't know how it would ultimately work out. No one knows for sure how anything will work out. Sometimes all we have to go on is a hunch. But sometimes that is all we need.

The Doorway to Infinite Potential

The most valuable thing in the world is not an object, but an idea. Every object you see came from an idea. An object is finite, limited, and can come and go. But a good idea contains within it the seeds of untold possibilities, including not just the idea at hand, but all the important ideas and products that may proceed as offshoots of the original one.

To believe in our ideas is to open the door to the infinite possibilities of our potential. To believe in ourself is to pave the avenue of success for our ideas. Do not shoot your ideas down before you give them a chance. Yes, some or even many of them may not work out, but the ones that do bear fruit will make it all worth it. Linus Pauling, the winner of Nobel Prizes for both Chemistry and Peace, declared, "The best way to have a good idea is to have lots of ideas." Gardeners plant many seeds and cull the best ones for further propagation. You must act as a gardener for your ideas, nurturing them all, removing the ones that are not helpful, and giving all the nourishment you can to the good ones. Then one day you will look at your garden, bless God for the inspiration, and honor yourself for following through on your original vision.

Dare to Be Original

1) List three original ideas that you have been waiting to put into action. What has stopped you? How can you follow through and create them?

2) Who are the people you most admire? What do you most admire about them? What do you offer the world that they do not?

3) Describe an experience in which you followed through on an original idea and then saw the universe confirm the importance of your idea and action.

4) What new ideas, products, or services can you create with materials at hand?

5) How do your best ideas come to you? Where do they come from?

DARE TO BE BEAUTIFUL

*Somehow I have to play my role in life as a gifted,
beautiful, happy, well-adjusted person.*

— Ashleigh Brilliant

It's a funny thing about beauty—if you don't know that you
are beautiful, you might as well not be. Your life and happiness
will not reflect the beauty that others see in you, and your
experience will mirror the lack you perceive in yourself.

Years ago I was dating a woman who was one of the most
beautiful women I have ever seen. Donna was a natural goddess,
bearing classic features that movie stars would envy and millions
of women spend fortunes and untold wishes to gain. The only
problem was that Donna didn't know how attractive she was.

I remember a conversation during which I invited Donna
to play a game with me. In this game we were to each write down
the ten best things about ourselves and read our lists to one
another. I was amazed to discover that Donna could not find
more than four things about herself that she was proud of. I was
even more surprised that Donna's physical beauty—which anyone
with eyes would acknowledge—was not on her list. Donna was
beautiful inside and out, but she did not recognize it.

I have known a number of other attractive women and men,
many of whom are successful models, actresses, and entertainers,
whose beauty earns them a living. To my great amazement, I
would say that many of them have had the lowest self-esteem
of all the people I have met. It seems, oddly enough, that there
is often an inverse relationship between outer beauty and inner
self-respect. I have found it to be a rare individual who knows
her or his own greatness, physically or spiritually.

Marilyn Monroe, one of the most ravishing beauties of the
century, was also among the most insecure. Her sad story reveals
a fantastically successful model and actress who was insatiably

desperate for validation. Although photos and headlines of Marilyn splashed the newspapers of the world daily, she could never get enough attention or approval. In the midst of Hollywood's greatest success story, Marilyn was dying of insecurity and depression.

While filming her last movie, *Something's Got to Give*, Marilyn told the producer that she wanted a new wardrobe with falsies because co-star Cyd Charisse's breasts were larger than hers. And when reporters asked Marilyn for her permission to print photos of a semi-nude scene Marilyn performed in that film, she consented on one condition—that they remove Elizabeth Taylor (by whom Marilyn felt threatened) from the covers of their tabloids. They did. Here was a woman who had empires falling at her feet, with some of the most popular and powerful men and moguls in the world ready to give her anything she wanted, but it wasn't enough. What Marilyn was really missing was an appreciation of her own self-worth, her own inner beauty. The outer world can never fulfill us as long as we are hungry inside.

Perhaps Marilyn is not so different from the rest of us. Perhaps her story symbolizes the part of us that offers great beauty and true worth to the world, but goes untapped because we do not recognize it ourself. It is not unusual that we are the last one to be aware of our greatness. Others can see it, but we have a blind spot which keeps us from knowing our gifts. And how powerful we are when we let the best in us shine! There is no greater purpose in living than to release our hidden splendor.

Form and Essence

Beauty is an essence which all of us embody. It is not a form; it is a spirit. I have know men and women who may not be considered beautiful by worldly standards, but who attract friends, suitors, and partners without the least effort. You see, it is not how we look that makes us beautiful—it is how we think about ourself. There is nothing in the outer world that makes us anything; it is what we are inside that determines who we are and what we create in our life.

Every person who lives is gifted with an inner beauty that is powerful, attractive, and uniquely lovable. The invitation before us is not to import more beauty through manipulating the outer world, but to release more radiance by opening to our inner world. We hold a vast untapped potential for fantastic excellence in all aspects of our life. To bring those unique qualities to the world is the gift that we came to bestow.

Dare to Be Enough

I discovered an attitude I was holding that was hurting me. There is a part of my mind that is never satisfied with what I do. No matter how much I accomplish, how richly I am acknowledged, or how deeply I am loved, there is a little critic in my head that tells me that I am not doing enough and I should be doing more. If I just did more, this voice tells me, then I would be enough. But the telling duplicity of this voice is that no matter how much I do, it's never enough. Like a phonograph needle stuck in the groove of a record, it just plays the same verse over and over again: "That's not enough."

The ruse of this disempowering voice became apparent to me when I noticed my attitude about the feedback I receive. Almost daily I receive loving letters of appreciation from people who have read my books or attended my workshops. These thoughtful people sincerely tell me how deeply they appreciate the work I am doing and how much my ideas and presence have changed their lives. Sometimes their heartfelt words bring me to tears. I treasure these testimonials, which I keep in a file in my desk.

Once or twice a year I would receive a letter from someone who was dissatisfied with a workshop experience. They would enumerate a series of complaints, some or all of which were designated as my fault. I felt disturbed by such letters and I mulled over them for a considerable time. They activated old unworthiness buttons inside me; I felt that I had somehow failed. The emotional vultures of fear and guilt swooped down and attempted to feed on old and limiting beliefs.

One day as I was pondering on such a letter of dissatisfaction, I opened my desk drawer and the file of loving testimonials literally burst at the seams and fell all over the drawer. I realized that there were literally hundreds of letters of deeply sincere thanks, any one of which would have been a good enough reason to be alive. There on top of the desk was one letter of complaint, to which I was giving a disproportionate amount of attention and emotional energy. My consciousness, I saw, was way out of focus. My old program of "I am not enough" had elbowed its way into my aliveness and, like a squid spewing forth a murky cloud of ink, totally overshadowed the love and beauty surrounding me. What a tragedy, I thought, if I was doing this great work and I didn't realize it.

I received a letter from my friend Rev. Anne Gillis, who assessed her "never enough" syndrome succinctly:

> I think I could resolve the war, write a best seller, and clear the national debt, and still a part of my mind would start going, "What about universal issues? You only healed one planet—what kind of God are you? You've only just gotten started!" One can imagine the clever innuendos of this inner critic when I am not succeeding in the world. I can also mention that the voice that speaks on my behalf is becoming clearer. I am grateful for my progress.

I met a man who introduced himself to me as a "reformed perfectionist." When I asked him how he came to see himself in that way, he told me, "I used to consider myself a perfectionist. But then I noticed that my perfectionism consisted of finding flaws. In the name of perfectionism I seized upon the faults I found in myself, others, and the whole world. My perfectionism was really bringing me down! Then one day I realized that if I was really a perfectionist I would be looking at the wholeness of things rather then the shortcomings. Since then I have trained my mind to find the beauty in all things, whether they are ostensibly perfect or not. Now I am finding the perfection that I originally said I was looking for."

If we believe that we are not doing or receiving enough, it is only because we believe that we *are* not enough. When we shift our focus from what we are not to what we are, we are well on our way to expressing and enjoying the beauty with which we are created.

The Truth About Our Beauty

I used to teach a yoga class in a convalescent hospital. My patients were elderly people with serious disabilities. All of the students came to class in wheelchairs and many of them were blind, paraplegic, and severely handicapped. My class consisted of light yoga exercises and guided meditation.

At first I came away from these classes feeling disheartened and depressed. I found it difficult to keep my spirits high in the face of the sorrow and sadness I saw in that hospital. By the time I got home after teaching the class, my joy battery was significantly worn down. Each week I became more and more dispirited by the pain I perceived there. One week, in my discomfort to deal with the suffering I looked upon, I literally forgot to go to the hospital to teach the class. The experience was a major challenge for me.

Then one day I realized that I was doing no one any good by forcing myself to go there and relating to the patients as unfortunate old sick people. I certainly wasn't inspired by my attitude, and I know they felt my fear. I decided that if I was going to teach there, I might as well bring them an attitude that would be helpful to them rather than oppressive. So I decided to take my attention off their problems and treat them like my friends rather than victims. I made it my goal to have fun with them.

The results were amazing! I laughed with my students, talked to them as equals rather than inferiors, and presented the class in a lighthearted way. By the end of the class I noticed that my spirits were vital and enthusiastic. And the patients certainly benefited from my transformed perception of them, and enjoyed me a lot more.

As the class went on, in time I began to revise the meditation

I was teaching them. I instructed them to see themselves as young, physically beautiful, strong, healthy, and energetic. I suggested that they visualize themselves running on the beach, dancing, or having any fun they could imagine with a vibrantly healthy body.

When I first began to guide them in this way, I was concerned that this was a cruel teaching method. I wondered if I was teasing them or perhaps insulting them by reminding them that they were disabled, as such fantasies of health were impossible for them in reality. I wondered if perhaps I was overstepping my purpose and I should rather teach a more conservative form of visualization.

Then I observed the students' faces as they were meditating. They were radiant! When I instructed them to visualize themselves jogging or dancing, they lit up and smiled. A surge of life rushed through them as they pictured themselves in their most desirable form. After their meditation the students shared that the visualization was their favorite part of the class. Many of the patients went on to describe vividly joyful scenes in which they elaborated in their mental movie. They loved seeing themselves as young, strong, and healthy.

From that experience I learned the power of seeing ourselves as beautiful. There is magic in attuning ourself to our highest vision of who we are. I believe that when we look upon ourself as beautiful (even if this image does not match the one we seem to be playing out physically) we are seeing ourself as we truly are. To behold the radiance of our soul is a gift of a lifetime.

Many psychics describe the spiritual appearance of people who pass on. As soon as they pass through the initial stages of the transition experience we call death, their light body becomes young and beautiful. Clairvoyants usually describe the departed one as they looked at the age of about nineteen years old. We would do well to remember the vibrancy of our true self even while we are in this life. We would bless ourselves richly by not waiting until we pass on to become nineteen again.

Through Adoring Eyes

In a world obsessed with criticism and imperfection, it indeed requires vigilance to hold the vision of our beauty. Especially in a culture that worships the youthful appearance of the body, we must stand tall in our appreciation of the beauty of a soul. Every soul is beautiful, but it is a rare individual who holds firm to the memory of the soul's reality in the face of the illusion that the body determines our attractiveness.

God, however, is not fooled by appearances. God beholds us always with adoring eyes and an appreciative heart. Like a loving parent who ever sees her child as the most beautiful on earth, Spirit knows us not by our acts, but by our essence. When we align our vision with God's view of our golden nature, we see ourself and the world anew.

It would be a powerful meditation and a supremely valuable gift to the planet to simply behold the beauty in all things. Magnificence is always present, waiting for us to find it. The first object of our appreciation must be ourself. Unless we acknowledge the qualities we already embody, we shall not gain them elsewhere. The world can mirror no more beauty to us than we find in the face that looks upon it. And our face is beautiful indeed, if we are willing to let it be so.

You will be amazed at the changes that take place in your life when you shift your focus from loss to splendor. Every lesson you undergo is in some way related to this critical shift in perception. You will discover the world as God created it, beaming with perfection. Then you will see that the ills of the world are created not by God's error, but by our blindness. That blindness is healed not by criticism, but by seeing. Accept your own Godliness and you will become a light that reveals the innate beauty of everyone who has forgotten their own. There is no greater gift you could offer the world than to restore God's vision to it, and renew His presence in the hearts of all who have forgotten it.

Dare to Be Beautiful

1) List your ten most beautiful attributes (more if you like).

2) List the five most beautiful people you have known, and describe why you chose them.

3) Note the attributes that you have that are similar to these people, and the situations in which you display(ed) these qualities.

4) What would you be doing differently if you were satisfied with yourself now?

DARE TO
TAKE YOUR POWER BACK

Your mind will tell you that you can live like this,
But your heart can't; it's about to explode.
— Charley Thweatt

*W*illow is the story of a young man in medieval times who wants to become a wizard. Every year the village wizard conducts a competition during which an apprentice is chosen. Willow is among three hopefuls, and he ardently wants to be accepted.

The day of choosing arrives, and the wizard calls the three applicants before a gathering of the townspeople. There he gives the would-be apprentices a test. The wizard holds up his hand, extends his fingers and asks, "In which finger does the power lie?" A hush falls over the crowd. The three young men ponder and meditate. Their hopes and ambitions rest in their answer. The first applicant lifts his hand and points to the wizard's index finger. There follows a pregnant silence. All eyes are on the wizard. Slowly he shakes his head.

The second candidate takes a deep breath and reaches up to indicate his choice of the wizard's thumb. Again silence. Again the master shakes his head.

The focus turns to Willow. If he makes the correct choice he will be taken into the wizard's tutelage and taught the secrets of mastery over the elements. If he chooses incorrectly he will go off to war with the other young men. The moment of truth is at hand. Willow points to the wizard's ring finger. He peers deeply into the master's eyes, hoping to get some glimmer of a response. The wizard shakes his head. "There will be no apprentices this year," he announces, and the throng disperses.

Willow is crestfallen. How badly he wanted to learn from

this great mentor! "What was the right answer, anyway?" he wonders.

The tide of Willow's life moves him to leave the village and set out on an extraordinary series of adventures. He becomes a soldier, faces many trials, and overcomes his deepest fears. In the process he grows in wisdom and inner strength. The boy becomes a man.

When he returns to the village, Willow visits the wizard. The sage asks him, "When I gave you the test of power, what were you thinking?"

"I wanted to say that the power lies in my own hand."

"Why, then, did you not say that?"

"I felt embarrassed," confesses Willow. "I thought it would be an arrogant response."

"That, my son, was the correct answer."

"I know that now. As I have fought my battles and stood for my truth, I realize that the power lies within me."

"Then you have indeed become the master."

Cause, Not Effect

One of the greatest tragedies of our culture is that we give our power away daily. We believe that there are forces in the outer world that control our fate, while the abiding truth of our life is that we create our own destiny. We choose other people as objects of romance and credit them with making us happy, and then when they leave we blame them for hurting us. A check comes to us in the mail and we feel abundant; the next day we receive an unexpected bill and we become upset. The sun shines and we feel elated, and then the rain comes and we are depressed. We act as if our happiness or misfortune is dealt to us by any hand except our own.

Could such capricious tides be the rulers of our destiny? We are children of a creative God, choosing and chosen to be here to act as cause, not react as effect. Surely we have a greater purpose than to bob helplessly on whimsical waves of circumstances. Although the world would have us believe that we are powerless, there is a strength within us that does not depend on other people, the economy, or climatic conditions. Our strength issues from a Source deep within ourself.

The Lord and the Landlord

I have given my power away to all kinds of people and things outside myself. I used to have a real authority problem with landlords. When I was living in a house with some other people, one day the landlord came to talk to me about several house-related matters. After one of my housemates observed my conversation with the landlord, she gave me some feedback. "You usually hold your power," she told me. "But when you talk to Marvin, you shrivel up. You become like a little boy. You don't speak to him with nearly the same presence or conviction that you hold with most people. What do you think is going on?"

Her observation really woke me up. I realized that I had put the landlord in a box of my preconceived judgments. I decided that he was someone to be feared. Seen clearly, I recognized that this was not a decision I would ever consciously make. Obviously there were some subconscious programs running me. I decided to stay awake, present, and remain in my power with him. I saw that Marvin may have owned the house I was living in, but he did not own me. He had dominion over the building, but I had dominion over my happiness. I wanted to relate to Marvin as a brother, not some dark figure from my childhood. From that point on, our relationship changed. Whenever I spoke with Marvin I purposefully held my ground and I came to see him in an entirely different light. I learned to relate to him as an equal rather than fearing him, and that made all the difference.

Pedestals Always Fall On You

We hurt ourself terribly when we put someone on a pedestal or allow ourself to rest on a pedestal of someone else's construction. During the last few decades we have seen many revered figures in politics, religion, and entertainment topple from

217

their gilded thrones before our eyes. One of the lessons behind this massive purge is for us to learn our divine equality. It does not serve us to see ourself as higher or lower than someone else.

When I first went to one of Patricia Sun's workshops I developed a crush on her. Patricia was physically attractive, she bore the wisdom of a sage, and she emanated great love and compassion. These were all qualities I admired, and I set her up in my mind with an aura of worship.

Although I spoke of Patricia in glowing terms, all the while I felt a gnawing emptiness. The emptiness issued from my sense of loss in disowning my strength in order to look up to her. I believed that Patricia had all these wonderful qualities and I did not—a classic formula for idol worship. My belief system was couched in a costume of admiration, but the net effect of my idolatry was debilitating to me.

The turning point came when I was invited to be a co-presenter with Patricia on a trip to the Soviet Union. When I saw her name on the roster I was excited at first, and then I began to feel anxious. Here I would be in close contact with my idol. What would I do? What should I say? Would she like me and approve of me?

When we finally did spend time together I felt terribly awkward in Patricia's presence. Every time I got near her I became extremely self-conscious, wondering if I was saying or doing the right thing, and hanging on the ways that she paid attention to me or didn't. My primary memory of our interaction is that I was very uncomfortable with Patricia and I didn't enjoy being with her at all.

None of these feelings, of course, were caused by Patricia or what she was doing. She was the same wonderful Patricia that she always was. My discomfort had to do with my projections of power, beauty, and wisdom that I had overlaid on her. I brought separation into the relationship, and true to its painful fruits, fear undermined my sense of peace in being with her. Idolatry replaced intimacy at the price of joy.

But there was a great gift in that experience. After the trip I assessed my time with Patricia, and I realized that I had robbed myself of enjoying her presence (and my own) because I had put her on a pedestal. I realized that I had hurt myself by seeing the God in her and not in me. My experience with Patricia was so uncomfortable that it brought me to the realization that no one and nothing in this world is worth idolizing at the expense of my own joy. Since that time I have not held anyone above me in the same way.

We cannot afford to deny our divinity in order to find it in someone else. Divinity is a package deal; we all have it together equally. To see more God in one person than another is not to see clearly. God sees all of us as equally beautiful and honors us as such. To see ourself as God sees us is to touch the highest vision possible.

Burn This Book

Just as we may renounce our power for the sake of another person, we can give it away to a method of learning. Any tool of awakening is valuable only to the extent that it lifts you from where you are and helps take you to your next step. If, out of fear, you try to hang onto where you are and resist moving ahead, the universe will nudge (or kick) you up the ladder to your next rung of empowerment.

In the film production of *The Razor's Edge*, Bill Murray dramatizes the journey of a spiritual seeker. Larry leaves a plush and sheltered English lifestyle to face the horrors of World War I, and then sets off to India to find enlightenment. Larry is an avid reader who seeks for the answer in many books. But his search has left him unsatisfied.

Larry finds his way to a temple near the top of the Himalayas, where he meets a wise guru. "What do you seek, my son?" the master asks him.

"I want to know how to live." Larry explains.

"Very well then," the sage tells him. "Do you see that hut at the top of the mountain?" Larry's eyes scan the snow-covered peak. He spies a tiny lean-to near the summit.

"Take your books and go up to the camp. Stay there until

you find the answer you have been searching for."

Larry's eyes open wide with excitement. Here is his chance to gain the truth for which he has yearned. He gathers his volumes and hikes up to the hut, which is nothing more than a flimsy shelter made of four wooden posts and a cloth roof. He makes a campfire and sits down eagerly to read. This is the moment Larry has been waiting for.

Larry goes through days, then weeks of reading. Each succeeding scene reveals him looking colder and more frustrated. The stubble on his cheeks grows into a beard. Despite his intense efforts, Larry definitely does not look any closer to enlightenment. In fact, he looks pretty discouraged.

After a few weeks at the campsite, Larry is freezing. Snow is falling, the winds are howling, and tiny icicles cling to Larry's moustache. If he doesn't do something soon, he will learn about enlightenment from the next world.

The fire dwindles and there is no more wood. But Larry is still reading voraciously, perhaps even more intensely than when he began. He's determined to find his answer. And he does. Against the backdrop of the cold night, Larry's eyes wander from the book to the diminishing fire, back to the book, and then to the fire. A spark of real understanding begins to glow in his eyes. The answer has come. Proudly Larry stands up, tears a few pages out of the book, and tosses them into the campfire. The flames rise and Larry delights in the warmth. An impish smile crawls across his face. He tears out a handful of leaves of the book and commits them to the blaze. Larry's smile turns into a muted giggle, and then howling laughter. Raucously he rips out the rest of the pages and chucks them into the flames. Then, as quickly as he can, he takes the rest of his books and hurls them into the bonfire. The flames soar skyward, casting light and warmth to the far reaches of the camp. From a distance we see Larry standing at the top of this dark mountain, enfolded in a bright orange glow.

The next morning Larry walks triumphantly down the mountain to the base camp. He his happy, conspicuously free of his reading material. Larry has found his answer, and it was not in a book. His answer was to live; to do whatever was required to make life fulfilling and joyful in the moment. Enlightenment was not to be found in escaping into words or suffering in the cold. He took the challenge before him and met it with the resources at hand. And he could do this only by being fully alive and aware in the moment. The answer was not somewhere out there. It was right here.

Sacred Sight

Some of us have had a tendency to believe that some practices, places, and events are closer to God than others. We may even believe in chosen people and sacred sites. It is important to remember that we are all chosen and God is present everywhere. Sanctity is not something we make a pilgrimage to visit; it is a quality of being we carry within us. As we walk with God we bring beauty, power, and harmony wherever we go, and there we shall find these virtues as well.

Linda Johnson is co-director of Youth Ambassadors of America, an organization which arranges citizen diplomacy tours for young people. She and her husband Ed regularly take American children to the Soviet Union to meet, share with, and develop supportive relationships with their Soviet peers.

One of the Youth Ambassadors' tours occurred at the time of the Harmonic Convergence. This was a day which many astrologers, ancient religions, and seers designated as a turning point in planetary history. Many groups joined for prayer, ritual, and celebration at sacred sites such as Mount Shasta in California and Machu Pichu in South America. Many of those who gathered came with the intention to focus positive healing energy for this planet. Others came because soothsayers had predicted that this auspicious day would bring cataclysmic upheavals, including earthquakes, tidal waves, and numerous catastrophes in which a large portion of the world's population would be destroyed. Some believed that these special locations would be safe from disaster.

These Apocalyptic prophecies instilled fear in the hearts of some of the children on the Youth Ambassadors' tour. Linda gave this account of a conversation she shared with a girl on her plane who was afraid she would be among those struck down by God:

> *Karolyn, a little girl in our group came up and asked, "Could our plane crash?" Her eyes were full of fear.*
>
> *Then it hit me: a legacy of good and evil beliefs our children inherit from us! All wrapped up in rituals and buried in sacred sites.*
>
> *"No, our plane will not crash," I responded. "Karolyn, I will tell you a secret: This entire world is a sacred site. Yup, God said the whole thing is good, and there is never more of God on a special day or a special place. God is everywhere right now. Can you imagine God saying, 'Karolyn, I'm not going to be on the plane with you today? I've decided to spend the day at Mount Shasta because it's a power point and much more sacred.'? God lives inside of you, loving you and protecting you, which makes **you** a power point—a moving, wonderful power point named Karolyn."*

Like Karolyn, we are *all* power points. Meister Eckhart described God as "a circle whose center is everywhere and whose circumference is nowhere." We must reclaim the power that lies within us. We may be attracted to certain people, places, or pathways that bring us inspiration and in whose presence we feel closer to God, and that is wonderful. We must pursue anything that links our mind with the divine, for that is the purpose of our coming here—to remember our spiritual nature. But we cannot afford to find God in one place at the expense of another. We cannot believe that a select group of persons or places is worthy of more love or protection than another. That is the very pitfall into which so many of the world's religions have fallen. Most of the wars that have been fought on the planet are called "holy" wars, in which each party believes that God is on their side. This cannot be so. God is on the side of love, and love does not go to war. Neither does love visit certain geographical locations and boycott the others. Love is present everywhere. Just as it disempowers us to find more God in one person than another, we cannot blind our sight to worship a site.

The Only Real Power

When Jesus was taken before Pontius Pilate after being accused of crimes he never committed, Pilate threatened him, "Don't you realize that I have the power to crucify you?" Jesus' response was clear and strong: "You have no power but that given you by my Father."

A sharper truth has never been spoken. No power exists except the power of God. In our child's game of earth we make up rules, regulations, rewards, and punishments, but all of these are meaningless to one who understands that the only real power lies in Spirit. No man or woman has any power over another unless we give it to them. Each of us is one with an all-powerful God, creating our universe moment by moment, giving strength to what we believe and dismissing what we do not. Our life is not ruled by people; it proceeds from Spirit. Our food is not the bread of the earth, but the Love of God. Our sustenance depends not on the paper strips and metal disks we trade, but on the infinite mercy of the One who created everything we believe we trade for. Be careful that you do not trade the awareness that your Source lives within you. To ascribe power to anything less than love is a poor bargain indeed.

Beggars or Kings?

There is a story about a man who takes his lantern and goes out in the night to his neighbor's house to borrow a match to light a cigarette. Upon hearing his request, the neighbor begins to laugh. Perturbed, the first man asks him what is so funny. "Look in your hand, sir" the neighbor suggests. "Your lamp already has a flame for you to draw from! The same light that guided you to come here could have given you what you need right at home."

A more modern metaphor reminds us that "the helping hand you are looking for is at the end of your own arm." And as Kabir said, "I laugh when I hear that the fish in the water is thirsty."

All of these metaphors point to a major life lesson that most of us need to practice and learn: *God, help, and healing are always available to us, for our Source lives inside our heart.* All of our adventures, even unto the ends of the earth, even unto lifetimes, lead us but to the same conclusion. Like Dorothy in *The Wizard of Oz*, we ultimately find that we never had to leave home to find what we are searching for.

Whether we journey to Oz, Mount Shasta, or the farthest star, we will find the same lesson waiting for us. The power that gives us life lies not in the hand of another, but our own. Willow went off to many adventures to learn the truth he already knew. The power lay always in his own hand. And so does our power reside with us exactly where we are. God is the Force that created us, the Home to which we return, and the Strength that we carry with us. We walk the world like beggars, while we are Children of a King. Let us together claim our Kingdom, and wield the power of love. Then shall our strength live as it was intended to be expressed.

Dare to Take Your Power Back

1) To whom or what do you give your power? In what situations do you hold your power? In what situations do you lose it? How do you feel in each case?

2) What do you believe other people or things can give you that you cannot give yourself?

3) Whom do you put on a pedestal? Who puts you on a pedestal? Describe the feelings and results that accompany each situation.

4) Describe several truly powerful people you know. Where does their strength lie? What do they ascribe as the source of their power?

DARE TO SAY NO

*Remember the "yes" behind your "no"
and focus on what you are moving toward
rather than what you are leaving behind.*

The entire spiritual path consists of learning which voice to listen to. God is always speaking to us, and so is our ego. We are here to learn to choose between love and fear. Guilt is the ego's henchman. It finds fault where there is innocence and tries to convince us that we are evil rather than good. If we listen to the inner attorney for the prosecution, we will sentence ourself to loss. Guilt will keep us cornered until we wake up from the dream of reprehensibility and reclaim our identity as children of a loving God.

If you feel guilty when you say "no," you have stepped onto fertile ground for healing. Let's explore the power of saying "no" so we can speak the word with conviction.

Two Sides of the Coin

To say "no" to one alternative is to say "yes" to another. To turn down a request to work overtime on the weekend is to give yourself the gift of relaxation and renewal. To refuse to give a child ice cream when she has had enough is to contribute to her health and well-being. To leave someone with whom you are in a sick relationship is to affirm that you deserve a better one. Remember the "yes" behind your "no" and focus on what you are moving toward rather than what you are leaving behind.

Make Space for What You Want

The universe abhors a vacuum. When you let go of what you don't want, you make space for what you do want to enter your life. We need to clear out undesirable elements that fill our space so we can use it more efficiently and enjoyably. You cannot work on the weekends and have time to play as well. The first step to enjoying a new wardrobe is to discard the old one. You cannot hold onto an old relationship and attract a new one. If we divide our psychic energy between the old and the new, we dissipate our power to manifest what we truly desire, and end up with two halves that don't make a whole. We must keep ourself open to our highest good. If we are clinging to a security blanket, our hands are not free to accept richer blessings. Saying "no" to something that is not working for you is a very positive affirmation that you are willing and ready to accept something better, and you trust the universe to supply you with the good you deserve. Our part is to know our worth and act on it; the great synchronicity of life will take care of the rest. In this sense, saying "no" is actually a powerful affirmation of faith.

When in Doubt, Don't

Do not allow yourself to be pressured by an inner fear or an outer agent to do something that you are not ready to do. Regret is the unmistakable offspring of panic, and can be avoided by allowing our decisions to proceed from peace rather than pressure.

A surprising number of women have confided in me that they inwardly knew they were not supposed to marry someone to whom they had said "yes," but hadn't really meant it with all their heart. I am astounded by the clarity of the guidance these women received and did not follow. Some of them had very lucid dreams that their marriage would end in disaster and yet, in fear of causing upset, went ahead with their plans in spite of their intuition. After the fact, they wished they had heeded the still small voice. (The good news is that they all learned valuable lessons in the process. But we can also learn gently, without following through on decisions that violate our integrity.)

It is always easier to say "yes" after you have said "no" than to say "no" after you have said "yes." There is a wisdom in waiting. An honest "No, I don't feel ready or able now" will set dynamics in motion that will move you closer to the truth of your being. If after deeper consideration you come to the realization that you want to say "yes," you can and will do so with real conviction. The results of your honest "yes" will be much more powerful after you have had time to consider it and proceed from choice rather than intimidation. Entering into a situation with a real "yes" in your heart will ultimately bring greater reward than if you had gone ahead with nagging doubts and fears.

I am a great believer in destiny (which we create by our soul's calling). I believe that if something is important for us to do, the universe will keep moving us in that direction. We will receive signs and indications—sometimes to the point of almost being hit over the head with our answer—as to our right place or action. We have every right—moreover, responsibility—to take the time and caring to watch for those signs and heed them when they appear. Even if you miss one opening, you will have the opportunity to choose again. No one flunks out of the university of life. If you fail a test, you are always given a chance to take it again. And you will remain in school until you pass. Because there is only life, there is no place else to go for summer school.

Let Peace Lead

I had a major lesson in learning to choose from strength rather than fear. I was shopping for a new car around the time of the oil shortage in 1977. While I was looking at a Honda, the salesman told me that I had better buy the car now, since that night President Carter was televising a speech during which he would announce oil restrictions that would limit the supply of gasoline and raise its price significantly. "Tomorrow," the salesman warned me, "there will be a long line of people wanting to buy the car you're looking at now."

A wave of panic churned in my gut. I imagined being unable to get that car or having to pay more for it because I missed my chance before the President's speech. I was tempted to accede to the salesman's ploy. But then another voice spoke within me. It, too, had a warning. It told me not to act out of fear. This voice, tranquil in contrast to the salesman's threat, reminded me that panic is not the path to obtain what I want; if I proceeded from peace rather than hysteria, the universe would give me what I needed. The inner guide advised me not to fall victim to scare tactics. When I tried that voice on for size, it felt a lot more real than plunking my money down that moment because the salesman was trying to frighten me into it. After a few moments of reflection, I decided to trust the voice of strength. I told the salesman that I wanted to shop around some more.

That night Jimmy Carter made his speech. The next day, contrary to the salesman's prognostication, there was no line at the Honda dealer. I took another week to shop around, and after intelligently comparing Hondas with the other cars I saw, I went back and bought a Honda. But the important difference was that my choice arose from wisdom, not woe. As I signed the sales agreement I felt proud of myself that I had chosen the car from a source of calm clarity rather than fearful self-protection. Now whenever someone outside me or a fearful voice within me attempts to cajole me into acting before I am ready, I remember the day that I chose to act rather then react. I have never regretted that decision, and I have gotten even more mileage out of the lesson than I did from the car.

From Enabling to Empowerment

Fear, true to the terrorist tactics it employs, threatens that we will be outcast if we say "no." In order to keep our friends, the ego advises, we must say "yes," even to requests that we do not want to comply with. What the ego forgets in its blindness, however, is the kind of friends that lying keeps. What value is there in a friendship that asks you to deny who you are?

A man in one of my workshops told the group, "Most of my life I have been afraid to say 'no' because I feared that I would lose my friends if I did. But then I discovered that I didn't have any friends because no one knew who I was."

Real friendships can handle "no." If your relationship cannot survive honesty, it is not a real friendship. Friends can disagree and yet love and respect one another. True caring requires realness, the willingness to be who we are. A friendship based on anything other then sincerity is a guilt bargain—two people selling themselves out for approval, and not acknowledging that their heart is aching to share more. In a way, many of the world's friendships are like the story of the emperor's new clothes. The ills of our world hold power only when we are unwilling to tell the truth in the face of illusions. Darkness cannot stand the light, and illusions cannot endure in the face of the truth. Dedicate your friendship to truth, and you will be amazed at the peace and satisfaction it brings you. If a friendship is not big enough to survive your "no," you don't want it anyway. The real strength of a true relationship lies in our willingness to speak our honest thoughts and feelings. Do not settle for anything less.

"No" is a very loving word to say, especially to someone who would be hurt by your saying "yes." To give liquor to an alcoholic, drugs to an addict, money to a borrower who will squander it, sex to one who does not honor it, false security to a codependent, help to one who is not interested in receiving it, or advice to one who is unable to hear it, is to add another shackle to the chain from which their soul is crying for release. Do not further bind someone who will hurt themself with your "yes."

The Gems of Truth

We find ourself on a journey in a far country ruled by laws that are foreign to our nature. Those who live under the dictatorship of separation make decisions to appease the gods of guilt and fear, beguiling despots of merciless rule. Let anyone challenge the lords of darkness, and he is branded a fool or disposed of as a threat to the regime of shadows. It is indeed difficult to make a stand for sanity in a world caught in the jaws of madness.

Yet the seeker of truth holds two gems in his hand which

have the power to vanquish darkness and shed precious light on the path of the heart. These sparkling jewels reflect the wisdom of Heaven and disburse clouds of confusion from the soul who would walk the journey to healing.

The first precious stone is the discernment to not be fooled by appearances. When confronted with terror of any kind, the student of truth calls upon a higher vision to pierce through the veil of drama and behold the holy presence, no matter what the outer forms indicate. Healing is impossible to those who look upon limits and agree to their formidability. Vision is the sage's most worthy companion; it will serve him well when all other comrades have fallen aside.

The second gem is the willingness to turn within for guidance. After a point on the journey, decisions proceed from the heart rather than an outer authority. *There is no outer authority.* There is one authority, which lies within. Everything we see in the outer world is but a refection of the dynamics of spirit that unfold within us. The true warrior of the heart takes refuge in the temple of the soul and draws sustenance from the flame of grace which burns eternally on its holy altar. All of his strength, guidance, and vision spring forth from this hallowed beacon.

If that inner guide advises us to say "no," then we must trust its wisdom. The astute seeker realizes that he sees but a minuscule portion of the great mosaic of which any situation is but a tiny tile. But there is One within him who does see the entire map of the journey, and when that One answers "no," there is a reason. And while the reason may not be obvious at the moment, it will be shown in due time.

When we hearken unto Spirit's "no," we do a great service to ourself and the world. Present your "no" with the dignity of the gift that it is. If you apologize for saying "no," then you do not believe in the voice that guides you to say it. The power of integrity lies in having the words of your lips be one with the wisdom of your heart. Blessed by the power of truth, your "no" to that which does not belong to you is a testimony that your good lies elsewhere and you shall have it.

Dare to Say No

1) What is the hardest thing for you to say "no" to? What are you afraid will happen if you do?

2) Make a list of the issues, invitations, or people you would like to say "no" to, but haven't. Next to each item, write down what you are saying "yes" to instead.

3) Do you have any friendships in which you feel unable to say "no"? Note how this withholding of truth diminishes the quality of the relationship. How could you help your friend by saying "no"?

4) Note any situations in which you feel pressured to say "yes." What is the worst thing that could happen if you postponed your answer until you are sure? What would be the best thing that could happen?

5) Describe a situation in which God said "no" to you, which turned out to be a blessing.

DARE TO SAY YES

The winds of grace are blowing all the time.
We have only to raise our sails.

Near the Puna district of the Big Island of Hawaii, Kilauea volcano has been steadily erupting for over eight years. Daily half a million tons of molten lava spew forth from bottomless caverns and pour in rivers of fire down ashen slopes to an equally restless sea. Since the eruption began, hundreds of square miles of forests and beaches have been destroyed, including over a hundred homes. To behold the entire mountainside covered with freshly hardened lava is an awesome sight.

At times I have felt sadness over this massive destruction. Huge tracts of pristine rainforest have been burnt and buried. Jungled pools of natural hot springs have been filled and covered. The quaint and picturesque village of Kalapana, once a haven of splendor and tranquil respite, is now but a memory. Why, I wondered, would God destroy such an Elysian terrain?

One night I ventured out to behold the lava flow at midnight. As I watched the steaming orange liquid congeal before my eyes, a newfound excitement stirred within me. I realized that something new was being created. The volcano is actually building fresh land. The island is growing daily. A new firmament lives on the face of the planet. Yes, there is destruction, but at the same time there is creation. The eruption has brought an abrupt end to what was, but it also marks the beginning of what is to be.

As I took a last look at the fire rolling down the hillside, considering the play of annihilation and resurrection, a voice within me tugged at the hem of my limits. "How did you think this island got here in the first place?" it asked. Then I understood.

Volcanic eruptions were the avenue by which these exquisite islands were born. At one time *all* of Hawaii looked black, bleak, and desolate. Seen from a broader vista, the desolation was the foundation for future abundance.

So nothing is entirely bad. (Even a clock that is stopped is right twice a day.) My lesson with Kilauea volcano was to learn to say "yes" to it. Until that night I had been resisting it, judging it as negative and hoping the destruction would end soon. But it is not really bad. There is great good in it, as there is in everything.

Command What Is

It is said that if we want to be truly powerful we need but command what is happening to happen. While there is a humorous note in this advice, there is also a profound wisdom. We are most powerful when we are aligned with the flow of the universe. To deny what is, would be like running out on your front lawn in the morning and commanding the sun to reverse direction and set in the east. No matter how strong your wish for this to be so, your chances of succeeding are very slim.

Our attempts to make life other than it is are just as foolish and ineffectual. To try to change people to suit us or fight against unchangeable situations is debilitating and useless. If something cannot be changed, our most powerful position is to go with it and find a blessing that we could not see when we wanted to be in charge.

I conducted a retreat during which it rained for eight days. We saw the sun for about one minute out of the entire time we were together. You can imagine the disappointment on the part of the participants, who had visions of basking in the warm tropical sun. After a few days I gave up expecting the sun to come out, and I considered what deeper purpose there might be in the weather conditions. I realized that there was a tremendous amount of inner growth that occurred during that retreat. Because we couldn't go out, we had to go in. As we discussed our frustration about the weather, we uncovered a vein of the disappointment that ran through our lives. There were many important feelings and reactions that came to the surface during that week, awarenesses that we never would have had the opportunity to look at and transform if we had been playing in the sun more. We did not get the retreat we expected, but we did get a major life lesson in discovering deeper truths about who we are.

Living in "Yesness"

I work with an assistant who inspires me tremendously. She is willing and enthusiastic to serve and get the job done, which is a real asset and blessing to me and the work we do.

One day I called Joan to ask her to look up some records. As soon as she heard my voice on the telephone, she brightly said, "Yes! Just tell me what you need, and I'll be happy to do it." Needless to say, I was delighted. As an employer, that is about the most positive response I could receive.

Joan would not do anything outside of her capability or integrity. She has simply chosen to practice one of Og Mandino's keys to success: *Throw yourself wholeheartedly into the task at hand.* Joan has adopted a "yes" attitude about her life, which makes all the difference in the joy and success she experiences in her work and spiritual path.

Joan's willingness inspired me to think about how we empower ourselves and those with whom we interact when we have a "yesness" about us. Some people seem to walk around with a big "No—don't bother me!" over their head. Out of fear and pain such heavily defended people create a psychic shield around themselves which keeps others from invading the territory they feel they need to protect. Others radiate, "Yes—I'm willing to play and win." These attitudes may not be communicated in words, but because we are all intrinsically psychic, we can pick up each other's life script statements instantly. Emerson noted, "Who you are speaks to me so loudly that I can hardly hear what you are saying."

It is no accident, then, who wins at life. Those who say "yes" to life enter into a miraculous adventure which brings the richest joy and blessings. "Yes" is one of the most powerful words in our language. It is right up there with "I am." Practice saying "yes" as much as you can, and you will enjoy a surge of newfound energy that will overcome seemingly insurmountable obstacles. Put the word to work for you. Remember that the universe always says to us what we say to it. "Yes" is the key to everything your heart desires. All that you wish to have and be is waiting for you to accept it, and "yes" is your claim check.

The Power of an Open Heart

One evening after presenting a workshop I found my friend Vaughn waiting for me, standing against the exit door of the building with his arms open wide. He had appreciated my presentation and he wanted to hug me.

I was struck by the visual image of Vaughn with his arms outstretched. In order to embrace me, he had to expose his heart. To really give and receive love, we must make ourself vulnerable. When we uncover our heart to embrace someone, they may be right there to receive and return our gift, but they may also leave us standing there alone. That's the chance we take when we open our heart to make contact. When we say "yes" to life, we open ourself to all the experiences that life has to offer. In the process we may feel hurt, rejected, or misunderstood. But we may also get hugged. That's the way intimacy works. You can't get hugged if your arms are folded.

The only thing more dangerous than being vulnerable is being absent. If we open the doors to let other people and life in, we take the chance of losing, but if we close the doors, we are lost. Fear's "logic" advises us that staying shut down will keep us safe, but a higher wisdom shows us that it will make us dead. We are most powerful when we put aside our defenses and let life flow through us.

If you don't know what to do with your life, just show up. If you are willing to follow leads, experiment with the unknown, and not write off people or experiences before you give them a chance, you will find the gate of the garden of innocence. This is the state of childlike wonder that Jesus told us we must live in if we want to enjoy Heaven. We are not asked to be saints, just to be open. A little willingness can make a big difference.

"Yes" is not just a word—it is an attitude. It is a state of mind and heart that we bring to life. Living in "yesness" is the all-important key to your heart's desires. Say "yes" to life, and life will say "yes" to you.

Dare to Say Yes

1) What have you been resisting saying "yes" to? What fear is stopping you?

2) Who or what would you like to say "yes" to you?

3) Is there something you have wanted that you believe God has denied you? How might you be saying "no" to yourself?

4) How could you liberate more peace and energy for yourself by accepting rather than resisting something you cannot change?

5) Write down three aspects of your life that you will experiment with saying "yes" to:

Dare to
Move Ahead

DARE TO MOVE AHEAD

*Once we pass this point, Marty, there's no
turning back—It's the future or bust!*
— Emmett Brown, *Back to the Future*

L ooking out the van window onto the darkened streets of
Tulsa at 6 AM, I wondered if I would get a flight out. The
reservations agent had told me that the flight was sold out,
but my intuition advised me to go to the airport anyway. Pulling
up stakes with the intention of getting a seat on that plane was
an act of faith.

While I rapped with the van driver, in my mind I was
preparing to ask him if he would wait for me in case I couldn't
get the flight. I certainly didn't want to be stranded at the airport.
If I had him wait for me, at least I would be assured of a ride
back to the hotel.

Then another voice spoke within me. This voice was bold
and to the point. "Do you plan to get on this plane, or don't
you?" it asked. Well, I hoped I would.

"That won't quite do," this instructive train of thought went
on. "This is *your* movie. There are no forces outside your own
mind. If you choose to get on this flight, you will. If not, you
might as well turn around now."

Well, that set the choices before me rather bluntly. I decided
to proceed as if I was going to get on the plane. The van stopped
in front of the United terminal, and off I stepped with my
suitcases. Here was my moment to act. I could chicken out and
play it safe, or go ahead with the expectation that I was going
to get what I wanted. I tipped the driver and bade him a good
day. It felt good to choose my intention and live by it.

I walked up to the counter and asked the agent if I could
get a seat on today's flight. He checked the computer. "No
problem," he told me, and on I went.

No Turning Back

In the wars of olden times, armies would often burn the bridges they crossed into enemy territory. The action was a clear statement of intention. There was no turning back. The only way to go was ahead.

Sometimes we need to burn our bridges to step into our new life. Our ego, which is ruled by fear and insecurity, wants to have something safe to fall back on, such as our past. But the gaping delusion the ego conveniently overlooks in its warped belief system is that the past to which we are attempting to cling did not work for us, or it no longer serves us in the way it did. If our past was worthwhile to be our present, we would be continuing to enjoy its productive rewards. But those "rewards" either never existed or they have ceased to be of value to us, which is precisely the reason we feel called to move ahead. But the ego doesn't want to hear this. Its investment is in clutching to the known, even if the known doesn't work.

We cannot cling onto the old and enjoy the new at the same time. We cannot be the person we were and the person we are to become. The caterpillar must entirely let go if its former life to emerge as a butterfly.

The Answer to the Voice of Death

When I was writing *The Dragon Doesn't Live Here Anymore*, I had the strangest sense that I was going to die. I felt that I had about six months to live, and I envisioned that the book would be my parting gift to life. I could not fathom where this sense was coming from, as I was in good health and I had no reason at all to expect that I would die.

As I further investigated the feeling, I realized that there was a part of me that was indeed dying—my old self. I was used to seeing myself as a rather mediocre fellow with not many important things to say and no great power to contribute to improving the world. As I recorded my ideas in that book, however, I felt a tremendous strength stirring in the depths of me. In the writing I was elevated to a higher consciousness and I sensed that once the book came out, my life would change dramatically. In those chapters I was revealing some of the most intimate experiences of my life and making a stand for some very potent principles. I was aligning myself with a significantly greater identity. There was no way that the old me and the new me could coexist. (As they used to say in the old westerns, "Pardner, there ain't room enough in this town for both of us.") I was shedding an old and limiting skin to become a bigger person spiritually. That was the death I was undergoing. As I came to realize what was happening, I knew that I did not want to be the old me—or at least my old image of me—anymore. "Let it die, then," I said to myself. And it did.

Since that time, I have had the "inner death" experience several times, and when it arises I bless it. Now I realize that the process is not bad at all; to the contrary, it is very positive. It means that I am about to leave something old and no longer useful behind, and step into a new life. What could be more glorious?

Sometimes people tell me they feel like they are dying. "Congratulations!" I tell them. "Now you are really getting somewhere!" And so they are. They are not dying, but getting ready to enjoy greater living. Death is not bad because it does not exist. It is but a changing of form, a letting go of what was in order to embrace the next step in our adventure.

When You're Ready

Another way that fear deludes us is to tell us that we're not ready. Will Rogers noted that "if you wait until you're ready, you'll wait forever." If parents waited until they were ready to have children, there would be no children. Very few parents, if any, are completely prepared to raise children. But they learn to become parents through having children. Remember that this world was not designed for the comfort of perfectionists; it was created as a schoolroom for us to learn by doing. The best way to learn something is to start doing it. You will master the challenge far more quickly and deftly if you throw yourself into the task at hand than if you sit around and analyze how it might be if you tried doing it. You may be a lot more ready to take your next step than you realize. Take advantage of the opportunity at hand.

Lean In

If you are unsure about whether or not to make a certain move, you can get a better sense of the correct choice by leaning into direction. You can take a gentle step onto the path you think you might like to travel and see how it feels. Making a choice in life is like shopping for a car—you need to take it for a test drive. You can try a possible next step "on for size" without committing the whole hog to it. If you "lean in" with an open and receptive attitude—and *if you honor the deepest voice that speaks to you through your heart*—your next step will be made known to you.

Remember not to let yourself be pressured or intimidated into thinking that you must make an all-or-nothing, totally committed choice if you do not feel ready to do so. When you are ready, you will know it. If deep in your heart you do not feel ready, you are not. Sometimes you have to really say "no" before you can really say "yes." (Often a solid "yes" is uttered at the top of a ladder of "no's.") If you do not feel ready to make a decision, you have every right—actually, a responsibility—to wait, watch, and ask for clearer guidance. It will come.

Don't Sit on the Track

Freezing is not helpful. As Will Rogers warned, "You may be on the right track, but if you're sitting down, you'll get run over." To avoid acting because of fear is not the answer. (To postpone action because you recognize a need for prayerful introspection is a conscious choice, and such a practice will usually yield very positive results.) But to do nothing because you are afraid to make a mistake gives power to illusions and postpones the blessing you will receive when you summon the wisdom and courage to make a choice that is true to yourself.

Indecision is a killer. Going back and forth incessantly over alternatives is fear's way of keeping us from claiming our greater good. You cannot learn without doing, and you cannot do without learning. The greatest lessons of life are mastered through trial and error. Thomas Edison made two thousand attempts to invent a light bulb before one succeeded. Mel Fisher, the explorer who discovered a sunken Spanish galleon containing millions of dollars worth of gold and jewels, searched for the capsized vessel for fourteen years. In the process he went though all kinds of setbacks, but one day he found the treasure. If you have tried something many times and "failed," you are in good company. But in truth there are no real failures. The knowledge you gain with each mistake brings you closer to the success you desire. And then it is all worth it.

Remember Sister Martha's tombstone—"No Runs, No Hits, and No Errors." She didn't lose, but she also didn't score—and what's worse, she didn't even play. God is not looking for stars; He is looking for players. If you are willing to show up and play, God will turn you into a star. (We already *are* stars, but we do not acknowledge our power to light the night.) If you sit on the bench and watch, your potential is untapped. Your potential is the one bank account you can always cash in on, for it never runs out. You can lose everything in this world but you cannot lose your potential. Your capacity to be great is Spirit's investment in you, and no one on earth has the power to take it away from you. It is the door that is always open to actualize the unique gifts that lie within you, waiting for you to bring them to life. Don't sit on the bench, the track, or your gifts. God has plans for you that you haven't even dreamed of. Dare Spirit to change the world—starting with *your* world—through you.

No Place for Complacency

Rev. Jack Boland advises us, "Don't let good be the enemy of better." Don't rest easy with what you have and forget that there is more available to you. We must bless what we have and appreciate our accomplishments, but we must also remember that the adventure of life is an ever-unfolding miracle. If we are not expanding with life, we are not living up to our full potential. God's plan for healing our life is founded not on what we have been, but what we are to become. What we have done may be great, but it is not as great as what we are yet to do. There is no end to the gifts that we may discover and deliver if we keep moving with the flow of life.

It is a noble quality of character to be continuously asking and striving for more good. Rabbi Shlomo Carlebach told me, "Unless you do something better each time you do it, you are not doing it correctly." Unless we are receiving greater prosperity, richer beauty, and more rewarding depths of relationship, we are not accepting all the gifts God wants us to enjoy.

It is a very dangerous thing to sit back and think you have it made. You do have it made, but you need to master the lessons of living which bring the knowledge of your wholeness home to you. Do not succumb to the temptation to believe that you have seen or done it all. No one has seen or done it all, and no one ever will. If you are not changing, growing, and deepening in your sense of wonder, you are probably spinning your wheels in a routine or you have painted yourself into a corner. Spirit cannot long survive in a box. Be careful not to mistake stagnation for safety. There is more security in living at risk then there is in camping out on one square on the game board. You can camp for just so long, and then it's time to move on. Greater riches await you.

Be daring enough to keep moving ahead. The happiest and most vital people I know are those who are willing to let go of everything to follow an inner call. A raft is an excellent tool to take you across the river, but it is an awful burden if you try to carry it on your shoulder once you have reached the other side. Every tool and path in this world is temporary, but each one ultimately leads to the infinite. Walk the path with love, dignity, and commitment, but let it go with the same conviction when the time comes. There will be a wider and brighter path, and you won't walk it alone.

Dare to Move Ahead

1) What bridges might you do well to burn?

2) Have you ever had the feeling that you were going to die as you entered a new phase of your life? What were your feelings? What were the results of your step ahead? Who or what is it that died?

3) What would you like to do that you don't feel ready to do? Might you be more ready than you have believed?

4) Describe a choice you must make that you could facilitate by leaning into one direction. What could you do to take an exploratory step?

5) Are you sitting on any tracks now? What is the fear that is keeping you from moving ahead?

6) On the left side of a sheet of paper, describe "Where I Am." On the right side, describe "Where I Would Like to Be." Draw a bridge between the two columns, and on the bridge list the steps you can take to make the transition.

DARE TO RISK

A person who makes no mistake
does not usually make anything.
— William Connor Magee

What do you think would be the toughest risk facing a national football hero? The acclaimed quarterback of the San Francisco 49'ers, Joe Montana, shares this account of his bid for the highest stakes:

> Many people think my toughest moments are at Candlestick Park with a wall of beef—guys like Kevin Greene of the LA Rams or Lawrence Taylor of the New York Giants—coming straight at me. But the truth is the riskiest play I ever called was in the Marina Green park in San Francisco. It was do or die, and I was all alone. No defenders. No one running interference. And it was the biggest play of my life. I was asking the woman of my dreams to be my wife.
>
> The year was 1984. Jennifer and I were going to meet some friends at Alfred's for dinner after a game. But I suggested we go for a little walk first, down to the Marina Green, at the water's edge, where sailboats anchor and joggers run. Jen couldn't figure out why I was taking her out of our way. What she didn't know was that I had hired a friend to fly overhead in a plane with a streamer tied to its tail. Nothing fancy. It simply said, "Jen, will you marry me?" [1]

To succeed in life, you must allow yourself to be vulnerable.

---

[1] *Vis a Vis* Magazine, November 1990

You must venture into uncharted territory without a promised or calculated result. You must step out of the safe zone and trust that the universe will take care of you, even if you do not see how that will happen. The real adventure of life lies in going beyond the seeming security of the familiar, bolstered by the realization that you are made safe not by your own defenses, but by a power grander than the feeble charade of self-protection. Our true self is always safe.

An acting teacher told me, "To be a good actor, you must be willing to be the fool." This principle applies to all of life; only those who are willing to make fools of themselves can make heros of themselves. The Tarot card deck depicts the fool as a young man walking gaily over a cliff, whistling. There is a controversy over whether this card is the lowest card in the deck or the highest. It is both. There is blind foolishness in which we hurt ourself because we do not pay attention to the signs warning us of danger. But there is also a divine foolishness in which we heed an inner voice guiding us to action that may look ridiculous to the world, but actually proceeds from deep wisdom which leads us to great good.

Most of the great change agents of history were called fools. Albert Einstein failed arithmetic and Thomas Edison was expelled from school at the age of thirteen, labeled "addled" (confused). Unbeknownst to those who judged them (and perhaps even themselves), these outstanding creators and many others like them were marching to the beat of a different drummer. They were not part of the mainstream, and blessedly so. If everyone followed the mainstream, the stream would stay exactly as it is, and the world would never improve. Give thanks that you are not like everyone else and that you have the inclination and opportunity to explore untrod paths. Spirit needs your courage to make the world—at least your world—a better place.

Beyond the Boulder

There is a fantastic book which captures many lofty and inspiring principles in a short parable. *The Knight in Rusty Armor* by Robert Fisher is the story of a knight who is so busy hiding behind his flashy armor that he gets stuck in his suit of iron and doesn't know how to get out. The knight is so enamored with dashing off in all directions to crusades that he doesn't realize that he has become a prisoner of his shiny wall of protection. When his beloved wife and son leave him because he is so distant from them, his heart is broken and he sets out on the path of truth. On this path he must confront himself and, as he opens his heart, he gains the wisdom and strength to let go of his armor.

At one point on his journey of awakening the knight encounters a huge boulder blocking his path. There is no way he is going to get over or around this massive obstacle. The knight finds an inscription on the boulder: "I cannot know the unknown if to the known I cling." The boulder symbolizes the knight's tremendous investment in clutching to the familiar for security. His identity, beliefs, and judgments now act only as an impediment to reaching the summit of truth. The knight recognizes that if he is to become totally free, he cannot hang onto the known; he must let go of all that has been and embrace the unknown. The knight chooses to let go of the world as he has known it, and as he does he is transported beyond the seemingly insurmountable rock.

The analogy here is clear: we cannot cling to our history and arrive at our destiny. Every step ahead on the path of truth involves the release of the steps we have taken to arrive where we are. Remember that every adventure we undertake empowers us in two ways: once, when we commit ourself fully to it, and again when we find the strength to release it. Stagnation is not living. If we think we know it all, we block ourself from knowing more. We must empty our hand to receive a greater gift than we have known. There is always more love to be enjoyed.

Insanity and Healing

Insanity is defined as doing the same thing in the same way and expecting a different result. If you always do what you have always done, you will always get what you have always gotten.

If you expect to improve your life, you will have to do something different than you have been doing. At the very least, you will need to think about what you are doing in a different way, from a higher viewing point. Change usually requires a risk. Risk is the first step to healing, which always occurs outside the safe zone. The great Paramahansa Yogananda described the world as a huge insane asylum. Everyone here, he maintained, is crazy. Each of us hangs out with other people who are crazy in the same way we are. We agree on a reality defined by our madness, and then we support each other in living it and defend ourselves from other forms of insanity by maintaining that they're crazy and we're not. It is only a truly sane person who can admit his insanity. I saw a t-shirt that declared, "Being crazy is the only thing that keeps me sane."

Look at the condition of the world as a result of the institutions and beliefs we have upheld. Are these the fruits of wisdom? The history of this world is a long dark saga of fear and our attempts to defend ourself from the ravages it threatens. In our preoccupation with protecting ourself we overlook the truth that we are safe, and we perpetuate attack by our defenses. The nuclear arms buildup is a clear example of the foolishness of believing that more defenses will make us safer, when they actually bring us closer to destruction. The best defense is the knowledge that we do not need to hide or protect ourself from a force greater than we are. There is no force greater than we are.

Only those who go beyond fear can free our world from it. The most powerful way to dismantle hell is to approach its gates and call its bluff. The true hero walks right up to the throne of Satan, looks him in the eye, and discovers that he is but a shadow. What we call the devil is a template onto which we have projected all of our fears and disowned selves. Satan seems powerful only because we have invested him with the life we have renounced because we have forgotten that we are born of God. Evil has no power because it is not of God. But we, as children of God, have given it power with our minds, and when we believe in something that is not real we must face the effects of our thoughts until we learn to redirect our creativity in alignment with Spirit's reality.

Risk is the corridor to true transformation. We must go beyond our history to arrive at our destiny. We cannot be the person we were and become the person we are to be. We must remain willing to let it all go in order to let more come. Security blankets can keep us warm on a cold night, but they can also smother us and keep us from seeing if we hold them over our head. It is not crazy to trust. The world teaches us that it is crazy to love and wise to fear. As with so many other elements of truth, the world has it topsy-turvy. It is not crazy to trust. It is crazy to cling to a drop of water when we have a whole ocean to swim in. The most powerful energy we can embody is trust.

Danger and Opportunity

The ancient Chinese knew the harmony and integrity of all life. Their philosophers and martial arts masters understood how to embrace challenge and make it work in their favor. Even their language displayed this high awareness. The Chinese character for "crisis" was a combination of two other characters: "danger" plus "opportunity." With every danger comes an invitation to make a change that will make our life stronger and ultimately easier. Thus risk is not seen as simply a danger, but a doorway to greater living.

Can You Not Do It?

A friend of mine was considering taking classes toward becoming a minister. For months and months she pored over the idea, very much wanting to undertake these studies, yet feeling fearful and hesitant about setting out on a new direction in her life. The notion got stronger as time went on. Then one day there came a turning point. "An inner voice asked me a question that led me to the answer," she explained. "The voice asked me, 'Can you *not* do it?' The honest answer was that I couldn't not do it. The idea was just too strong and it wouldn't go away. Besides, I didn't want it to. My heart was calling me to my next step, and I decided to surrender. That day I registered for the classes, and my life is changed for the better because of it."

Now when I seem to be drawn to an action or a path, and the intuition or inclination keeps knocking at the door of my heart, I ask myself, "Can I *not* do it?" If I get a "no" in response, I go right ahead. What's the use of fighting or postponing something my spirit is guiding me to do?

Usually if something is right for you, you will keep getting signs and indications from the universe—inside and out—that this step is for you. God is very patient and compassionate. She will send you plenty of invitations to be yourself, even if you lose or misplace the first few, throw them away, or believe that they are for someone else. You have a date with destiny—a very good one at that—and you may be able to postpone your good, but you will not escape it. Be sensitive to the calling you are receiving, and don't fight your urge to grow. It will make you great.

Playing for the Critics

If you avoid acting because you are afraid of being criticized, you have traded your creativity for worldly approval. You will never win in such a poor bargain. You may be able to manipulate other people to approve of you, but you will learn to hate yourself in the process. You came to earth to express your unique gifts; to withhold them because you are afraid other people may not like them is to deny your own purpose here. Do not allow opinions to rule your life. They change with the capriciousness of the wind. Let your destiny be rooted in your heart's desire, and your actions will bear fruit to nourish generations to come.

The great irony of taking a risk is that the thing you feared to lose is usually what you end up gaining. Do not shy away from offering your creative expressions because you think people will criticize them. If your gifts are truly worthy, you will not alienate people, but ultimately serve them. Yes, some people may laugh, criticize, or challenge you in the process, but that is a sign that you are really getting somewhere. It is only when everyone agrees with you that you are in trouble. The great Christian mystic, Thomas Merton wrote:

If a writer is so cautious that he never writes anything that cannot be criticized, he will never write anything that can be read. If you want to help other people you have got to make up your mind to write things that some people will condemn.

You cannot cling to the status quo and make the world—especially your world—a better place. The pain of the world is the offspring of fear. Billions of people over all of history have attempted to bottle the river of life and keep love stockpiled in their basements. But when water is not allowed to keep moving, it becomes stagnant and unhealthful. Water is a symbol of spirit, and we, as spiritual beings, must keep flowing with the river of our life, which is a tributary that ultimately flows into the Great River that is God's Life. To be fully alive, we must fully flow.

The Illusion of Risk

All risk is illusion. We are spiritual beings, and our identity with God is inviolate. There is nothing we could possible do to lose the only thing of value, which is our divine nature as whole and wholly lovable beings.

It is only in the world of appearances that we seem to be able to lose. It appears that we can lose things, people, and love. Much of our energy is devoted to protecting ourself from the loss of our worldly treasures. But remember Jesus' admonition to "Lay up your treasures in Heaven where moth and rust do not corrupt and thieves do not break in and steal." Jesus was telling us to value the things that are eternal, so we do not fall into fear of loss. No one can take the gifts of God from us. Love, joy, and appreciation are treasures that we own because they are a part of who we are. We have the capacity to enjoy all the gifts of God wherever we are, no matter what is happening around us. Our purpose is to remember these gifts in all situations and teach ourselves and the world that there is indeed nothing of worth that we can truly lose.

The most tragic thing that we could lose is our experience

of peace. When we give way to fear, we have already lost. Anything we could lose in this world is meaningless in comparison to the loss of our inner joy. When we worry about losing something, we have already lost a great deal. There is a *Course in Miracles* lesson which reminds, "I could see peace instead of this." If I find myself worrying or my mind starts wandering into dark caverns, I remind myself, "I could really be enjoying myself right now if I so choose." When I stay in the present moment, I am empowered. To worry about the future is to deny and lose the beauty of the now. In no present moment is fear justified. Fear is always of the future, which never comes if we are living in the now. Freud said, "All thinking is preparing." You cannot prepare anxiously for tomorrow and be fully alive today.

Jesus said, "I came to bring you life more abundant." We cannot have a life more abundant unless we leave the life less abundant behind. Even if what you have is good, remember that you are capable of having even more. I am not preaching dissatisfaction here; I am staking a claim for the deepest satisfaction we deserve. I am speaking of the greatest spiritual riches. Our birthright and destiny is to enjoy peace of mind, perfect health, and fulfilling relationships. If you are living with less than these gifts, you are not really living. You are compromising, settling for less than you deserve. Keep going ahead. Keep challenging anything that is less than love. Keep asking for more strength and vision. Risk the loss of fear and pain to gain love and strength. Set your sights on the top of the mountain and don't stop until you get there. There lies a great treasure with your name on it. When you are home, you will know it.

The chief danger in life is that you may take too many precautions.

—Alfred Adler

Dare to Risk

1) What would you like to do that is a risk? What might you lose? What might you gain?

2) Focus on a particular risk you are considering taking. What is more frightening to you: Taking the risk, or staying where you are?

3) Consider a venture that has been calling to you. Can you *not* do it?

4) Recall several risks you have taken in the past. What lessons did you learn from them?

DARE TO
WALK THROUGH FEAR

Do it trembling, if you must, but do it.
— Emmett Fox

F ear is not our enemy. Seen rightly, fear becomes our best friend. Because there is nothing to fear in the entire universe, when we experience fear we have the opportunity to free ourself from an illusion that has been holding us back from living the life our heart desires. Fear is not a monster, but a signal that we are at the doorway to healing. Our purpose as awakening souls is to walk beyond fear and find love where we once saw danger. Fear is nothing more than an invisible membrane beyond which we *believe* we dare not step. There are no true limits except those we accept into our mind.

High Stakes

Do you know how elephants are trained? A young elephant is tied by the foot to a rope which is attached to a stake in the ground. After it tries unsuccessfully to dislodge the stake, the elephant accepts that it must stay within the circumference inscribed by the rope to which it is tethered. The animal gives up its efforts to move out of this circle. Now here is an amazing fact: As the elephant grows larger and stronger, it becomes quite capable of uprooting the stake. But because it has long since accepted that it is impossible to free itself, it doesn't even try to escape. The elephant is bound not by a physical object, but by an illusion. It is limited not by an outside source, but by a memory. Insubstantial as it is, that one thought is sufficient to keep a mammoth animal captive. Illusions, as *A Course in*

Miracles tells us, are as strong in their effects as the truth.

Fear is like an invisible rope attached to a mental stake that entraps us in a little circle of apparent yet meaningless security. While acts that proceed from fear appear to keep us safe, there is one major error in fear's "reasoning." The ego, in its insane drive for security (which it never truly accepts) overlooks the fact that the wall we have erected to keep the world from hurting us keeps us imprisoned. The more we protect ourself from life, the less life there is for us to enjoy. Fear is truly the devil's bargain: the *illusion* of safety at the expense of being fully alive—a poor deal by any standard!

Fear hurts us by creating results exactly the opposite of the benefits it pretends to bring us. Fear promises us strength, while it is debilitating; it offers us security, yet leaves us feeling terribly vulnerable; and it dangles independence before us, while it unconsciously binds us with invisible handcuffs to the thing that we feel we must protect ourself from. Ironically, we are the most powerful when we are undefended. Protection out of fear weakens us. To anxiously build a defense affirms that we are vulnerable, and that erroneous premise denies our perfect security in Spirit.

Allowing life to bless us is largely a matter of not fighting to keep life from hurting us. The optimist, we are told, expects the best and is sometimes disappointed, while the pessimist expects the worst and is never disappointed. You can numb yourself to pain, but in so doing you cut yourself off from happiness. There is no happiness in a void, and neither is it truly safe. A void is exactly what it sounds like—nothing. But we, as Children of God, are something—and a very good something, at that. As such we will never be satisfied with nothing. Therefore it behooves us to relinquish our attempts to take refuge in the void. We must stop gyrating to "a void-dance." The essence of life is love, and we cannot turn our back on one without losing the other. To be separate is not to be safe; it is to deny love's brilliance as the inherent majesty of our soul. Life is eternally seeking to bless and heal us. The greatest contribution we can make to the fulfillment of our destiny is to let ourselves be loved.

Then, fully accepting our grandest gift, we are fully capable of giving it.

Unfair Performances

Popular singer Bobby McFerrin, who brought a bright and much-needed message to the world with his hit song *Don't Worry, Be Happy*, describes a period in his life when he was stagnant in his music. After the phenomenal feat of winning five Grammy awards in 1988, Bobby dropped out of sight for sixteen months, during which he spent quality time with his wife, played with his two young sons, listened to music, read the Bible and biographies of great creative people, and studied conducting.

Why did Bobby McFerrin stop in the midst of the kind of success for which other musicians would trade their soul? He explains, "Conventional industry wisdom dictates that once you have a hit, you play it to death, pound the pavement, and sell all the albums you can. But I was soooo tired. Touring had become a bore and a chore. My solo concerts were stale, not challenging. I wasn't nervous anymore, I wasn't scared. It wasn't fair to an audience that I was so flat creatively. Although my audiences were enjoying the performances, I wasn't. I was on autopilot. Here I was singing a song and thinking about something else. It was time to chill out."

So what did Bobby do? Exactly what excited—and scared—him the most. He began training a choir to sing in his unique *à capella* style. He performed *Peter and the Wolf* with the San Francisco Symphony Orchestra. He gave a duet concert with famed Japanese cellist Yo-Yo Ma. Bobby plunged into the endeavors that made him feel most alive and creative, even though they were frightening and not necessarily guaranteed of success. (But remember that healing always occurs outside of the safe zone.) After his creative juices were flowing, Bobby went on tour again. This time he was in joyful integrity because he was fully present.

Here is the test to know whether or not you are in your right place: Ask yourself, "Am I living creatively? Am I following my joy voice? Do I feel challenged?" And (you might be surprised at this one) "Am I afraid? Am I allowing life to push me out of my safety zone into a bigger ballpark?" The answers to these questions will provide you with the direction to your next step through and beyond fear.

Security is a popular disguise for death. You may appear to have your life together, but you may be dying of stagnation or boredom. Do not fall prey to coasting on your former accomplishments. Like Bobby McFerrin, do not cheat your audiences—whoever you meet—by sitting on your laurels. If you are not vitally alive with the power of each new moment, you are missing the show and probably not giving a very good one. Achievements are not the top of the mountain—they are steppingstones to a higher peak. Our quest is to follow love's lead rather than stop at fear. I respect Bobby McFerrin for stepping out of stagnation and doing the thing that made him nervous. It probably saved his life.

How to Escape from Fear

The world is filled with people running away from fear. It is awesome to consider the web of addictions that rule our society. Anne Wilson Schaef has analyzed our cultural psyche in her book, *A Society of Addicts*. Millions, perhaps billions, of people on the planet are attempting to escape from the challenges of life by diving headlong into addictions that serve only to distract us from the fears we do not want to face.

Brendan Francis has a prescription to master those fears constructively. He suggests that "the best way to escape from a problem is to solve it." Problems keep recurring, usually in stronger degrees, until we face them. What we resist expands and persists. No problem has the power to hurt us if we stand up to it and face it. Ironically, problems hurt us only when we run from them.

The key to walking through fear is to remember that problems are gifts. Richard Bach, in his masterful book *Illusions*, explains that "Every problem comes to us with a gift in its hands."

When we accept the gift (the empowering lesson the challenge is inviting us to learn) the problem disappears. To keep running from the problem magnifies its power over us and delays our receiving the gift it came to deliver.

It is a very useful practice to eliminate the word "problem" from your vocabulary and replace it with the word "project." A problem seems dark, heavy, and victimizing. A project, on the other hand, has the ring of a challenge, an invitation to succeed, an opportunity to create something new, exciting, and rewarding. In truth there are no problems, only opportunities for deeper healing.

Great Overcomers

Many of the people who have made the most profound contributions to humanity had to walk through major fears to deliver their gifts to the world. Often the greatest heros had to face the greatest fears. Mahatma Gandhi was so nervous as a young lawyer that when he presented his first case (a ten dollar lawsuit) he became tongue-tied and was literally laughed out of the courtroom. Barbra Streisand, who has one of the most powerful and hypnotic voices in contemporary music, was so shy to perform in public that she hardly ever gave a concert. If you feel blocked by a fear, study the biographies of successful people and you will discover that they became great not in spite of their fears, but because they grew strong in learning to overcome them. Approached consciously, our fears propel us forward.

Fear as a Guide to Healing

A Course in Miracles teaches that our purpose is not to seek love, for that is what we already are. Our purpose is to seek and find the obstacles to our loving, so we may release them and express our true nature more fully. We can bless fear when we recognize it as an opportunity to see where we are stuck. Remember that this world is a school. To truly learn, we must bring to consciousness the areas where we are unconscious, so we can begin to dismantle our limits. Where there is a fear, there is a limit, and as children of a free God we cannot afford to be bound in any way. To discover that we are afraid of something is to hit paydirt. We have come upon a sure sign that we are losing out on life somehow. Becoming aware of a fear is like discovering a booby trap, a land mine that will blow up if we step onto it. The good news is that we carry within us the power to defuse it through observation, willingness, love, prayer, and practice. No fear can stay alive in the face of the consciousness of Spirit. We make a major contribution to our spiritual growth and that of the planet when we face fear and invite the hand of God to lift us beyond it.

Ask God For Help

When nothing else you have done seems to be helping you to walk through a fear, there is one method to which you always have recourse: *Ask God for help.* Simply say to God (in whatever form you understand or believe in Him), "God, I just don't see any way I can do this by myself. I open my mind and heart and invite you to step into this situation and do through me and for me what needs to be done to bring about real peace for all concerned."

I assure you that a prayer like this, sincerely spoken, must be heard and answered. You are admitting that you need help and acknowledging that God has the power to do for you what you cannot do for yourself, which He most certainly can do. God cannot fail to come to the aid of one of His children whose heart is open to receive healing.

A Course in Miracles invites us to visualize holding the hand of a spiritual guide as we move past dark clouds toward the light. The Course assures us that such a visualization is no idle imagining. When we invite the presence of a higher power to guide us, the law of the universe dictates that it must do so. Love is uncompromising in its willingness to lift those who invite its presence.

Later in the Course we are told that God is willing, able, and happy to substitute for our ego in any situation into which we call Him. I have called upon God time and time again to stand in for me when it seemed as if my little self had failed to bring about positive results through its plan. I say, "Dear Higher Power, would you please enter into this situation and take charge of it. I allow you to replace my small self and act for me to bring about the highest result here." Then I take a deep breath and release the situation to the hands of love. Such an invitation has never failed to bring about healing, and I can recommend this method with the highest confidence.

Do not feel embarrassed or ashamed if you feel afraid or need to ask for help. If you were entirely fearless, you would not be here in the first place. This world is not a place for people who are free of fear; it is an arena in which those who have fear can learn to overcome it. Be assured that no one conquers terror alone. Our sense of aloneness is the cohort of fright, and when we come to terms with one, we diminish the other. Know that you are accompanied by unseen companions, and you are well on your way to victory over dark dreams.

Dare to Walk Through Fear

1) Fill in the blank at the end of this sentence: If I were not afraid,
   I would _____ .
   (Repeat with different responses.)

2) What old emotional programs still hold power over you? What
   situations and feelings imprinted these programs? What is the truth
   about who you are and what you can do now?

3) Are you giving any "unfair performances" — cheating yourself and
   others by hanging out in a familiar but boring pattern because you
   are afraid to try something more challenging? Describe what you
   would like to do that is more exciting.

4) List several fears you feel and describe how they are actually spurring
   you on to greater strength and healing.

5) Take a few "problems" you face and describe them as "projects."

6) Ask God for help with one or more specific situations which you
   seem to be unable to handle yourself. Write each request for help
   on a piece of paper and place it in a Bible or other book of wisdom
   and inspiration.

DARE TO COMMIT

*When you're interested in something, you do it when
it is convenient. When you're committed,
you accept no excuses—only results.*

— Dr. Kenneth Blanchard

"What are we going to do now?" we wondered. I and
my partners had a retreat scheduled, and here it was
a month before the retreat was to begin, and we had
only two people registered. We had never found ourselves in
this predicament before. We were counting on a minimum of
twenty people, and just a few had enrolled.

We dove into a deep and soul-searching staff meeting. For
hours we went back and forth on the merits of cancelling the
retreat versus carrying through with our original intention. Every
half hour we arrived at an opposite conclusion; at certain
moments it was clear to us that we should cancel the workshop
while there was still time, and then minutes later we were just
as sure that the right thing to do was to go ahead. After several
hours it seemed as if we were getting nowhere.

Finally one of the staff suggested that we just get quiet for
a moment and listen for Spirit's guidance on this question that
we obviously weren't able to answer with our rational processing.
I closed my eyes, became still, and asked God to tell me what
I needed to know. After a few minutes of delving inward, I heard
the words, "Remember the vision."

I thought back to the time a year earlier when we began
the retreats, and I recollected the enthusiasm we had for offering
spiritual healing, relaxation, and celebration amidst the magnificent natural beauty of Hawaii. As I remembered that vision I felt
a spark in the middle of my chest, which was the purity and
potential of our original idea. The flame felt warm, comforting,

and exciting. It was clear to me what path we should take.

We opened our eyes and I spoke first: "I believe we are being asked to remember the vision upon which we founded this work in the first place. We love presenting retreats, we do it well, and many people are uplifted and transformed though our services. My guidance is to do what we aspire to do, even if the number of people is not what we had hoped or expected. Let us consider this retreat to be an investment in living the life we love."

My partners both smiled. "We got the same answer!" they happily told me. We hugged and affirmed that we felt good about our decision, knowing that Spirit was guiding us.

The next day we received a call from our registrar. "Four more people have signed up," she informed us. Within a week we received five more registrations. By the time the retreat began we had twenty-two people present, and we went on to have one of the most powerful healing retreats I can remember.

The last night of the retreat everyone in the group spoke of the gifts they had received from our time together. I told the gathering, "It is hard for me to even imagine this retreat not happening. There were so many life changes that blossomed among us which would not have taken place if our staff had not followed through on our intention. I am so glad that we chose to hold fast to our vision, even when the circumstances didn't seem to be supporting it."

The turning point for that retreat was the moment our staff joined and said, "We're going through with this." I believe that such a commitment opened the door to attract more people and the right people for that retreat. As I discovered through our decision-making process, *the world we see is always reflecting our intentions.* Because we harbored doubts about going ahead with the retreat until we made our agreement, the universe responded with a faint enrollment. We were mugwumps—we had our mug on one side of the fence and our wump on the other. So that is exactly the kind of results we got—neither here nor there. You cannot have a half-hearted intention and get a whole-hearted result. But if you invest your whole heart in anything, the universe will respond.

Use Results to Discover Your Intention

Here is a fascinating principle of self-discovery which, if you have the sincere desire to master, will help you tremendously. *To see what you are asking for, look at what you are getting.* We get exactly what we ask for—no more and no less. If life does not seem to be supplying you with your needs or desires, it is not because the universe is malfunctioning; it is because on a subconscious level you are asking for or expecting something other than what you believe you want.

For example, you may attract a series of relationships with men or women who are unavailable. Someone in a victim consciousness might blame God or the universe for a poor supply of eligible partners, but the truth is that you are not fully available. If you were, you would surely attract someone who wanted to connect with you at that level. There are plenty of available people in the world, and if you were ripe and ready for such a meeting, it would happen. If you consistently attract people who are not very open to you, you must look into your heart and mind, and discover what are your fears about intimacy.

This method of observing results to discover true intentions is a very challenging path of growth. If you choose to use it, your ego will probably rile up and present a thousand reasons why you are not fully responsible for what you are attracting. Don't believe a word of these arguments. Making a case for your powerlessness is exactly the line of "reasoning" that keeps us in victim consciousness. If you are willing to tell the whole truth about your inner feelings, you are well on the road to major transformation. Use this method of inquiry for your healing. Take advantage of the mirrors that the world and your relationships offer you.

What Would Someone Have to Believe?

A good question to ask yourself if you are stuck in a pattern of any kind is, "What would someone have to believe to keep attracting situations like this?" For example, if you have a hard time making ends meet financially, you may be harboring a belief that there is not enough supply in the universe to take care of you, or that you don't deserve to have the things you want, or that life is a struggle and you must sweat and strain for your good. If you can't get people to like you, you may believe that you have to prove yourself to be lovable. If you have a challenge with chronic tiredness or disease, you may believe that living is a chore, or that pain offsets guilt, or you might see life as a threat and feel too afraid to face it and move through it.

None of these world views are true, but if your parents or early role models demonstrated such dark scenarios and you tell yourself lies long enough, you can create circumstances that painfully reflect your beliefs. It is possible to go through life as if you are bound, when in truth you are not.

The first step to reprogramming a limiting belief is to become aware that you are holding it. It is not our conscious beliefs that hurt us; when we see something consciously we can choose whether or not we want to continue the action or attitude. The crucial factor in whether our ship will sink or stay afloat is the iceberg of thought patterns, the majority of which lies beneath the surface of our awareness. Observing results as a mirror of intention is the psychic sonar that allows us to become aware of the thoughts that are creating our world from the factory beneath the surface of our usual vision.

The good news about opening ourself to the truth reflected to us is that ultimately we will see that we are powerful and loved. Yes, we may become aware of a number of ways that we have been hurting ourself, but as we peel away the layers of fearful thinking we discover that there is a lot more good and beauty within us than we had imagined. Many of us have feared to look in the mirror because we were terrified that we would behold an ugly or evil person, too horrible to be loved or healed. That fear is but another trick of the ego, which will do anything it can to keep us from having a good look at ourself. The ego, which is fueled by fear and separateness, knows that if we truly beheld our beauty, we would immediately withdraw our investment in attack and defense, and the ego would soon be out of a job. The more we ask and discover the real truth about ourself, the more we unveil a being of such comely grace that we will wonder why we ever avoided discovering the jewel of our true identity.

We must further acknowledge the reflections of the positive results we create. The good that comes to us is a sign that we are loving ourself. We can look about our life and find loving friends, great beauty in art and nature, health, and spiritual growth, and recognize these blessings as affirmations that we must really love ourself to attract and receive such golden gifts into our world.

What would someone who has dear friends have to believe? That he or she is worthy of trust, support, and friendship. A parent who appreciates his playful children must enjoy an equally vibrant child within himself. To take a vacation indicates that you know you are deserving of rest and play. We must honor the mirrors of kindness, forgiveness, and well-being that we draw to ourselves out of self-appreciation and the celebration of our goodness. And many of us have been doing that more than we realize.

Who's in Charge of the Show?

Several years ago I presented a workshop which, to my surprise, had a very low attendance. While I and the organizers were hoping for a large group, only about a dozen people showed up. I felt discouraged and disappointed. I didn't feel much like presenting a program, and my energy was conspicuously low.

On the same program there was a duo of singers who taught me a lesson that changed my life. This couple, a husband and wife team, gave one of the most dynamic performances I have ever seen. They dashed up on stage to start the program and pounded out a dazzling opening number. To my amazement, their level of enthusiasm and energy was as if they were singing for a stadium of forty thousand enthusiastic listeners. I was astonished. With each number they sang I became more and more inspired and excited, and by the time I was called on stage I felt very present and enthusiastic.

This duo was not inhibited by the small crowd. They were not about to let the size of the audience dictate the level or quality of their performance. They were there to share their gifts and create the kind of feeling in the room that they wanted. That night was a turning point for me. I realized that I can and must be the creator of the atmosphere around me, not a subject to it.

Those singers bestowed upon me a precious lesson in the power and importance of commitment. They were committed to their art and their vision, and they did not allow outside circumstances to dampen their fire. That is the kind of commitment it takes to be a success in any field. You are in charge of your own show, and the results of your performance are not based on who sees or hears you or how your audience responds. Your results are based on what you give.

How the World Works Better

The simple value of commitment is this: your life and the world usually work better when you do what you say you are going to do. Human relations go a lot easier when we can count on each other. When we don't have to worry about whether or not we can trust each other, we have a lot more energy to be creative and produce the results we desire.

When you keep your word, you and your word become very powerful. Living up to your promises will bring you great inner strength. To say we are going to do something and then not do it weakens our integrity and, like the boy who cried wolf, makes us and others wonder if we are telling the truth. Remember that "in the beginning was the word," and the creative power of the word continues unto its completion.

Be careful not to make any promises that you are not certain you can keep. (On *Yom Kippur*, the holiest day of the Jewish year, the most sacred prayer, "*Kol Nidre*" is a plea to God to release us from all promises we may make during the year to come.) In the enthusiasm or passion of a moment we may make a promise with the full intention of fulfilling it, but when the elixir of the excitement of the moment wears off we find ourself with a vow that will be difficult to fulfill. In such a case it would be better to promise only what you know you can do, and then if you can give more as the project or relationship proceeds, it will come as a welcome gift. Your partner will then be pleasantly surprised rather than disappointed.

When dealing with commitments, allow for the possibility of change. Sometimes it is not possible to do what you said you were going to do. As we noted in "Dare to Change Your Mind," you may have made a commitment in an unconscious way, and now that you have grown or awakened you see that it is not honest or realistic for you to follow through. In such a case integrity would dictate that you acknowledge the change openly and clearly with the person with whom you made the agreement. Integrity is based on honest communication. You honor yourself and the other person when you tell the whole truth.

The truth of change also behooves you to give someone else space if they need to break a commitment they made with you. Their life may have changed sufficiently to warrant such an action. It usually does not work to try to force someone to be committed. You cannot make someone be responsible; they have to choose it. It is useless to try to manipulate someone into doing what you want them to do. Sometimes you just have to let go, trust, and free the other person as you would like to be freed if you were in their position. As spiritual beings we seek relationship, not puppetry. Regarding codependent behaviors, it is said that "we do not have relationships; we have hostages." What person with any mature consciousness would want a wife or a business partner by coercion? What value is there in being with someone who is acting out a role they don't feel from the inside out?

The thing to remember if someone breaks an agreement with you is that there must be a higher plan that you are not seeing in the moment. Remember that the person or your contract with them is not the source of your good. You have a much higher contract with a much higher source. When you feel disappointed in a human being, you a have a fertile opportunity to remember that God is in charge. I have found that when someone breaks an agreement with me, there is usually something better in store. At such a point we must let our human mind go and allow our divine knowingness to come forth.

If we have a challenge with other people breaking their commitments with us (leaving us, disappointing us, or not living up to their agreements), we must acknowledge the pattern (once is an accident, twice is a coincidence, and three times is a pattern). Such a consistent motif is an invitation for us to look into our own psyche to see why we are continuing to attract such disappointing circumstances. It is not other people's commitments that we must transform, but our own. On some level we are committed to loss, mistrust, and/or disappointment. This important self-discovery is a call for us to make a new commitment. We might commit to release our fear or past programming and draw to ourself people who will stay or honor us. Once again we see that everything is a lesson in personal awakening and expanded vision and power.

Fear and Commitment

One of the great gifts of approaching a commitment is the arousal of fear. As long as we are sitting on the fence, our ego is not threatened, for we can always fall back on the status quo if we need to. But commitment usually means change, and change is one thing the ego doesn't like. The ego wants everything to stay just as it is (even if it's terrible), because the way it is is a known quantity, and if things change the ego might have to let go of being in charge.

Considering a commitment, whether it is to a marriage, a child, a new job, or a new home, forces us to look at issues we never would have faced otherwise. This is always good. The lessons of life revolve around us discovering and mastering deeper levels of our nature. Commitments bring things to the surface that we need to see. Many of us walk around with fears that run us as we are entirely unaware of them. To bring a fear to consciousness is the beginning of its healing. Thus the process of making a commitment is a powerful healing method in itself.

How to Avoid the Devil

The Bible tells us, "Say 'yes' or say 'no,' but don't say anything else, for all else is the work of the devil." Translated into less hellish terms, this teaching means that we function most powerfully when we make a stand. To hang out in "maybe," "I don't know," or "tomorrow," weakens our spirit. To be non-committal is to disempower ourself.

My acting teacher told our class, "Make strong choices." He was advising us to choose how we will interpret a character and then dive into it whole-heartedly. There are a thousand ways an actor might portray a character or a line. It does not work to avoid acting because you are not sure which angle to take, or to try to depict more than one characterization, or to flounder back and forth between several of them. It works to choose and act.

We might apply the same principle to our daily life: *Make strong choices.* Strong choices require commitment. Choose one path or another, but don't try to straddle the fence. When you commit, you may make a mistake, but at least you will know it and you'll be able to move on with the benefit of what you've learned. If you don't act, you won't make any mistakes, but you also won't learn.

The invitation to commit is one of the grandest portals through which we may walk in a lifetime. God is entirely committed to being God, and when we commit ourself to a noble path we reflect and live in the majesty of the divine. Even to commit yourself to a path that is less than noble is to live more powerfully than to make no commitment at all. Whatever you choose to be, embrace it with strength, conviction, and a whole heart. Be whatever you really are, and go all the way with it. If there is ultimately a higher path for you, action with conviction will lead you to it. Make strong choices. Make and be a strong statement to the world. Don't apologize for your dreams and desires. Make up your mind. Step ahead. Dive in. And if you commit with a loving heart, your life will be different forever.

Dare to Commit

1) What areas of your life are calling for a deeper commitment? What would help you to be more committed?

2) Look at some of the painful patterns or results you have attracted. What would someone have to believe to create such a pattern?

3) Look at some of the positive and rewarding patterns or results you have attracted. What would someone have to believe to create such a pattern?

4) In what ways are you a mugwump? Write down a few strong choices that will help you get off the fence.

5) Is there anyone with whom you are incomplete about a commitment that was made but not resolved? What could you say or do that will complete it honestly?

DARE TO PERSEVERE

Come, my friend. It is not too late to seek a newer world...We are one equal temper of heroic hearts, made weak by time and fate, but strong in will. To strive, to seek, to find and not to yield.

— Alfred, Lord Tennyson

Let me tell you about a man who was plagued by defeat. In '31 he failed in business and declared bankruptcy. In '32 he lost an election for the legislature. In '34 his business failed again and he declared bankruptcy a second time. The following year his fiance died. The year after that, he suffered a nervous breakdown. Two years later, in '38 he was defeated in another election. In '43 he ran for the U. S. Congress and lost. In '46 he made another bid for a seat in Congress and he was defeated. In '48 he ran again for Congress and again he lost. Seven years later he entered a race for the U. S. Senate and he was defeated. In '56 his name was placed on the ballot for the Vice Presidency of the United States and he lost the election. In '58 he ran for the Senate and lost again. In '60—1860—he was elected President of the United States. His name was Abraham Lincoln. In spite of this incredible string of setbacks he went on to become one of the greatest statesmen of history. He said, "You cannot fail unless you quit."

If you persevere, you must succeed. The only time we fail is the last time we try. If you keep trying long enough, you are bound to attain your goal.

The famous Paramahansa Yogananda told this parable: "A and B were fighting. Both of them were tired and A decided to give up. B, however, said, 'Just one more blow' and he delivered it to win." Jesus taught the same lesson in his own way. He spoke of a judge who cared neither about God nor people. One day a widow came to him to ask for justice in a dispute she was having. At first the judge put her off, but when the woman persevered in asking the judge for justice, he gave in and granted her plea. Jesus asked, "How much more readily will your Heavenly Father grant you justice when you call on Him continuously for help?"

Truly there is a Force in the universe that responds to our sincere desire to attain a result. When we tap into that Source and learn how to work with it, it will bring us all the good we seek.

Always Time to Succeed

Time is not an obstacle to one who chooses to succeed. He is not stopped because his vision does not manifest in the time he initially wants or expects it to. It is the mortal mind that imposes deadlines on our dreams. When we see through the eyes of God, we realize that all of our dreams come true in their right and perfect time.

Do not use time as an excuse to be discouraged and run away from your ambitions. Be patient and hold firm to your vision. When your dream is at hand you will feel that the result is well worth the time it took to create it.

Ted Nugent is a rock guitarist who first attained notoriety when he played with a group called the Amboy Jukes in the sixties. Several of the band's songs made their way to the charts; the highest they climbed in the ratings was number 33.

The group disbanded, but Ted kept singing and playing. He joined various bands, none of which became very famous. Later he went on to do some solo recording. Then in 1989 he had a hit song that made it to the top ten. Now Ted Nugent holds the record for the longest time between an artist first making it to the charts and scoring a top ten hit—twenty-two years.

A lot of other people might have given up without more consistent rewards. But Ted kept his heart open, his dream alive, and he kept creating. You never know when you will hit it big. Achievement may come sooner or it may come later, but be assured that it will come. Each of us has a right to success in some field of endeavor. No matter what is your chosen arena, one thing is for sure—whatever you invest your heart in will bring you the greatest reward.

Today's the Day

Remember Mel Fisher, who spent fourteen years searching for a sunken Spanish galleon off the Florida Keys. I knew a woman who was a scuba diver for Mel's company. Every day the crew went out and kept looking for this elusive ship. Many wondered if they would ever find it, or if the ship was even there. Mel had a motto which kept the crew inspired: *"Today's the Day!"* He had t-shirts made for the entire crew bearing that maxim. Then one day today *was* the day. They found the sunken treasure containing millions upon millions of dollars worth of gold and jewels. That day the entire fourteen years was worth it. Mel's perseverance and that of his supporters paid off.

Did you know that the Beatles were turned down by several record companies before Capitol signed them? Can you imagine what the world would have missed if those four gifted creators had given up after a few unsuccessful auditions?

We may also recall Sir Richard Attenborough, who spent eighteen years in the production of his motion picture on the life of Mahatma Gandhi. Sir Richard had to go to incredible lengths and conquer many setbacks to obtain funding and complete the film. But when he made numerous trips to the stage to accept the Academy Award for the Best Picture of the Year and many other Oscars, the universe confirmed to him that his energy had been well invested.

God wants our dreams to come true. She will do everything to fulfill our heart's desires. Our job is to cooperate, do what we can with our means, and trust that Spirit will provide what we cannot. We must keep the door open until the final result is manifested. Often it is just one more step that makes all the difference. Imagine that the step at hand is the most important one, for it is; every step is the most important one.

Beyond First Blush

Integrity is the ability to follow through on a project long after the initial enthusiasm has passed. Often the idea phase of a project is the most exciting one. We are inspired, enthusiastic, willing, ready, and sometimes starry-eyed. Then, to our great surprise, work sets in! We see that achieving our dream may not be as easy as we had envisioned. We may bump against unexpected challenges or setbacks. We may encounter people who do not cooperate with our plan in the way we had hoped or expected, or even as they said they would.

Any of these obstacles may tempt us to turn around and give up. But it is precisely at these times that we must remember the initial vision and the purpose for which we are working. Your purpose must be bigger than the obstacles you encounter. If you keep your highest vision in mind, you will find the strength and the means to keep going. As you overcome each hurdle, you and your project will grow stronger and more real. In fact, when you look back in retrospect after the project is complete, you may feel that the lessons you gained in overcoming the challenges were even more important than the project you set out to complete. In a sense, the project was a vehicle for you to master some strategic life lessons. If that has happened, your efforts have been well worth your investment. We are here to learn and grow, and every adventure is a valuable opportunity to practice the dare to be ourself.

Perseverance, Not Foolishness

A wise aspirant must be able to distinguish between persevering until a goal is reached and naively chasing a dream that will not come true. There are situations in which wisdom would lead us to let go rather than attempt to force another person or situation into a position in which they are not willing to fit.

We are not required to persevere at the expense of our happiness. Relationships are a fertile laboratory for such mistakes. One partner hangs in there seemingly forever, wishing, hoping, and believing that the other person will come around someday and finally realize they love the one who is waiting. In the name of noble romance the hopeful partner puts up with all kinds of abuse and untruth, while there is little substance to the relationship outside of the dreamer's hope. Hope is a valuable commodity, but it is not a sufficient foundation for a relationship. Hope is like a pilot light on a gas stove. You can have a good spark, but if there is not sufficient fuel to make the flame rise, you will never get the fire hot enough to cook a good meal. To live only in hope is not a healthy attitude to create a relationship or any real success. True love is not blind.

We see a similar misappropriation of perseverance in relationships involving addictive personalities. One partner or family member puts up with the addict's alcoholism, drug abuse, sex abuse, obsessive work habits, or other debilitating activities, hoping that one day the partner will change. In such a case the partner of the addict would do well to be instrumental in bringing about the desired change by confronting his or her partner with the truth rather than indulging their addiction. You do not help a beloved by allowing him to continue to hurt himself. You help your partner by standing on integrity rather than succumbing to fear.

To persevere is to remember your purpose and let it bolster you to pass beyond obstacles. Your mission here is to be true to yourself and honor your spiritual nature. Remember this objective and you will be guided in all situations.

Your Good Cannot Be Stopped

There is a radiant couple who attend some of my retreats. Murray and Leslie are very much in love, and they have a beautiful family. To look upon them is to see that their bond is very alive and empowering for both of them.

At a workshop session, someone complimented this couple on the strength of their connection. Murray laughed. "I haven't always been like this," he shared. "This is my fourth marriage. Each time one of my previous marriages ended, I felt like a failure and a loser. I wondered if I would ever enjoy the kind of relationship I wanted. At times I felt like giving up. Then when I met Leslie my heart opened and I knew this was the kind of relationship I had always wanted and knew I was capable of having. And its beauty and wonder have grown over the years."

We are living in unusual times. It seems that everything is speeded up. In one lifetime we may go through several marriages, many jobs, numerous homes, and untold classrooms of learning on our spiritual path. It is as if we are on an express train that winds and turns through many cities and open country en route to its final destination.

During such an odyssey we may be tempted to give up because of the apparent instability of our life. But perhaps there is another way of looking at our journey, a way which empowers rather than discourages us. Perhaps we are to be commended for taking an advanced course. Perhaps we chose to learn as much as we can in the shortest time possible so we may maximize our growth and usher the planet to its next level of healing. Real learning requires trial and error, and to be sure we have had many trials and made many errors. But equally surely, we have learned and grown, and we will continue to do so.

Our good cannot be kept from us. We must and will receive what God has appointed for us. Our job is to not give up. Discouragement, doubt, and despair may arise to try to intimidate us like the dragons that guard the doors of oriental temples. But we are bigger than those feelings. There is a place in our heart in which we know that the goal is still available. Now faith is required. Like the knights of old, we are on a quest for the Holy Grail. The grail is not but a physical cup; it is the knowing that we *are* the grail, the chalice into which God pours His holy essence, from which we may drink and then offer sustenance to other thirsty travelers. Beloved Child of God, your destiny awaits you. Persevere. Hold firm to your truth. Do not stop until you reach the summit of loving. There you will celebrate every step on the path as you meet yourself and embrace your splendid beauty. What has been hidden shall be revealed.

Dare to Persevere

1) Describe a situation in your life in which you feel like giving up. What keeps you persevering?

2) If you were assured of success in a dream or project, what would you set out to do?

3) By what kinds of obstacles do you tend to be stopped or discouraged? What do you need to remember to overcome them?

4) Describe a project on which you succeeded due to perseverance.

5) What would you tell a child who wanted to give up? Write yourself a note using the same message.

DARE TO SUCCEED

It is within your ability to take everything that happens to you and make yourself a winner out of it. Yet there is a price you must pay, and you must decide if you are willing to pay it. The price you must pay to become a winner is your self-concept as a loser. This includes any idea of victimization, sacrifice, or sense of powerlessness. It means letting go of any notion that someone or something outside yourself is responsible for your success or sorrow. Your decision to succeed may mean changing your whole perceptual view of who you are and where your good comes from. It may mean becoming an entirely new person.

To become a winner you must see everything that happens to you as a gift, drawn to you in wisdom by your higher self for your healing. Make one exception to this law of higher learning and you will quickly plunge yourself into the world of losers. You must choose, once and for all, whether you are powerful or powerless. You must declare who you are and what you want to be. You must recognize that winning is not a quirk of fate, a coincidence, or a circumstance—it is a choice.

The Winning Edge

I love the character, Skip, played by Gene Wilder in that outrageous movie, *Stir Crazy*. In the story, Skip and his partner Harry (played by Richard Pryor) are thrown into prison for a crime they did not commit. In the penitentiary the warden and the other inmates attempt to break Skip and Harry into the prison mold. Harry continually appeases his peers and superiors, while Skip finds endless ways to be happy. Skip's cheerful attitude irritates his foes to no end, and they set out on a campaign to burst his joy bubble.

To begin, the guards hang Skip by his wrists for several days. When they return, the guards expect to find him grimacing in pain, begging for mercy. Instead, Skip radiates a blissful smile, exclaiming, "Oh, thank you, thank you! My back problem of eleven years is finally healed!"

Next, the prison officials lock Skip in the hot box. Out in the brutal summer sun he is contorted into a little tin box like a sardine. "This should do it," the guards snicker; "If the darkness doesn't get him, the heat will!" When the guards return five days later, they wonder if Skip will still be alive. As they open the door they find Skip beaming and joyful. "Oh please, oh please— just one more day!" Skip begs, "Let me stay in here just one more day. I was just beginning to get into myself!"

Finally the warden pulls out the heavy artillery. He casts Skip into a cell with Grossburger, a 300-pound crazed murderer. This is a man who strikes terror in the hardest of hearts; whenever he enters the prison cafeteria, all the inmates run the other way. To be locked in a small cell with Grossburger, it is commonly agreed among the inmates, is tantamount to suicide. The guards toss Skip into Grossburger's cell, lock the door behind them, and walk away with smug smiles on their faces. You can imagine the guards' bewilderment when they return the next day to find Skip and Grossburger sitting on the floor together playing cards, laughing and patting each other on the back. Skip is a man who refuses to be unhappy, and he invites everyone around him into his world.

You may know people in your life who, like Skip, find happiness wherever they go. Remember Abraham Lincoln's declaration that "most people are about as happy as they make up their mind to be." Emerson noted that "we may search the world for happiness, but unless we carry it within us, we will find it not." And then, of course, there is the *Far Side* cartoon showing a man whistling happily as he pushes a wheelbarrow through hell. Behind a rock one little devil remarks to another: "I just don't think we're getting to this guy."

You and I, too, have a choice about whether or not we will let life bring us down, or we will bring life up. Life was created to be a celebration, and so it is unless we are seeing through the eyes of fear rather than love. If we are not rising in love with every experience and relationship, we must move toward dissolving the clouds of limited thinking that we have allowed to obscure our vision. We must dismantle our fears, one by one, and burn the bridges to the past. We must commit ourselves wholeheartedly and unequivocally to win.

Look Deeper

Even if you have been committed to losing and misery for a long time, you can make a complete reversal in your life at any moment you choose. Even if you consider yourself a positive person, *look deeper*. How could you be happier? How can you win more? What would you like to have in your life, but don't believe you can? Is there a difference between who you are and how you are living? What is your next step to more joy, more success, more fulfilling relationships? These are the questions that will draw your soul to your next step of unfoldment. Look into your heart, tell the truth, and have the courage to act on what you know.

Room at the Top for Everyone

There is no competition in God. Your winning does not mean that someone else has to lose. Quite the contrary; when you truly win, so does everyone else. Your success does not take away from anyone else's success. It empowers others to be successful.

There are no losers—only those who do not yet see how they have gained. When you see yourself as a loser you teach yourself and the world that loss is a reality, and this is not so. Instead you can give the gift of your winning to the world. When you see yourself and others as winners, you inspire, encourage, and provide an example of success and fulfilled vision to everyone who sees you. If you believe that your winning diminishes anyone else's opportunity to succeed along with you, look again. Everything that comes to us comes not by the world's law of supply and demand, but by God's law of consciousness. We attract to ourselves by virtue of our thoughts, and so do those with whom we seem to be in competition. There is enough of everything for everyone, and we don't have to fight to have what we need. You will attract what you deserve as a result of your pattern of thinking, and so will your "competitor." You can both attract a great deal, or you can both attract very little. Your good is not dependent on the consciousness or actions of another, and neither is another's good dependent on you. That is why you cannot really hurt another and no one can hurt you—unless you both agree that it is so. Be careful not to ascribe an external power to your actions or experience, and do not fall into the dangerous position of seeing yourself as a victim or a villain. If you do, you enter a world other than God's and you will feel lost and powerless, two attributes that do not belong to you as a Child of an all-powerful Creator. You have no enemy other than your thoughts of war. You have power over your own consciousness, and that is all you need to be an enlightened being. You bless the world by remembering that each of us is free to create whatever we wish.

Jealousy Healed by New Vision

If you experience a sense of jealousy or envy about someone having something that you do not, you have forgotten that you are the creator of your world. At such a time you have renounced your destiny to the hands of circumstance rather than choice, where your strength truly lies.

There is a way to lift jealousy into healing, especially when you envy another for receiving what you would like. The way is simple, and it always works: *Bless their success as your own.* Because all that we see is a reflection of our own thoughts, you cannot see anything in the "outer" world that does not already live within you. When you see someone "out there" who has done well, you are looking at a part of yourself that has succeeded.

The most powerful way you can create more of what you want for yourself is to bless, support, and celebrate another's progress as if it were your own—for *it is*. When you acknowledge their good, rejoice with them, and support them in receiving even more, you will surely draw more of the same to yourself.

When my friend won six million dollars in a state lottery, I was thrilled to hear it! I did not feel envious for even a moment, and I did not think that her good in any way inhibited mine. To the contrary, I thought, "Wow! It's possible for someone to wake up one morning and be six million dollars richer! Now there's a demonstration of instant transformation. And it's someone I know—someone real, like me, with whom I can identify; not some fictitious character or remote subject of a news article. This is someone close to me; a miracle has touched my personal world. I must really be getting somewhere in my prosperity consciousness to manifest six million dollars though my friend. It won't be long now until I create something wonderful for myself!"

The word "envy" sounds like the letters, "N.V." "N.V." stands for *New Vision*—the vision of the good that you behold as another person receives it. Your old vision must have certainly been more limited, for you did not see this good manifested in your life. Therefore translate your envy into New Vision, and you are on your way to making that vision a reality.

To curse the success of others is to sabotage your own well-being and push your good away from you. To attack another's success is to deprive yourself of the same. We always receive more of what we celebrate and we push away what we are jealous of. Find joy in their blessing, and you enter the world that allowed them to receive the good that you desire, which is certainly also available to you. God did not create limits; we invented boundaries with our thoughts of lack. To return to the abundant world that God created, we need but change our mind about what we see. We will always receive more of that which we concentrate on, especially with strong emotion.

The Fear of Success

Strange as it may seem, some of us (or a part of all of us) are more afraid to succeed than to fail. To succeed means that we might have to change our life, claim a higher purpose, and let go of our "treasured wounds." Instead of glorifying the good and the miracles that come to us many times a day, we wear our sorrows, past misfortunes, and sense of righteous indignation like medals to be applauded by a world which worships loss and crucifies messengers of peace. Our investment in losing is far greater than we have recognized.

The time comes when we must wake up to our power and leave smallness behind. Goldie Hawn starred in a very funny movie, *Overboard*, in which she plays a wealthy and very spoiled heiress who terrorizes everyone she meets with her bratty attitude. One day she falls off her yacht, gets washed ashore, and wakes up with amnesia. She has totally forgotten her identity. The heiress is found by a poor carpenter whom she insulted and fired a day earlier. When he realizes her predicament, the carpenter decides to take revenge by bringing her home and telling her she is his wife and the mother of his four unruly children. Needless to say, this position nearly drives the heiress crazy; although she has forgotten her identity, she retains a memory of her luxurious life-style, and this is definitely not it. Her "family" lives in a funky hovel and her "children" are a band of screaming banshees. After a series of misadventures in which the carpenter and his children convince the heiress that she does indeed belong in Shanty Town (which pushes every pampered button in her psyche), she regains her memory. The heiress remembers that she does not belong in poverty. She has a great mansion, a yacht, and many servants in her charge. The heiress returns to her decadent lifestyle, but there is one problem. She has fallen in love with the carpenter and his children, and they with her. After trying to live without them, she realizes she would much rather live with them. Finally she joyfully welcomes them into her world. They have found a place in her heart, and they happily join her in her abundant domain.

The metaphor is a good one. Like the heiress, we have a

right to the entire kingdom of love and all of its reflections on earth, including joy, peace of mind, health, satisfying relationships, creative self-expression, and prosperity. And like the heiress, we have suffered under a case of amnesia. Our memory loss is that of our spiritual identity; we have forgotten who we are and where we came from. Moreover, we have been convinced by many other deluded people that we deserve to live in spiritual and material poverty. Misery loves company, and so do the illusions that create it. We may be convinced that we belong in a hovel and we may go ahead and act out the role, but there is a part of our mind that remembers that we have a higher home and we deserve better. And we will not stop until we are restored in full dignity to the Kingdom of our birth.

A New Agreement

To succeed is daring because living according to your own choices makes you a threatening exception to a world bent on denying the power that we hold. Religions, governments, and social institutions have thrived for millennia by teaching citizens, subjects, and groupies that they are guilty and powerless. Billions of human beings have suffered under the mass hypnosis that losing is our natural condition and our destiny. But this cannot be so. Powerlessness is perpetuated by agreement only, and at any moment we can change the agreement. Your life is your contribution to establishing a new agreement and breaking the spell of helplessness. Your vision is the key that opens the door to the healing of your life and that of the entire world. You are not being called upon to change yourself. You are being asked to be more of what you are. The invitation is bold, the stakes are high, and the outcome is certain. There is no choice but to leave smallness behind and stand tall. The path of strength is before you, and your job is but to take your next step. With that motion you will draw to you all means of support and assistance. Success is your birthright. Loss is impossible. Do what you came here to do. Be what you are.

Dare to Succeed

1) What would you like to succeed at doing? What fears seem to stand in your way? What signs do you receive that you can accomplish this?

2) Do you have any fears of success? If so, what are they?

3) How do you respond when someone around you succeeds?

4) How would you have felt or reacted differently if you knew that their success was a sign that you would be receiving the same?

5) List 3 things you are envious of. Do you believe there is enough of the same for you?

6) Make a list of the successes in your life and those of others. Add to the list daily.

DARE TO
DO THE IMPOSSIBLE

Think you can, or think you can't,
and either way you'll be correct.

— Henry Ford

A famous teacher of positive thinking had an eye-opening encounter with a man sitting next to him on an airplane. The man told the teacher a story that awakened his mind to even greater possibilities for abundant living.

When he was a senior math major in college, Alex's fervent hope was to win a coveted position as a graduate assistant. The only way to obtain the post was to receive the highest grade point average in the senior class.

Alex's grade hinged on the final exam, on which he needed to score a hundred percent to overcome the stiff competition among the students, many of whom had their sights set on the same graduate post. For weeks preceding the test, Alex studied ambitiously, burning the midnight oil and cramming as much as he could. He overworked himself so much, in fact, that on the eve of the exam he fell asleep at his desk and didn't wake up until minutes before the appointed hour.

Quickly Alex gathered his books and dashed to the examination hall, where the test had been in progress about ten minutes. He grabbed an exam booklet and began to work. As he moved through the test questions, Alex felt confident that he was completing the formulas accurately. Deftly he breezed through the problems, and despite his lateness he finished about fifteen minutes before the allotted time was up. When he stood up to hand in his paper, however, he noticed that there were two more problems on the chalkboard. Alex was stunned.

Apparently the professor had brought these questions to the class' attention during the first few minutes of the exam, when he had been absent.

There was no way Alex could complete these formulas in the time left. He sat down to try, but he could finish only one in the fifteen minutes he had. So Alex decided to appeal to the mercy of the professor. He asked the teacher if he could have some more time to solve the second problem. The professor told him that he could take the question home over the weekend and hand in his work on Monday morning.

The student wrestled with this last formula the entire weekend, and could not find a solution. As the deadline drew near, Alex's anxiety rose. He knew that there were many math wizards in the class, and any score less than a hundred would cause him to lose the assistantship he so badly wanted. As Sunday night became Monday morning, Alex went into deep despair. He fell back on his bed and stared despondently at the ceiling.

At that moment his mental fog was pierced by a loud knock at his front door. Puzzled about who could be calling on him at this late hour, he opened the door to find his math professor standing there with Alex's exam in his hands and an excited look on his face.

"Do you realize what you have done?" the professor inquired.

Alex was stymied. "Could I have done that badly on the test?" he wondered.

"Alex, you have made mathematics history!" the professor exclaimed.

"What are you talking about?"

"You have solved one of the classically unsolvable problems in mathematics!"

"How did I do that?"

"It was the first problem on the chalkboard."

"I thought that was part of the test."

"No, you silly boy," the professor laughed. "Those were two scientific enigmas that were left on the board from the previous class—and you are the first person in history to unravel one!"

"But nobody told me they were impossible to solve," Alex explained.

"Perhaps that is exactly why you were able to solve it." Needless to say, when the next semester began, the office door of the graduate assistant bore a sign with Alex's name on it.

The Fiction of "Can't"

Nothing is impossible. Nothing is beyond our reach unless we allow a barrier to stand between ourself and our dreams. The bricks of such a menacing wall are forged with thoughts of "I can't." "Impossible" is a concept that exists only in the mortal mind; it is not a part of the world that God created. God's world is one of endless possibilities. If we perceive a dead end to our potential, we have wandered into a perilous room of illusions. Never agree that limitation is real.

Aerodynamic engineers have analyzed the bumblebee, and after studying the size, mass, weight, and strength of the body and the wings, they came to the conclusion that such a creature is impossible. The size and strength of a bumblebee's wings, these scientists tell us, cannot support its body. Thank God no one told the bumblebee! I love those beautiful intelligent creatures, and I am glad that they never studied with the teachers who believe they are impossible!

Our great need is to turn our minds in the direction of possibility thinking. To see the potential rather than the problem is the all-important difference between those who ride the surf of life joyously to the shore, and those who flounder in the waves. As *A Course in Miracles* asks us, "Do you want the problem or do you want the answer?" Are you attached to being right about the dilemma, or are you ready to find a way out of it? As Richard Bach reminds us, "Argue for your limitations, and sure enough they're yours." Argue for your freedom, and sure enough you are empowered. The door to all the power in the universe is in your own mind. When asked where lies the key to the universe, a guru answered, "I have good news and I have bad news: The bad news is that there is no key to the universe. The good news is that the door has never been locked."

If You Don't Mind, It Doesn't Matter

There are some types of fish which, upon seeing the shadow of a net, believe they are trapped and remain in the shadowed area without even attempting to escape. Some clever fishermen, aware of this behavior by the fish, have ceased to use nets. They herd a great deal of fish into a catchment area simply by casting shadows. The fish respond as if they were caught, when they were free all the time.

We, too, give our power over to shadows. The past is a shadow, the future is a shadow based on our projections from the past, and many of our relationships are simply shadows of previous ones. We believe that we are seeing our husband, wife, child, boss, or president, when we are actually seeing but a veiled reflection of the issues we have not resolved with our parents or ourself. We allow ourselves to be herded by illusions of danger into little compartments of fear. And in our attempts to escape from nothing, we have done some rather foolish things. We have been prisoners of shadows.

But remember that a shadow has no power of itself. A shadow appears when something blocks our vision of the light. The proper response to a shadow is not to deny it, fight it, or run away from it. The way to relate to a shadow is to recognize it for what it is—an appearance only. Appearances may be very frightening, but that does not mean they are dangerous. You must learn to separate fear from danger. Fear is a response to apparent danger. But a response without a real cause is unjustified, and only serves to deepen the illusion that frightened you in the first place. Because there is nothing frightening about God, there is nothing worth fearing. Shadows cannot hurt you.

Sometimes I observe my parrots pecking at their shadows on the wall. They spend a lot of time playing with their shadows, fighting against them, and trying to make them go away. The humorous irony of their predicament is that it is they who are making their shadows all the while. They attack and defend themselves from the dark images that seem to come at them, while the forms they fear are but unrecognized projections of themselves. They are as empty and powerless as a mirror, and as foolish to defend against. So do we waste our time fighting shadows and protecting ourselves from dark dreams. We will never succeed in doing so because we are but fighting ourself in a disguised form. And there is nothing about who we are that requires battle. We do not need to bolster our ability to make war. We need to deepen our understanding as a step to finding peace.

The most direct way to release ourselves from the debilitating effects of wrestling with a shadow is to turn from the shadow and face the light. Fighting against or running from fear, separation, and death will not help us escape from such challengers, but will only make these shadows seem more real. To escape from the tyranny wrought by the dark and sinister forms that terrorize the theatre of our subconscious, we must turn up the light. To battle or deny a shadow is to give it power; to illuminate it is to diffuse it. That is what the entire spiritual path is about.

We are here in this world to peel away, one by one, the veils of fear and ignorance that have shrouded our spiritual sight. There is nothing wrong with your eyes, but it is quite difficult to see perfection through distorted lenses. Our role is to remove the heavy films of fear and guilt and learn to see clearly. What are these films made of? Ideas, and ideas alone. Ideas of lack, loss, limitation, and separation. Notions of "I can't," "I'm not good enough," and "maybe next year." Fears of "what if?", shackles of "I'm this way because...," and self-defeating prognostications such as "I guess I'll always be this way." I met a man who was melancholy because his astrologer told him he would be depressed for another eight years! That is quite a limiting belief to accept. We buy limitations too readily. We would do better to invest our attention in the truth of our freedom rather than submit to nets without substance.

Dare to Go Beyond Belief

"Most of our so-called reasoning consists of finding arguments for going on believing as we already do," explains

James Harvey Robinson. Dr. Wayne Dyer further elucidates, "You'll see it when you believe it." For centuries metaphysicians have been telling us in a million different ways that we see the world not as it is, but as we are.

Recently I had an experience that proved this principle to me in a very personal way. While visiting a tropical hotel, I was attracted to a beautiful Macaw parrot who had a perch in the hotel restaurant. Being a parrot lover, I approached the Macaw and began to talk to it. As I got close to this magnificent creature and reached my hand out to pet it, I was jarred by a shrill human voice: "Don't get too close to that bird!" a man interrupted. "He may bite you, and I don't want you to get hurt." I turned to see that it was the restaurant manager who was urging me to stay clear of the Macaw. Although I am confident with parrots, I decided to heed his advice, more for his sake than mine.

I stood and talked to the Macaw from a distance. Within a minute a waitress passed by and saw me with the bird. "Oh, he's such a sweet bird," she exclaimed, glowing as she looked upon the parrot affectionately; "he'll give you a kiss if you like!" The waitress came close to the parrot, extended her puckered lips to him, and sure enough he gave her a kiss. "What a darling!" she smiled as she went on to her service.

I stood there and laughed. "Isn't this the story of the world," I said to a friend. "One person is afraid of something, makes it into a threat, and passes the consciousness of fear on as if it were the truth. Someone else looks upon the same object, finds it beneficent and loving, and lives in an entirely different reality. What is the truth? Whatever we make it to be. Our experience will always play out our vision.

We do not believe what we prove—we prove what we believe. Don't limit God to your beliefs, but instead expand your beliefs to include all that God is. There is an infinite supply of all good things waiting to serve and support you if you just open your mind. Let go of the lesser to accept the greater.

Dare to Act As If

There is a divine form of pretense that God just loves. It is to pretend that you are great. To act as if you are worthy of all of your good. To claim the authority of one who is born of royalty. To honor your passions and deeds as if you love yourself. To forge ahead with the confidence that nothing is impossible.

This form of pretense is quite different than the charade of one who believes he is unworthy. To cast yourself as guilty is to uphold a lie and keep yourself downtrodden. Be careful of the role you take on, because you may become what you lead other people to believe you are.

You have been hypnotized into believing that you are less than whole. The messages of the world have told you that you can't, you aren't, and you won't. At one time you knew that you could, but you fell prey to an idea that you were less than divine. You have not sinned, but you have made one error that has cost you dearly: you gave up believing in yourself. You saw a shadow, mistook it for a net, and felt trapped by an invisible hand. But, no matter how lost you have felt, do not despair; your greatness has been held in trust for you until you remember it.

I know of a young man who was very shy. Leonard had a terrible fear of standing before people, and he was terrified by public speaking. Though he yearned to be more socially active, Leonard spent much of his time by himself. This was not his heart's choice; he was just too afraid of looking or sounding foolish.

One of Leonard's friends suggested he visit a certain psychic counselor for guidance. The counselor told him that he had been a great orator in a past life. In an ancient time, she described, thousands of people travelled many miles to sit in his presence and feast upon his words of wisdom. She went on to explain that the ability to awaken people's hearts through the power of eloquent speech was still with him.

Leonard was touched by this vision. The psychic's words awakened a profound feeling deep within him and stirred his innermost being. Her ideas moved him so much, in fact, that he wanted to pursue her guidance. Leonard joined a local chapter of Toastmasters and began to investigate his potential as a public speaker. The following month he volunteered to give a presentation at the office staff meeting. Though he felt nervous to stand before his peers, he also felt excited.

The results were astounding. Leonard received positive feedback from his peers, and he felt encouraged to further explore his newfound interest. He found more opportunities to speak in public and went on to take a Dale Carnegie course. Now Leonard is a well-respected and sought-after speaker for motivational meetings. He became the orator.

Was the psychic reading accurate? I cannot say for sure. But there is one thing of which I am certain: Leonard's willingness to put himself out there, to cast himself in the role that he wanted to play, was the first and most important step to becoming what he wanted to be. If Leonard had waited to change his life before he changed his self-image, that metamorphosis may never have occurred. But when Leonard got a glimpse of himself as greater than he had been seeing himself, his richer image brought about the desired change.

Sometimes you have to "fake it 'til you make it." It is not hypocritical to act like the person you would like to be. It is a greater deceit and deception to act smaller than you are. Whenever you act small, unworthy, or unloved, you deny your identity as a spiritual master. The Bible tells us that we, as human beings, are given dominion over the earth. This means that we have the power to create our world with our thoughts. Let us use the power of our mind and heart to magnify our beauty and walk in the dignity of our highest and most loving nature.

The Steppingstones and the Peak

We are not governed by any person or authority in this world outside of ourself. God created us unlimited, but it is up to us to recognize the perfection of our being so we may experience and enjoy it. We build a house of limitations with our thoughts and then we live in it. There are no walls to our life except those we inscribe by our beliefs.

Everyone in this world lives within the boundaries of his own belief system. The game of life consists of stepping beyond our old limits and replacing them with broader vistas. As we accept more expanded ideas of how gloriously we can live, we add rooms onto our house until we recognize that the entire universe is our home.

While walking along the shore one day, I found a beautiful seashell. A friend explained to me that the creature that inhabited this shell did not occupy it for its entire life. The "tenant" lived there for a period of time and then, when it had outgrown the shell, discarded this casing and went on to build and live in larger quarters.

It occurred to me that this is exactly how we grow through different beliefs in our life. We live in one house of understanding for a while, and sooner or later we outgrow it, let it go, and move on to a larger mansion. We enter into relationships, diets, religions, philosophies, and all kinds of belief systems, we learn and gain all we can from them, and then we move on. It would be foolish and unnecessary to stay in any room of learning longer than we need to. This world is not our final destination; it is a school through which we pass. Our belief systems are very helpful at the time we adopt them, as they give us a context to focus on specific lessons. But then we must let our belief systems go and move on to enjoy greater mansions.

I see now how every belief I have adopted has helped me and led me to the next one. I have been a baseball player, an orthodox Jew, a drug explorer, an encounter group leader, a chef, a college instructor, a meditator, a businessman, an author, a gardener, a builder, an orator, and I have played many other fascinating roles in all kinds of arenas. Each of these stages of learning has blessed me, bestowed gifts upon my mind and heart, and delivered me safely to my next station like a wave that has a destiny on a particular shore. Now in my current work I incorporate elements of everything I have learned. Nothing is lost and nothing is outside the curriculum of my healing and the gifts I came to share. All of my beliefs have been perfect in their own time and place, and it is perfect that something new is here now.

Beliefs are not the peak of the mountain of truth. They are steppingstones to the summit where we stretch forth our wings and fly. Be careful not to camp out for too long on any one plateau on the way up the mountain. You may get stepped on by the climbers behind you and you'll miss a breathtaking view from the top.

The Gift of Challenge

The universe has a way of pushing us to go beyond our limits. At first our challenges seem like curses, but in the end we learn to bless them. Challenge is God's way of getting us to wake up to the fact that we are bigger than we thought we were. God is our best friend because She remembers our potential even when we don't, and She will not let us slumber in the stupor of limited living. God is like a parent who takes us to buy a new outfit, and then laughs when we come out of the dressing room in a suit three sizes too small for us. Of course She won't buy it for us (or from us); She knows that we are so much more attractive and happier in an ensemble that suits us and honors our beauty. Challenge is an invitation to be great.

To become all that you can be, you must welcome into your life people who ask more of you than you ask of yourself. It is not healthy to surround yourself with people who always agree with you or play a game of littleness with you. A real friend values truth more than the charades that hold us back from shining as brightly as we can. If you shelter yourself from challenge, your spirit will wither and you will grow weak of will. Your creativity will be reduced to a trickle. You will become bored and wonder what you are doing here. Learn to recognize boredom as a sign that you must escape the shell in which you have become entombed. Let restlessness spur you to reach out and stretch to your next creative adventure. As Helen Keller said, "Life is a daring adventure—or nothing."

The Power of Agreement

I have a friend who bases his entire ministry on the power of agreement. He has created many wonderful miracles in his life by entering into agreements with other people that his desired results are possible. When his wife found a house that she really liked, Bill was concerned that he wouldn't be able to finance it. When he saw that he was laboring under fear, he sat down with a friend and asked, "Do you agree that I and my wife have a right to live in a beautiful home that we desire, and that I can finance this home easily and peacefully?" Bill and his friend closed their eyes and found the place within themselves that accepted that this was indeed possible. They shook hands and declared that they agreed this could come about. Soon Bill met someone who helped him with a financial plan that really worked for him. Now Bill and his family are enjoying their home and many other blessings of a life based on possibility thinking rather than fear.

I have experimented with the power of agreement, and I can declare from my own experience that it really works. I have an agreement partner with whom I have manifested many inspiring miracles. My assistant Noel is a dear friend who is willing to agree with me on the highest possibilities. One day my office laser printer needed a repair. When I called the serviceman and explained the problem to him, he sighed and with a heavy voice told me, "I hate to tell you this, but that is a very expensive part to replace. The piece you need is a part of a cartridge, and the only way to fix it is to buy an entire new assembly, which costs seven hundred dollars, plus labor."

"That's outrageous!" I thought. The entire printer, a sophisticated electronic device, costs only sixteen hundred dollars new. It seemed crazy to have to pay half of that just to replace a small roller about the size of pencil.

Upon hearing this dreary diagnosis I turned to Noel and asked her, "Do you agree that we can get this machine fixed for a lower price?" She quickly replied, "Of course I do!" and we shook hands. I called another repairman, who gave me the same story, but told me that he would charge me only the wholesale price of four hundred and fifty dollars for the part, plus labor. That still won't do, I thought. It was more than I was willing to pay or believed I needed to shell out for a small simple part.

I turned to Noel and asked her again, "Do you agree that I can get this machine fixed perfectly and easily for a fraction of that cost?" "Certainly!" she answered. We shook hands again.

I made one more call. This repairman told me he knew someone who could replace the part without the cartridge. I called this serviceman and he told me, "Sure, I do that all the time." I told Noel, "I think we have our man!"

This fellow came to my house (about a forty-minute drive each way from his shop), sat down, took out a screwdriver, took my machine apart, replaced the defective part, and put it all back together in about half an hour. Then he presented me with a total bill of only eighty-eight dollars—one tenth of the cost of the first estimate! Now the printer works perfectly.

I cherish this experience as a lesson that we don't have to accept the limitations or demands the world presents to us, and that we can invoke the power of agreement to obtain the results we desire. In a way, the entire experience was a challenge for me to see if I believed I could have my life work without paying an exorbitant price. The world will tell us that we have to suffer and sweat to earn happiness, but perhaps we are listening to the wrong people. Perhaps there is another outlook that would work better for us if we are just willing to accept it. Let us agree that we don't have to pay a high price for love and that our life can be a success without sacrifice. Love requires no price, but waits upon our welcome.

A Higher Agreement

At a workshop I was presenting in Texas, a young man stood up to speak. "This is an important day for me, and I want to tell you why:

"My doctor diagnosed me as having AIDS, cancer, and leukemia. He told me that I had about two weeks to live. He said there was no hope for recovery."

A hush fell over the room as we listened intently.

"I went home and began to think about my life. As a student of metaphysics, I know that I create my own experiences and circumstances. 'How, then, did I create this?' I wondered.

"I traced my thoughts back to the time when my lover of ten years was killed in an automobile accident. I remembered thinking, 'I don't want to live anymore. Without him, my life is worthless.' I felt that if I entered into another relationship, I would contract AIDS. After a while I began to see someone, and sure enough within six weeks I was diagnosed as having AIDS.

"I was astonished by the process with which I had set myself up for these diseases. It was perfectly clear to me that my desire not to live had invited illness to me. Here were my thoughts manifesting for me to examine through their effects. I felt that I was being given my final choice: Do I want to live or die?

"I began to reconsider my life. I recognized that I truly do love living. I cherish my relationships, and I want to be here. I reasoned that if I had the power to manifest these diseases, then I also have the power to manifest healing.

"So I began an adventure of appreciation. I began to love myself and value all the miraculous things about who I am and what I am doing here. I decided that everything I did would be an opportunity to give myself and others love.

"Almost instantly I felt a wave of healing energy flow through my body. I began to feel stronger and more excited about participating in life. I knew that something good had happened, and that I also needed to continue with my program of self-appreciation.

"The two weeks turned into two months, and the two months into two years. I went to the doctor yesterday, and I am happy to tell you that he found no sign of any of those diseases in my body. By the Grace of God, I am whole."

A huge wave of applause and appreciation roared through the audience. A sense of awe welled up within me. I looked at this man, and he was radiantly healthy. His aura was shining, and the strength of his heart and body was apparent.

I felt humbled and inspired in this man's presence. Here was one who had stepped to death's door, and chose to turn back and enter life. He was a living demonstration of the principle that nothing is incurable and that health and happiness are not circumstances, but choices we make.

I had an intuition which I shared with him: "You have been healed not just for yourself, but for everyone else diagnosed with those diseases, and any other seeming limitation. Now, my friend, you must 'take your show on the road.' You must tell your story and demonstrate by your life and strength that we do indeed choose our path, and that self-appreciation is a most powerful way to healing."

He smiled and told me, "It's funny you should mention that—you're the third person to tell me that. I think I will."

Anyone with any life-threatening disease or any illness at all needs to see that disease is not a punishment, but an invitation to look deeper and open to richer living. If you are subject to fear of any kind you must recognize that God has not limited you, and that you are capable of going far beyond your ideas of what you can't do. God does not share such thoughts of lack, and therefore they have no power. Nothing is impossible to God, and as His perfect child, nothing is impossible to you. "If," "but," and "impossible" are the language of fools, and even if you have been fooled in the past, you are smarter than your history. We may have dreamed that we are small, but dreams have no power in the face of reality. Your reality is divine, and nothing can stand in the way of a soul with a vision and the confidence to achieve it.

Only those who see the invisible can do the impossible.

Dare to Do the Impossible

1) Make a list of the things you feel you cannot do. Beside the list write down the reasons you believe you cannot do them. Next to that list make another list supporting why you could do them. Practice arguing for your success rather than your limits.

2) Name three things you thought you could never do, that you have done.

3) What desired behaviors could you "act as if" you had mastered them? What would you be doing differently?

4) Who challenges you to be bigger than you are? How do you react to them?

5) Invite someone to be your agreement partner. Choose three projects on which you would like to succeed, and ask them to agree with you on the possibility of your success.

DARE TO LIVE YOUR VISION

*Go confidently in the direction of your dreams!
Live the life you've imagined.*
— Henry David Thoreau

There was something about his face that was different. The other people interviewed in the magazine seemed drawn, tired, and overworked. This man's face, by contrast, was radiant and childlike. Although he was in his sixtieth year at least, his countenance was by far the youngest and happiest in the magazine.

I had to find out more about who this man was and what he did. Below his photo I saw the name, Charles Schulz—creator of the *Peanuts* cartoon strip. "Aha! This man looks young because he thinks young!" I surmised.

I had been feeling overwhelmed with my work for longer than I cared to admit. Obligations and responsibilities seemed to be piling up around me. I felt squeezed from all angles. I was stressed to be spending most of my time doing things I had to do, and almost no time doing the things I wanted to do. I had been praying for an answer that would help me escape this dilemma.

Toward the bottom of the Schulz article, the interviewer asked him why he is so successful. "It's simple," Charles answered. "I do the thing I love to do the most and best, which is to draw cartoons. I don't bother myself with anything else. I don't even have a checkbook!"

I dropped the magazine in my lap and said, "That's it!" aloud. Here was my answer. This man had the courage to do the thing he loved and let all else go. He may not have a checkbook, but he had millions upon millions of dollars in accounts that other people manage for him. He has listened to his heart, made other

311

people happy, and the world has rewarded him for his gifts. And he is happy.

Schulz has followed his dream. How many of us can say the same? Have we had the courage to set out on the path that our heart guides us to follow, and believe in it rather than worship the false gods of guilt and fear?

Do you remember your dreams? I am not referring to the reveries we undergo while sleeping at night. I am referring to the vision you had when you chose your life's path. You and I aspired to do and be wonderful things, feel fulfilled, and enjoy the support of the universe in the process. There was a place in our heart that knew if we were true to ourself, the world would be a better place and we would not want for anything as we expressed our creative desires.

Yet somewhere along the way many of us traded in our vision because we became afraid. We read a newspaper headline heralding disaster. We felt the pain of our relatives who believed they had to struggle. We were offered a surefire way to make money that was less creative than we wanted, and decided to take the certain reward instead of reaching out and trying for the gold ring on the merry-go-round. And it may have been a practical thing to do at the time. But perhaps there remains a place in our heart which wishes that we had taken the path of greater adventure. Perhaps we wince when we see someone doing the thing we would love to be doing. And then we wonder if maybe we could still do it. Perhaps we can.

The Thread of Life

Sometimes the only thing we have to cling to is our dream. Sometimes it seems that all else has fallen away except our dream, and we hold fast to that vision like a life raft on a stormy sea.

Several years ago I came up against one of the hardest times in my life. My mother was in the hospital, not recovering after cancer surgery; my girlfriend and I had parted painfully; I developed a staph infection that knocked me into bed; and I was snowed in at the nadir of a cold New Jersey winter. Wherever

I looked I saw only bleakness and darkness.

As I was trying to recover from the infection, I listened to a cassette tape of instrumental music by my friend Maloah Stillwater. Instantly my heart was drawn back to a time when I visited Maloah and Michael Stillwater at their home in Kula, a breathtakingly beautiful area on the island of Maui. My friends lived high up on the slope of a ten-thousand foot dormant volcano that shapes one half of that magical island.

As Maloah was preparing dinner that afternoon, I stepped outside to enjoy the view—and what a vista it was! Before the backdrop of the setting sun I could see the silhouettes of no less than five Hawaiian islands standing in humble yet majestic dignity. I heard a thousand birds singing their sunset song, felt the sacred breeze wash over my cheeks and arms, and I filled my lungs with the cleanest air I have ever imbibed. I stood on top of a hill, opened my arms, and shouted, "Yes! Thank you, God! This is paradise!" More than ever before in my life, I remembered the purity and magnanimity of all creation, and felt God's presence with me on the earth. For me it was a vision of Heaven on earth.

Now, a year later, buried in the frozen darkness of a bleak winter without and within, this memory pierced my sorrow like a shaft of light penetrating the morbid casket in which I felt entombed. Somehow the remembrance of that brilliant moment still lived within me, and it bore life enough to nourish me. As I began to recall the feeling on the mountain in Kula, I felt a surge of life charge through me. I remembered that there was something worth living for. Life was not entirely painful; there were rays of hope. A helping hand of Spirit reached through the storm and touched my own.

I played the tape over and over again as I consciously focused my mind on my memories of my day at the Stillwaters' home. That was the key to my healing. It was the turning point. From that moment on I began to feel better and my health and life improved. That vision was my lifeline, and I will never forget it.

Oh yes—the following year I moved into the home in Kula, where I have enjoyed the air and the sunset from that day on. My vision became my reality.

Now is the Time

Don't wait until it is too late to live your vision. You never know how much time you have in which to do what you want to do. Therefore do the most important things now; don't leave them until the end. Don't let your life be like a postcard on which you write trivial things in big letters and then have to squeeze what you really wanted to say in little letters all around the margins.

My friend Ric received word that his father had died suddenly of a heart attack. As he drove frantically down to the hospital to meet his family, Ric was beset with the agony of all of his unfulfilled desires for his relationship with his dad. There were so many things Ric wished he had said and done with his father before he left this world. The young man's heart sank in despair as he considered that he would never again have the opportunity to be with his father in the way that he hoped they would grow to enjoy one another. Never had he regretted anything more than the unspoken words and undone acts with his dad, whom he dearly loved, but had not admitted in word or deed.

When Ric arrived at the emergency room, he was astounded to learn that his father was not dead. He had been unexpectedly revived, and he was going to survive. You can imagine the relief and release that Ric felt to learn that he would have another chance with his father. "From that day on, my relationship with my dad has been entirely different," Ric told me. "Now I appreciate him, tell him everything I want to, and I no longer regret not expressing my unspoken love. I thank God that I have had more time to heal and celebrate my relationship with my father."

Og Mandino offers a powerful method to improve the quality of our relationships: Imagine that the person you are with will not be alive after midnight tonight. How would you be with them differently? How would you want them to remember you? What would you overlook that you are complaining about now? What do you want or need to say that would help you to feel complete with them? In the answers to these questions lies the key to healthy, satisfying relationships.

Living our vision is the one thing we cannot afford to postpone. Actualizing our dreams is the one goal we will regret not accomplishing when we review our life. Make every moment count, starting with this one.

Leave the How and When to God

You never know how or when your vision will be manifested. You just need to know that if it is a good dream, God will help you make it a reality. Until then, just carry on what you are doing with the faith that the wheels of the universe are operating even when you don't see them.

A friend of mine is the minister of a church that does a great deal of service to the community. One day a young woman walked into the church service and informed the assembly that the house she had just built belonged to the church. She and her husband had been guided to build a beautiful estate on a large parcel of pristine forest. The couple had prayed and attuned their design and construction with the Native American way of building in harmony with the natural surroundings. She offered to sell the house and land to the church at the price of eight hundred thousand dollars.

The minister and the church were not in the market for a house, and they certainly did not have eight hundred thousand dollars to spend on one. But they decided to take a look at the place anyway. When the church leaders stepped onto the land they felt a powerful healing energy and they sensed that it would make an excellent retreat.

The minister's family began to explore ways to raise funds to purchase the house. Arduous research led them to the conclusion that there was no way they could finance the purchase with their resources. After exhausting all of their ideas and going through considerable emotional struggle about how to fund this project, they decided to just let it go. If God wanted them to have this house, they agreed, He would find a way.

The next week the minister received a telephone call from one of her friends, a wealthy entrepreneur. In the course of the conversation, the minister mentioned the church family's adventure with the house. The two parties hung up, and that was the end of the issue—for the moment. The next morning the minister received a call from her friend. "Go to the bank on Monday morning and the money for the house will be in your account," the entrepreneur told her.

Sure enough, on Monday morning the minister's account was fatter by eight hundred thousand dollars. The house was purchased for the church, and I had the delight of staying there when I did some programs for the church. A wonderful feeling permeated the estate, and my time there was more enjoyable for the fact that the retreat came as a gift from God.

Seeds and Flowers

Sometimes we plant the seeds of our vision in one season and we see them sprout in another.

Around the time I began my citizen diplomacy missions to the Soviet Union, I saw an article in the newspaper about a man who had received a lot of criticism for flying a Russian flag next to an American flag in front of his house. The man wanted to make a statement for world peace through honoring both nations. His neighbors, however, were offended by his display and he was the subject of insults and threats.

I was so inspired by this fellow's vision and courage that I sent him a letter telling him that I appreciated his efforts on behalf of peace, and that he certainly had my support. I enclosed a copy of my book, *The Healing of the Planet Earth*.

Five years later I was presenting a workshop in Philadelphia, during which I asked if there was anyone in the audience who wanted to share anything with the group.

A man in the center of the auditorium stood up and announced, "I'm Len Fredricks, the man who flew the Russian flag in front of my home. I caught some flak for that, and although I believed in what I was doing, it was a challenging time for me. I came tonight to tell you how much your letter and book meant to me. It gave me faith and inspiration to carry on. I will never forget your kindness."

Len paused and noted, "I feel especially joyful that today, the day of President Gorbachov's arrival in the United States, Russian flags are flying all around our nation." A burst of applause rang through the auditorium. The audience was cheering for the courage to sow the seeds of our vision, even if we have to wait to see them sprout.

Dare to Get Real

Never underestimate the importance or the power of your dreams. Our dreams are actually much closer to reality than the world we usually accept as real. The Chinese Patriarch Chuang-Tsu told his students, "In a dream I saw myself as a great butterfly. Now I am not sure if I am Chuang-Tsu dreaming I was a butterfly, or I am a butterfly dreaming I am Chuang-Tsu."

Be careful not to allow the world to convince you that your dreams are not valid. Often when someone tells us to "get real," what they are really saying is, "get limited." Like those around Jonathan Livingston Seagull, Jesus, and so many saints, sages, and seers throughout history, many people are threatened by one who presses against and beyond the edges of the reality into which they have gotten comfortable. But if there is a bigger world to live in, why not go out and find it?

Prophets are customarily ostracized in their own time and then canonized when they are not around to pose a threat anymore. Vincent Van Gogh sold only one painting in his lifetime, for a pittance. Now four of his paintings are among the top ten highest valued paintings in the world, and one of his works recently sold for a record eighty-three million dollars. Mozart was buried in an unmarked pauper's grave. The list goes on. Current recognition is not an indication of greatness or ultimate contribution to humanity, and lack of recognition by no means indicates lack of worth. Worldly acknowledgement is a very poor index of truth.

That is why you must have a greater investment in your vision than in the accepted reality. Accepted reality is usually an illusion, and dreams are the doors through which the illusion is escaped and replaced with a larger domain. Dare to walk through that door.

Your intuition will show you more than your outer senses, and bring you to truth more quickly. Descartes, considered to be the father of the scientific method, reported that the method came to him in a dream. The entire foundation of modern science, based on empirical observation by the five senses, came to earth by way of intuition. The method by which we have developed the technology to produce all of our amazing cars, computers, and medicine arrived in a dream. Truly there is a higher way of seeing, a divinely ordered faculty which will help us abundantly if we are open to receive its gifts.

Dare to Imagine

Real outer change springs from inner vision. Patricia Sun, a brilliant psychologist and educator, maintains that half of elementary education should be devoted to constructive daydreaming. (A lot more than half of current education is already devoted to daydreaming, but it is not constructive. A survey of the sketches and statements written and carved into school desks and lavatory walls demonstrates that students have many things on their minds other than the lessons at hand.)

Imagine an educational system in which children's minds are allowed and encouraged to soar beyond the norm. The word "education" comes from the Latin *educare*, "to draw out." Unfortunately, we have interpreted and practiced education not as drawing out, but pounding in. We must admit that when it comes to stimulating creativity, our educational system is generally a failure. Most of our schools are little more than babysitting centers in which students learn more about what they don't want in life than what they do; more about what their parents and teachers expect of them than what they are.

We cannot say that we have truly educated a child unless he becomes more of a person and less of a template upon which the prevailing societal fears leave their stamp. Unless a child is more in touch with his heart's desires by the time he graduates from a program, he has not learned anything of value. Yes, technical skills are important, but they are useless unless there is a spiritual or moral component toward which the gained expertise can be directed. What good is a world in which everyone's computers work, but their hearts don't? Our machines are healthier than our souls, and if we expect to make any progress as a civilization, we are going to have to bring our spirits up to the efficiency level of our imported automobiles. If we are going to change our educational system for the better, we need to teach our children in an entirely different way. The first step to our cultural healing is to honor our children as human beings and draw forth their inherent greatness by giving them a chance to exercise it. Then we will replace deadening with creativity, and be on our way to rebuilding our world on the foundation of caring rather than robotics.

Dare to dream, and dream big. Linus Pauling, the Nobel Laureate in Chemistry and Peace, suggested that "the best way to have a good idea is to have lots of ideas." Do not censor your ideas before they have a chance to blossom. A good gardener sows many more seeds than will ultimately mature. The lesser seedlings will be thinned away, and the best of the crop cultivated. Give your ideas a runway to take off without criticism or evaluation. As you open up the pipeline of your creative impulses, it will remain an open channel and you will be amazed at how many more ideas you generate, many of which will go on to become reality.

Use your imagination. Albert Einstein, one of the great scientific geniuses of the ages, proclaimed that "imagination is greater than knowledge." Ernest Holmes, founder of Religious Science, declared that "what the mind can conceive, man can achieve." The seeds of greatness lie within you. Cultivate them. You can and will become as magnificent as you allow yourself to be. Point your mind toward the stars, and let your arrows fly.

Hold the Vision

I met an actress who enlightened me about the process of movie-making. "Most people don't realize how much technical work goes into creating a film," she explained. "There is so much more that makes a good film than the acting. In fact, there is very little continuous acting on a movie set. Usually only a few lines are spoken before the action is stopped and the actors, cameras, and crew are repositioned. When you see two people in a film having a discussion over dinner, for example, the conversation is not filmed at one time. One person says his lines to an empty chair, and then everything stops and the camera is moved to shoot the other person saying her lines to an empty chair. Most of a typical day on a movie set is spent waiting while scenes are prepared and the technicians make their adjustments.''

I went on to ponder the other factors in producing a film. Scriptwriting, financing, casting, set construction, takes and retakes, coordinating hundreds or thousands of artists and technicians, repairing equipment malfunctions, dealing with temperamental actors and personality conflicts on the team, facing moral and ethical issues regarding content and themes, and on and on. A two-hour movie represents an amazing amount of work, challenge, and creative endeavor. The motion picture is truly a monument to human ingenuity.

Then I began to consider the kind of vision, faith, dedication, and commitment required to bring a quality film to birth. Amidst this fantastic maze of technical, financial, and emotional details, someone has to hold the vision. Someone has to remember what the movie is for and keep in mind and heart the feeling and results the film is intended to create. This requires clear and vigilant focus on the bigger picture as all of the little pieces are moving in place.

We, too, must hold the vision for our life. While we have a lofty goal, there are many details that contribute to bringing this dream to reality. It is rare that anyone wakes up one morning and finds that their life's dream has magically become a reality overnight. Usually there are many nuts and bolts that must be put in place before the dream can fly. These steps are often tedious, time-consuming, and frustrating. We must work with other people and face the challenges of human relationships. We experience setbacks, delays, and what appear to be failures. Sometimes we must go all the way back to the drawing board and start from scratch. Sometimes there seems to be plenty of good reasons to throw in the towel and give up.

But there is one awareness that gives us the energy and power to keep going and make our dream come true: *Remember the vision.* Remember why you decided to do this in the first place. Remember the excitement and enthusiasm you had before things got tougher. Remember the gift you want to deliver to the world, and the way that only you can deliver it. If you remember the vision, you will have all the power you need to complete the project and triumph over all kinds of adversity. Fear would tell you to quit when hurdles confront you, but wisdom will give you the strength and the energy to surpass them.

No hurdle is as high as your dream. Quitters turn back when fear says "boo!" and winners keep their eye on the finish line. Hold the goal first and foremost in mind at all times. You will arrive there, and you will be very glad that you didn't let shadows stop your run. In the end, we only face ourself. When we remember our vision, it is our self that we find.

The future belongs to those who
believe in the beauty of their dreams.

—Eleanor Roosevelt

Dare to Live Your Vision

1) What vision empowers you to continue toward your goal?

2) What dreams seem beyond your reach? How might you still be able to attain them? How might the universe be working at this moment to make your dream come true?

3) What kinds of obstacles have stopped you? What goal can you remember that would help you move beyond your fears?

4) Close your eyes and take a few minutes to let your imagination soar. Fantasize doing all the things that you would love to do. Do not restrict your thoughts in any way. Write down as many images as you can recall.

DARE TO BE DIVINE

Our birth is but a sleep and a forgetting,
The soul that rises with us, our life's star,
Hath had elsewhere its setting,
And cometh from afar;
Not in entire forgetfulness,
And not in utter nakedness,
But trailing clouds of glory do we come
From God, who is our home.

— William Wordsworth

Recently I met a gay singer at a spiritual conference. She had just returned from performing at a national gay convention. This courageous woman told me that before she went on stage to perform, the organizers of the conference called her aside and told her, "Please do not sing any of your spiritual songs." This request surprised her. She thought for a moment, and then responded, "You and this movement for gay liberation have taught me for many years to be able to stand before spiritual audiences and admit that I'm gay. Now I think I should be able to stand before a gay audience and admit that I'm God."

You and I, too, need to have the courage to claim our spiritual identity in the midst of a world afraid of light. We don't need to flaunt our spirituality, argue about it, or attack anyone who does not see or agree with it; we just need to live it. The path of mastery does not require us to convince anyone else of anything; it simply asks us to remember who we are and be it. When we know that we are born of God, heirs to all the spiritual riches of the universe, the dilemmas of life give way to a deep sense of confidence that our destiny is one of great good.

Perfect Reflection

Because you are divine, you can have no attributes other than those of God. God is love, and therefore by nature you are

323

a loving being. God is eternal, and so you have all the time in the world and beyond it. God has all the resources of the universe available at the command of His word, and so do you. God is the only power in the universe (What could threaten Spirit?) and therefore you have nothing to fear. Affirm that all that is good belongs to you, and slice away anything that is unlike love. Lack of any kind is unbecoming to the child of a beneficent king.

Imagine a circular room with a wall of sheer mirrors. The entire wall of mirrors reflects what is in the room. In the center of the room stands a crystal table, so clear and pure that it is almost invisible. On the table stands a crystal vase which is also translucent. In the vase rests a beautiful red rose. This rose is perfect in every way. Behold this magnificent flower in its richest blossom, with its velvety petals fully open. Every aspect of the rose is healthy, radiant, and vibrant with life. Take a moment to close your eyes and clearly visualize this image.

Now observe the reflection of the rose in the mirror. The mirror reflects the rose and only the rose. Each portion of the looking glass captures a different aspect of this glorious flower. The mirror is perfectly smooth and accurate in its reflection; the only image that exists in the room is the rose in many different facets of splendor. Focus on this vision in your mind as a meditation.

The rose represents the perfection of God, and we are the mirror. God's absolute perfection cannot be fully replicated in this world, but it can be reflected in such clarity that God is seen and known here. When we open our heart and mind to real vision, we find God walking among us, as us. As offspring of God, we carry His attributes only and always. Without the distortion of fear and its progeny, the smudge of guilt, we recognize that God lives fully in us. Because God is the truth of our being, our nature is to express love, kindness, joy, compassion, and gentleness. All else is unlike ourself, and springs from illusion.

The Power of the Word is Yours

The most powerful words in our language are "I am." "I am" is the creative seed thought of God's power on earth and in Heaven. The Bible tells us that "in the beginning was the word." All that we create begins with our word—specifically, the words, "I am."

Be careful how you complete the sentence that begins, "I am . . ." In your completion you will found your reality and conceive your destiny. With this sentence you will literally sentence yourself; you will choose whether you will live in strength, power, and dignity, or in the weakness of fear. These are no idle words. Your statements, mental and verbal, conscious and subconscious, are the key to all you will ever become.

When you speak the words, "I am," you must tell the truth. If you say that you are lost, unworthy, or unloved, you have uttered a great untruth. You will have to live out the experience of these false identities until you discover that you are greater than you have thought or spoken. If, however, you align yourself with your divinity and affirm that you are a powerful Child of God unto whom is given infinite power, the richest abundance, and undying love, you call to expression the mightiest—and only—force in the universe. With your decree you summon the power and presence of every great soul who has reached the mountaintop of life and discovered God to live in his heart. Be aware of the mighty forces you set into motion with your words. Your words will make you or break you. Let them be of God, as you are.

Choose Once Again

Each time we speak "I am" we stand at a fork in the road of our destiny and we choose the direction we will go. If we utter a demeaning untruth, we cast ourself onto a dim and rocky byway. There we will wander in fear until we return to the same fork and choose once again. And we will have the opportunity to choose again. We must keep facing our unconsciousness until we become aware of the light that we are. This is a blessed path

325

indeed, for Spirit will not let us wander forever in darkness. There is no way home but through self-discovery. Our destiny of love is ensured.

Sow a Thought

There is a poem which captures the essence of our power to create our world:

> *Sow a thought, reap a word;*
> *Sow a word, reap a deed;*
> *Sow a deed, reap a habit;*
> *Sow a habit, reap a character;*
> *Sow a character, reap a destiny.*

Behold the formula by which our thoughts shape our destiny. Make no mistake that this is the process by which we create our lives. It is supremely important that we are vigilant about the ideas we sow in the garden of our consciousness, for from them springs all we are to experience.

In our words lies the formative power of God. Many of us have abused this power for lifetimes by entertaining thoughts of victimization and defending morbid self-images with our words. Amazing as it sounds, we have used our creative power to be attorneys for our own prosecution. And because we are also our own judge, we have convicted ourselves by believing the witness of our fears and sentenced ourselves to lack, loss, and death.

Could this be the lot and destiny of the children of the King of the Universe? Certainly not. Thoughts and experiences of emptiness are but dark dreams and delusions. The telling feature of a delusion is that it is unlike reality. Amnesia may change our experience, but it cannot change the truth. Our unconsciousness may have put us through some horrid experiences, but it cannot undo the certainty that in love we are invulnerable.

It does not matter how unconscious we have been or how long we have been asleep. What matters now is that we wake up. The process of awakening begins with even a brief moment's consideration of the possibility that we are divine. The instant we enjoy even a fleeting taste of the golden knowledge that the God of good lives within us and offers Himself to us completely, the door to healing opens. If you peer through the keyhole of the universe, you will recognize a familiar world. Step beyond the gate of fear and you will hear a comforting bell echo in the temple of your heart. It is said that "the Spirit within us loves to hear the truth about itself." To behold our life through the eyes of God is to see ourself as we are. That knowledge will not be lost. Unlike the incomplete love we have known in this world, the knowledge of God is the one awareness that only increases with time and experience.

Experience Versus Identity

We are spiritual beings going through a material experience. We are always bigger than our circumstances. What happens to us is nothing compared to who we are. In our adventure on earth we have opened ourselves to experience the gamut of human emotions and affairs. Daily we walk amidst a symphony of pathos, change, challenge, heartache, and ecstacy. In a day or a life we may rise to heady peaks, struggle in shadowed valleys, and find ourself teetering between paths divided. Yet all the while there is One within us who knows that we are magnificent far beyond the scope and limits of our experience. No matter what drama we log in the journal of our days, our connection and relationship with our Source remains intact. Then, when we tire of the game of earth, we fold up the game board and put it back in the box, remembering that any given day or life is but a mosaic in a grander tapestry. It is the bigger picture we seek to know, and know it we shall.

Dare to Be Divine

The Bible tells us, "You are gods." There is a strong taboo in our culture against saying, "I am God." This is so because we believe that we have offended God and are deserving of punishment for trying to usurp His throne. God is not offended, and His throne cannot be undermined. Love cannot be exiled, for there is no place in the universe untouched by mercy's presence. Love is the abiding quality of our being, the glory we carry with us unto eternity. It is not punishment that awaits us, but awakening. Beloved ones, the time has come to put aside the toys of earth and take up the purpose for which we were born. We came to learn that we are of God, and express this great truth in all of our activities and relationships.

We are not greater than God, but neither are we lesser. Within each of us dwells the spark of the divine. In the emperor and the scavenger God lives. In the prostitute and the saint, the villain and the hero. This life is but a masquerade, a passing but poignant scene in a vaster play. Our moments of illumination here are like diamonds twinkling atop a moonlit sea, reflecting a light that emanates from a source far beyond the world it bathes. Our brightest moments recall the brilliance of the home we left to wander and learn. One day, perhaps soon, we shall stand atop a craggy rock on a high cliff overlooking a measureless sea, and we shall bless our journey. We will laugh the release of the ages, and weep the tears of all humanity. We shall forgive our birth, find compassion for our errors, and embrace our passing from this world as we recognize that its slings and arrows cannot puncture the heart God set gracefully in our breast. We are the masters of our experience. We walk with God, and we walk in majesty. There is no description too great to bestow upon those who bear the light of Spirit. And there is no purpose higher than to recognize the beauty within us and share it.

The dare to be divine is the final challenge of the great dare to be yourself. Our quest for identity ultimately ends with the realization of divinity. All of the other dares lead to this one. This is not a book about self-indulgence; it is a map of self-discovery. Every step we have taken along our way has brought us closer to awakening our memory of our spiritual nature. Nothing matters unless it draws us nearer to our Source, which rests at the center of our self.

The remembrance of our divinity is the only knowledge that will bring us true peace. We have journeyed through years and lifetimes of searching, experimentation, and philosophies. We have lived in many lands, experienced the giddy heights and painful depths of myriad relationships, and walked the paths of religions ancient and modern. We have trod barren deserts in which the wind of adversity blew our own pain like coarse sand against our face and whittled our arrogance into humility. Seeking comfort, we have lain in the arms of angels and charlatans, drenched our lips in nectar, and recoiled from stinging poison. Yet all of our searching has but led us back to ourself, where all the answers have awaited us. To seek greatness outside ourself is to miss the treasure within. Our sojourn in the world of mirrors has shown us that everything we behold points us back to ourself. At the center of ourself is God. We have no source of strength other than Spirit. This is the grand truth we came to discover; it is the final piece of the puzzle that fits into its perfect place.

We are living at a time unlike any other in history. This is the time of the dissolving of fear and illusion on the planet. It is the moment of the great awakening, and we are a part of it. What an auspicious time to live! How great is our contribution as we find the strength to offer our gifts!

If these words have touched you, then go forth and live them. Your spirit's vision is needed here. Your presence in this world is more important than you have realized. The earth is crying out for healing, and your love is the gift that will restore dying creatures to life. Be sure that your light does not flicker. Nourish your heart. Touch the hearts of others. Forget not that we are all born of the same God. Your vision of love is the same one that God has for you. You will find the courage to dare to be yourself.

About the Author

ALAN COHEN is the author of nine popular inspirational books, including *The Dragon Doesn't Live Here Anymore*. His monthly column, "From the Heart," is syndicated in newspapers and magazines throughout the world.

A sought-after lecturer and workshop leader, Alan's moving presentations have touched and transformed the lives of many thousands who have found the courage to believe in themselves and follow their dreams.

Mr. Cohen lives in Maui, Hawaii, where he conducts retreats in spiritual awakening and visionary living.

For more information about
Alan Cohen's books, tapes,
videos, and workshops, write to:

Alan Cohen Publications and Programs
P.O. Box 5030,
Port Huron, MI 48061–5031
or call 1-800-462-3013.